Michael Moorcock
Elric
OF MELNIBONÈ

Credits

Author
Lawrence Whitaker

Additional Text
Aaron Dembski-Bowden

Editor
Richard Ford

Cover Art
Chris Quilliams

Logo & Map
Iordanis Lazaridis

Proofreading
Ron Bedison

Interior Illustrations
Black Sheep Studios, Leonardo Borazio, Martin Hanford, Ryan Horvath, Phil Renne & Chris Quilliams

Playtesters
Nathan Baron, Simon Bray, Mark Billanie, Jason Denton, Colin Driver, Darran Driver, Mark Galeotti, Mark Gedak, Tammy Gedak, Daniel Haslam, Mark Howe, Thomas Howe, John Hitchinson, Andrew Lamburne, Alan Moore, Pete Nash, Daniel Rothman, Mark Rowe & Michael J Young.

Publications Manager
Ian Belcher

Production Director
Alexander Fennell

Special Thanks
Michael Moorcock, Pete Nash & Richard Watts

Additional Thanks
Ian Kaufman & John White

Contents

Copyright Information

1

INTRODUCTION

For ten thousand years the Bright Empire of Melniboné has ruled the Earth, the shadow of its Dragon Lords reaching far and wide. From the icy fjords of Tarkesh to the Boiling Sea and sands of Dorel; from the Marshes of the Mists and the forests of Jharkor to the Ragged Pillars separating the empire from the unknown, unmapped East; across the oceans to take in the Isle of the Purple Towns, Pan Tang and the mist-shrouded Sorcerers' Isle. Melniboné, greatest of empires, has reached that point all empires inevitably reach, when decadence overtakes sense, and the corrupting influence of power undermines confidence and control.

This is the time of the Young Kingdoms. This is the beginning of the End of the World.

A storm approaches. Its architect is Elric, last emperor of Melniboné. An albino Prince of Ruins: a weakling and a mighty sorcerer, a poet, a lover, a kin-slayer and a pawn of the Lords of Law and Chaos. The agents of the world's destruction are the capricious Dukes of Hell and a sinister, sentient runesword forged to destroy a race of gods, but destined to destroy this cycle of time and herald the start of new empires, though none will ever come close to the majesty or influence of fading Melniboné.

Yet, despite the cataclysm, this is a time of adventure, intrigue and romance. Against the backdrop of Melniboné's decline, new nations are emerging and seizing control of its fragmenting empire. This is the time of men and, whilst brief, it is no less bright than the Empire of Melniboné, and as the Earth approaches its darkest hours, humankind can, and will, make a difference.

This book describes the world of Elric of Melniboné and the Young Kingdoms. It details its lands, its peoples, its possibilities and its doom. It offers an insight into the schemes of the Lords of Law and Chaos and provides Games Masters and players with the tools to adventure alongside Elric, Moonglum, Rackhir and Myshella. Adventurers can aid, thwart or ignore the grand designs of the Lords of the Million Spheres and can carve for themselves quests, legends and even their own empires.

This is the time of the Young Kingdoms. This is the beginning of adventures at the End of the World.

Dancing at the End of Time

The spotlight in the world is firmly on Elric, as noted in both Michael Moorcock's stories. That is to be expected from the works based on Elric's life, but there is still room for Games Masters and individual characters to make a difference. That is where this book comes in.

Elric's saga spans ten or so years of Young Kingdoms history, from the time Elric leaves Imrryr to travel for a year, through his many years of wandering the world and other planes, culminating in the final battle that reshapes the Young Kingdoms. This book describes this decade, referring to events in the recent past, those occurring, and in the near future. Elric is abroad in the world, Theleb K'aarna hatches his schemes against the southern continent, Myshella and Tanelorn, and the Sea Lords gather to plan the razing of Imrryr. So the default setting for this game is during the time of Elric, but no precise date or period is given. Games Masters may choose any point in the ten years of the saga, using the momentous events Elric causes, as either a backdrop to their campaigns, or to include the adventurers in them. There is still time for many adventures in the years before Elric wields Stormbringer in the great battle against Chaos. Although the fate of the Earth is set by the stories not everything is set in stone. Characters can still trek across the Weeping Waste, heavy blades held in tired hands as they keep alert for signs of bandit ambush; or stalk through the forests of Jharkor, ever-aware that they are being preyed upon by otherworldly monsters.

Some Games Masters will lead their players through the intrigue-laden, cold-hearted court of Imrryr the Dreaming City – plotting, scheming and duelling their way to both glory and infamy while their empire dies around them. Other characters may find themselves clutching axes as they sail to the Dragon Isle, ready to topple the towers of the Dreaming City and slaughter the inhuman race that lives there. *The Seventh Dark* chapter,

Elric is one of *the* icons of fantasy fiction, his story spanning over forty years of superb writing, including short stories, novels, comics, music and the spoken word. Familiarity with Michael Moorcock's Elric milieu is presumed, but, for a condensed overview of this fine body of work, see *Synopsis of the Elric Saga* beginning on page 135.

beginning on page 126, provides some additional ideas on placing campaigns before Elric's birth; either at the Bright Empire's height, during the war with the Dharzi, or in the aftermath of that war at the very start of the time of the Young Kingdoms.

What Is In This Book?

Elric of Melniboné deals with the world of Michael Moorcock's infamous character, the albino sorcerer-swordsman Elric. This book presents Games Masters and players with all they need in order to create and run adventurers set in the Young Kingdoms.

Elric of Melniboné contains the following chapters.

The Young Kingdoms

An introduction to the world and each of the major nations, powers and races in the Young Kingdoms at the time of Elric, including Melniboné and Pan Tang.

Character Creation

Creating a Young Kingdoms adventurer; full rules and guidance on generating characters for *Elric of Melniboné* games, using the *RuneQuest* engine.

Skills

Full rules for utilising and developing skills in the Young Kingdoms.

Equipment

Detailing currency, weapons, armour and adventuring gear required for survival in the world of Elric.

Combat

Full rules for melee and ranged combat.

Adventuring

Details movement, fatigue, healing and other necessary aspects of adventuring in the Young Kingdoms.

Lords of the Million Spheres

Cults and religions found in Elric's time.

The Silver Grimoire

A detailed examination of magic in the Young Kingdoms, including rules and guidance for allegiance with a particular cosmic power and treading the Moonbeam Roads.

The Seventh Dark

A section for Games Masters, offering notes and advice on running *Elric of Melniboné* campaigns, including an overview of the Elric saga.

Creatures

A Young Kingdoms bestiary and guide to the demons and supernatural beings of the Elric saga.

Heroes & Villains

Descriptions and statistics for the key players in the Elric saga.

About Michael Moorcock

There are few living authors as prolific as Michael Moorcock. Born in 1939, he published his first novel in 1961. Throughout the 1960s and 70s he was the editor of the hugely influential *New Worlds* magazine, which actively championed ground-breaking fantasy and imaginative fiction. Michael's Jerry Cornelius novel *The*

What is Needed Besides this Book?

Elric of Melniboné uses the *RuneQuest* game engine but is otherwise self-contained. The *RuneQuest Companion* and *RuneQuest Monsters* may prove to be of use although they are not essential to getting the most from this book.

Condition of Muzak, won the 1977 Guardian Fiction prize, and he has been accorded no less than three 'Lifetime Achievement' awards. In 2002 Michael was inducted into the Science Fiction and Fantasy Hall of Fame.

Elric is his most famous and enduring creation. The albino began life as a reaction to both the brawny heroes of Sword and Sorcery fantasy and the detailed epics of JRR Tolkien. Michael reversed the traditional clichés, questioned the role and nature of the 'hero', and delved into the psychology of his most famous character in ways unseen in fantasy literature. Despite killing Elric at the end of only the second book concerning the albino's exploits ('*Stormbringer*'), he continued to revisit the saga over the course of the next forty years, adding to it, enriching it, and delving deeper into philosophical ideas concerning love, betrayal, and the meaning of existence. Elric is, as a result, one of the most detailed and best-drawn fantasy characters ever created. As the Elric stories have progressed, Michael has explored the roles of myth and their interpretation, creating an even deeper body of work that continues to provoke and astound in equal measure.

Michael has never confined himself to one medium. Elric has been the subject of music, poetry and graphic novels (Elric: The Making of a Sorcerer being the most recent exploration of the saga). Michael is highly respected as a writer, editor, thinker, and chronicler of the fantastic. He has never shirked from tackling controversial themes in his work and remains as active, and as influential, as ever. The shelves of book stores might groan under the weight of epic fantasy trilogies, each penned by a succession of 'new masters of the genre'. But Moorcock was there first: but for his efforts, those shelves would have more meagre offerings.

THE YOUNG KINGDOMS

There came a time when there was great movement upon the Earth and above it, when the destiny of Men and Gods was hammered out upon the forge of Fate, when monstrous wars were brewed and mighty deeds were designed. And there rose up in this time, which was called the Age of the Young Kingdoms, heroes. Greatest of these heroes was a doom-driven adventurer who bore a crooning rune blade that he loathed.
– *Stormbringer*

Prehistory and the Birth of Melniboné

The Young Kingdoms predate our own world. When Elric blows the Horn of Fate he signals the end of his time and the beginning of ours; time begins anew.

This is not, however, the first such cataclysm. A full cycle of time has passed already, although little is known of it. What Melniboné's scholars do know is that the world was created by the Lords of Chaos and with it all life. The first sapient life was a race known as The Doomed Folk and they grew to hate their world with such intensity that they brought about their own destruction.

In the new world that arose from the ashes of the Doomed Folk, several non-human races established themselves. These included the Older Ones, worshippers of the Lords of Law and now long forgotten; the winged people of Myyrrhn, the civilised descendents of the ape-like clakars; and, in the Silent Lands, a strange inhuman race that were distant relatives of the Myyrrhn. The Elemental Rulers: Grome, Straasha, Lassa and Kakatal, vied for power and inevitably came into violent conflict. Twenty thousand years ago the world was reshaped again, this time into the continents of the Young Kingdoms, when Grome and Straasha battled for supremacy over land and sea. The imposing geographical features of the world, such as The Ragged Pillars and the Roaring Rocks, are the result of this supernatural struggle and not plate tectonics.

Then appeared the race that would come to be Melniboné: the Mernii. Their true origins are unclear, even to Melniboné's own scholars. Some claim that the Melnibonéans were Nomads of the Time Streams whilst others argue that they were natives of the Earth and interbred with the Older Ones. Certainly Melniboné's first seat of civilisation was not the island of Melniboné but the city of R'lin K'ren A'a, now hidden in the jungles beyond the Boiling Sea. When a race known as the Dead Gods sought to challenge the Older Ones, the Older Ones responded by forging the twin runeswords Stormbringer and Mournblade to slay their enemies. The war between the Older Ones and the Dead Gods resulted in the destruction of both races, and the Mernii inherited the world.

At this time the Mernii were allied with the Cosmic Balance and they left R'lin K'ren A'a and settled on the series of islands that became Melniboné. But the sinister powers of the Lords of Chaos seduced certain Mernii, showing them how, through Chaos and sorcery, they could surpass any of the races that had ruled the world before. A vicious civil war erupted with the Balance-aligned Mernii fleeing the dreadful, Chaos-fuelled destruction of their city, H'hui'shan. The Chaos-worshippers who remained inherited the title of Melniboné. They learned to tame the great dragons of their island and built new cities, first and foremost dreaming Imrryr. The Dragon Lords, bearing Stormbringer and Mournblade, conquered the rest of the world swiftly and mercilessly, revelling in their power and new-found cruelty.

The Bright Empire was born.

Upstart Nations and New Oppressors

Melniboné ruled the world for 10,000 years. It did so through a mixture of fear, sorcery and economic might. Melniboné considers humans as an irrelevance; pathetic and uncultured barbarians fit only to be used as slaves or, at best, treated as harmless pets. Melniboné ruled alone, although the smaller, more distant empire of Quarzhasaat – the first truly human civilisation – arose in the north but was annihilated by Melniboné in a great battle in the Sighing Desert.

Nothing could challenge Melniboné's supremacy and nothing did until, approximately a thousand years ago, when the beast-worshipping Dharzi came from the east and sought to assert itself over the Bright Empire.

The ensuing war was disastrous for Melniboné. It was forced to call upon every resource it possessed – ancient pacts with the Lords of Chaos, the Elements and Beasts; its mighty, slumbering dragons; its huge, golden-plated Battlebarges and its thinly spread, decadent populace. Melniboné had conquered and grown complacent: it was in no condition to fight a war with an enemy seemingly as mighty as itself. Melniboné prevailed, but at huge cost. Its power was depleted, and large parts of the Bright Empire were left either ungoverned or ungovernable. It had no option but to retreat to Imrryr, the Dragon Isle's capital.

Into this vacuum stepped humans, those pathetic, uncultured barbarians, and they seized upon Melniboné's weakness, taking control of abandoned territories and forming their own societies free from Melnibonéan domination. The first was Malador, in the country known as Lormyr. Aubec proclaimed himself earl and established new boundaries and new laws. Earl Aubec's confidence was manifest in his ability to stride to the edge of the world and carve new lands from the miasma of Chaos, creating life and hope. Others followed: Vilmir, Dharijor, the Island of the Purple Towns, Filkhar. Melniboné's grip weakened with every new territory and, although it tried to assert its authority, it found itself impotent. Its dragons were spent and could not be roused. Where once a fleet of battlebarges would have razed any opposition, now it could barely muster a handful of ships.

This was the time of the Young Kingdoms and the start of the Bright Empire's demise, although Melniboné, with typical arrogance, chose to ignore its fate. Its cities in lands such as Shazar and Ilmiora were turned to rubble and new ones took their place. Melnibonéan nobles retreated from their ancestral lands, returning to Imrryr's dreaming spires and a retirement of drugs and decadence.

It is in the nature of empires to beget empires and the Young Kingdoms were no exception. Seeking to either spite, or emulate, the Bright Empire, Lormyr sought to carve its own from the southern continent, subjugating the new countries of Argimiliar and Filkhar. Further north, Pan Tang sought to replicate Melniboné's sorceries and seized control of the western continent. To the east, Vilmir, cleaving to the Lords of Law, set-up its own regime, firmly rejecting every aspect, good and bad, of Melniboné's legacy. The result was a constant state of war, and the rise and fall of countless city states and countries. Some, like the desert empire of Quarzhasaat, reached heights of true magnificence that even Melniboné was forced

The Dharzi

Little is known of the Dharzi, save that they were Beast Folk, worshipped the lords of the Beasts, and created terrifying creatures, such as their Hunting Dogs, a vicious cross between bird and huge hound. Although the Dharzi lost its war with Melniboné, remnants of its attempts to colonise the Young Kingdoms are still in evidence throughout the Silent Lands and the Marshes of the Mist, parts of Ilmiora and the Forest of Troos. These ruins contain ancient, terrible, Dharzi secrets and sorcerous machinery; a lure for the brave and foolhardy alike. Opish, the Dharzi language, is still used as a thieves' cant in Quarzhasaat.

to recognise, but fell just as quickly and became forgotten. Others, like Pikarayd, seemed to regress, becoming more insular and barbaric, despite the progress being made all around them.

After 400 years of struggles, petty wars and magical, political machinations, the Young Kingdoms have stabilised. Melniboné, whilst still an economic power, still feared by many, has almost fully retreated to Imrryr, rarely bothering to dabble in the affairs of men. Lormyr's southern empire has collapsed, and Argimiliar is the ascendant power. Vilmir has all but atrophied under its allegiance to the tenets of Law and the Ilmioran city states prevail. Only scheming, malevolent Pan Tang has sustained its claims to Melniboné's inheritance, with its vassal country, Dharijor, and its vicious pirate navies that prowl the northern sea-routes in search of slaves and sacrifices to the Lords of Chaos.

The Young Kingdoms as they are in Elric's time are described in the following pages. A general overview precedes the detailed descriptions, giving information on culture, daily life, language and trade. The kingdoms' descriptions are then gathered into their respective continents with the islands being treated separately.

Society

With Melniboné's retreat the nations of the Young Kingdoms have cast-off the isolation once imposed by the Bright Empire and have become a hive of social endeavour. Trade between nations, much of it sea-borne, flourishes with the great markets of Dhakos, Cadsandria, Menii, Old Hrolmar and Raschil being respected centres of trade. People sense the opportunities independence brings and seize them eagerly, either through dignified means or through the motivation of greed and the age-old practices of theft, duplicity, raiding and piracy.

There is a hunger for knowledge and discovery with explorers such as Duke Avan Astran and Smiorgan Baldhead undertaking ambitious voyages into uncharted territories and forgotten corners in search of wealth, magic and new markets. The rich grow richer at the expense of the poorer nations, and there is little sympathy for those who accept their lot and prefer a quieter life.

This is a time of great city-states, such as Ilmar, Karlaak and Bakshaan, as well as grinding poverty and depravation such as that of Nadsokor, Dhoz-Kam and Ryfel. The people of the Young Kingdoms still seek to make their mark and the

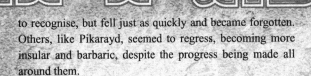

The Shape of the World

The Young Kingdoms occupy an area roughly the size of continental Europe and the British Isles. The world extends much further to the north, east and west, but these lands are only scantily described in the Elric saga and are not covered in this book. The unmapped East is the only area accorded anything more than cursory detail, with the countries of Anakhazan, Changshai, Eshmir, Okara, Phum and the Valederian Directorates being identified. It is believed that the Dharzi originated from lands even more easterly.

To the south lies the edge of the world, marked by the turbulence of pure Chaos. Save for Aubec of Malador, none have dared venture into it.

result is a constant succession of border disputes, territorial expansion, piracy and unbridled ambition, as epitomised by Pan Tang's desire to emulate the grandeur of the Bright Empire. Most scratch a living from the soil and lead a subsistence existence, but many more flock to the cities and ports to ply old trades and crafts or learn new ones. Society is rich with promise and the intrepid reap the rewards whilst the reticent continue to drudge and moan, almost as though they were still servants of Melniboné.

Culture

The Young Kingdoms are a melange of cultures. The richest states have raised great cities and aspire to a level of civilisation enjoyed by Melniboné. In this sense the Young Kingdoms could be considered to be urbanised with a cultural level equating to that of renaissance Europe. Yet sitting beside these centres of creativity and discovery are realms that have either failed to lift themselves from barbarism or have no desire to do so. The city-states might be controlled by noble families and dynastic traditions, with sophisticated social and religious practices, but elsewhere the tribe, the clan and the hearth still predominate bound by superstition, taboo and fear of the unknown.

This is certainly an age of great cultural achievement in the arts and scholarship. The famed University of Cadsandria claims to catalogue all human learning in its great libraries

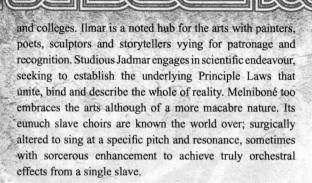

and colleges. Ilmar is a noted hub for the arts with painters, poets, sculptors and storytellers vying for patronage and recognition. Studious Jadmar engages in scientific endeavour, seeking to establish the underlying Principle Laws that unite, bind and describe the whole of reality. Melniboné too embraces the arts although of a more macabre nature. Its eunuch slave choirs are known the world over; surgically altered to sing at a specific pitch and resonance, sometimes with sorcerous enhancement to achieve truly orchestral effects from a single slave.

Slavery and serfdom are abundant across the Young Kingdoms. Whilst some enlightened nations shun the practice Dharijor, Pan Tang, Pikarayd and some of the Ilmioran city states actively trade in slaves. Of course, the greatest call for slaves is from Melniboné herself, and there are many nations who engage in trading criminals, enemies of the state, or even just the poor and dispossessed in the slave auctions of Gromoorva, Hwamgaarl, Ryfel and Imrryr.

The Young Kingdoms is a maritime culture. The finest sailing ships are built in Tarkesh but every nation with a decent, deep-water harbour builds solid, ocean-going vessels. Trade routes are well established but still prone to piracy especially in the waters surrounding Pan Tang and some of the more remote stretches of the southern continent's coastline. Privateers – legalised pirates – are supported by many nations, including Vilmir and the Ilmioran city-states, either as a way of inflicting humiliation upon an enemy or rival, or simply as a means of supplementing the economy.

Ships come in all shapes, sizes and types. Galleys, often slave-powered, are common, but masted merchant cogs, brigs and schooners ply the trade waters using speed and manoeuvrability to outrun lurking pirate vessels. And of course Melniboné maintains its fleet of golden-hulled Battlebarges, the size of small towns and powered by hundreds of slaves as well as sorcery, although their presence on the oceans is a thankful rarity.

Magic & Technology

Magic and sorcery in the Young Kingdoms is both powerful and rare. As it stems from Chaos, most magicians must bargain with Chaos to both learn and practise their art. Those who become sorcerers risk madness and death as they are forced to deal with powerful and malevolent entities of the various Hells that make-up the realms of Chaos. Even elemental magic, which poses less risk, is still a potent and

unpredictable force, and there are few brave (or foolish) enough to pursue that knowledge. Melniboné reserves sorcerous knowledge for itself and those humans who have gained some degree of magical mastery, such as the snivelling, love-struck Theleb K'aarna, have had to spend years in both search and study to attain their cognisance. By Melnibonéan standards, even the most accomplished human sorcerers are but amateurs in the art; and Melniboné has forgotten more sorcery than the Young Kingdoms will ever know.

As a consequence the Young Kingdoms view sorcery as something malicious and sinister. While this is primarily a fear born from ignorance and superstition, it is also an assumption not a million miles from the truth. Magic is seen as the purview of dark-hearted men and the decadent Melnibonéans. Sorcery's myriad possibilities and strengths are now largely viewed as foul and unhealthy by the people of the Young Kingdoms. Humanity has turned elsewhere for enlightenment and power, to exploration within the sciences. This prehistoric age will never see anything like the modern technology of our own world, but clockwork engineering

has been discovered and practically every human realm with some coins to rub together can afford to manufacture blades of clean steel rather than wield weapons of bronze or iron.

Language

The Young Kingdoms speak a common tongue (simply Common) derived from the Low Tongue of Melniboné, although much of the semblance between the languages has been lost over time. Regional dialects and unique vocabularies exist although it is easy enough to communicate with people of different nations and nationalities. Exotic cultures, such as the remnants of Quarzhasaat and the Weeping Waste, have their own native tongues not derived from Melnibonéan influence. Literacy levels in the Young Kingdoms are low with reading and writing being the preserve of those who can afford to educate their children and themselves.

Religion

There are many gods in the Young Kingdoms. First and foremost are the Lords of Law and Chaos, diametrically opposed beings standing for absolute adherence to unwavering progress or submission to the randomness of creation and destruction. The names of these lords are legion: Arkyn and Donblas of Law; Arioch, Chardros, Xiombarg, Mabelrode and Pyaray of Chaos. These are real gods with real powers, but kept in check by the presence of the Cosmic Balance which maintains that neither force shall hold sway, leading to destruction through either stagnation or perpetual, random change.

Chaos is worshipped by Melniboné, Pan Tang, Dharijor, and Pikarayd. Law is followed throughout Ilmiora, Vilmir, Argimiliar and Lormyr Chaos follows a haphazard ecumenical structure whilst the Church of Law is focused on Vilmir and follows a more rigid hierarchy.

Languages of the Young Kingdoms

Common Tongue. The lingua franca of the Young Kingdoms with considerable regional and national dialects. Derived from Low Melnibonéan and has a written form.

High Melnibonéan. Also known as High Speech this is the formal language of Melniboné and used for all official communications. It is also the language of sorcery (it is claimed that Slortar himself devised the language for communicating with lesser beings) and anyone wishing to work magic needs a good understanding of it. Given its nature, it is very difficult to learn and is structured like no other earthly tongue. In parts, its vocabulary and the demands made upon the voice to utter it, defy the traditional laws of speech and acoustics. When written, High Speech characters and runes seem to flow from one plane of existence into another.

Low Melnibonéan. Also known as Low Speech, this is conversational Melnibonéan and the basis for the Young Kingdoms' Common. It is deeply poetic in structure and almost borders on song. It has a complex written form combining a conventional alphabet with the runic characters sometimes attributed to the Older Ones.

Mong. The hard, brutish language of the Weeping Waste. Its terse inflections reflect the environment although it can, at times, be deeply moving especially when used in song. It has no written form.

Opish. The guttural, strained tongue of the Dharzi, a mixture of bestial grunts, mutters and perverse inflections. It has a rudimentary written form extrapolated from what few original Dharzi writings remain. It is used primarily in Quarzhasaat and Nadsokor where it is a thieves' tongue.

'pande. Spoken in the Unknown East. It seems to combine abstract poetry with rigid intonation and formal pronunciation. In its written form it is mixture of pictograms and flowing calligraphy. It bears some resemblance to both High and Low Melnibonéan, but little to Common.

The Elemental Lords, Grome (Earth), Straasha (Water), Lassa (Air) and Kakatal (Fire) are chiefly worshipped in rural, barbarian and primitive regions. The people of the Weeping Waste follow Grome and Lassa, and it is believed that some of the tribes of Dorel follow the sun cult of Kakatal. Straasha is worshipped heavily in northerly Tarkesh and in The Purple Towns. The elementals follow no formal hierarchy although certain cities have developed some codified practices surrounding elemental worship, but congregations tend to be small.

Other, minor deities exist. Ancestor worship in Oin and Yu, along with a curious form of animism centred on the concept of the country itself possessing a kind of sentience. In Filkhar, a land of bountiful harvests and rich vineyards, several nature spirits, reflecting the nation's bounty, are worshipped alongside both the Lords of Law and Chaos.

A very small cult is allied with the Cosmic Balance, that which keeps Law and Chaos in check. These mystics have achieved a certain degree of enlightenment and have come to comprehend the true nature of the opposing forces and the equilibrium the Balance represents. Their principle goal is to locate mythical Tanelorn, the city of the Cosmic Balance, or to build it anew in the hopes of averting worldwide destruction.

The Northern Continent

The vast northern continent includes the harsh expanse of the Sighing Desert, separating the remains of the Quarzhasaat Empire from the major lands of the Young Kingdoms; and the wind and rain-swept plateau-lands of the Weeping Waste. It is home to the great city states of Ilmiora, the lawful lands of Vilmir, the fetid ruin of Nadsokor and the sorcery-torn malevolence of the Forest of Troos.

The northern continent was the first region conquered by the Dharzi and it remained their stronghold for over a century, until Melniboné destroyed them with dragon flame and demon allies. Ruins of the Dharzi can be found by those with the bravery and skill to cross the lonely northern wilds and outwit the wily and territorial desert nomads who prey on the intrepid and unwitting alike.

In the north, the Sighing Desert dominates. The dry, unforgiving sands are home to the nomads who travel between the oases, keepers of secrets from the time of the Dharzi and other magics, such as dream theft. Lonely

Quarzhasaat, a crumbling edifice of pettiness and duplicity squats, half-hidden and maudlin, in the heat and dryness. South of the Sighing Desert are the city states of Ilmiora, vibrant, liberal communities where most trades, goods and services can be found, along with decadent indulgences of all kinds.

Seeming to react against the freedom of Ilmiora, Vilmir broods in the south of the continent. Irrevocably tied to the worship of the Lords of Law it has raised bureaucracy and state control to a high art, closely governing the thoughts and feelings of its populace with grim tales of doom that await those who do not aspire to the teachings of Lords Donblas, Arkyn and Miggea.

East of Vilmir and Ilmiora the land breaks and rises to the high plateau of the Weeping Waste, a remnant of the war between Grome and Straasha. This unnatural shelf of land is baron and wind-swept, plagued by an incessant drizzle that frequently breaks into torrential downpours, said to be the tears of Straasha, crying for his stolen realm. The nomads of the Wastes are a resilient, pragmatic folk tied to their land, their clans and their tribes, caring little for the events below their plateau.

Ilmiora

Ilmiora lies south of the Sighing Desert where the sands give way to temperate grasslands, rolling pastures, deep forests and gentle hills. The discrete city state kingdoms are civilised, cultured and liberal. Ilmiora is ruled by a hereditary caste of senators drawn from the city-states that make up the kingdom, with Ilmar the acknowledged capital. Each senator represents a noble family or a merchant clan of repute and power in the region and they rule over their respective city-states, occasionally feuding and warring among each other over matters of law and profit. The greatest rivalry exists between Ilmar and Bakshaan and this rivalry has come close to all-out war in several occasions over the past three hundred years. In the time of Elric the city states are at relative peace, but tensions are never far from the surface and easily exploited by the unscrupulous and power-hungry.

Great distances separate the city-states, leaving the wilderness open to banditry and brigands of all stripes who prey upon the many caravans that trundle overland between the trade-hungry cities. The Ilmiorans highly prize commercial acumen, but there is never a shortage of those who prefer to acquire their coin through more dishonest means. Beyond the merchant and noble classes, Ilmiora is

also a land of farmers, with great cattle herds grazing the grasslands or forming livestock trains from one settlement to the market in another.

The city states foster arts and crafts. Ilmioran leatherworking is especially valued both in and out of the kingdom, and even the humblest peasants often trade for (or create their own) high-quality leather clothing or goods for personal use. Leatherworkers with unusual skill can take their trade out to the Young Kingdoms and make a small fortune selling intricately-worked pieces to the appearance-conscious nobility of other realms. Both Ilmar and Bakshaan are patrons of the arts, and Karlaak is famed for its high quality steel.

Ilmioran City States

Bakshaan. Wealthiest of the city states, Bakshaan is the largest seaport of the northern continent and the envy of the other Ilmioran city states and neighbouring Vilmir. Its merchant princes and trading guilds are fiercely competitive and often driven by both jealousy and corruption. Assassins, thugs and thieves are easily found in Bakshaan, all of them eager to fill their pockets in any way they can, regardless of how many bodies they step over.

A resident of note is the merchant adventurer, Nikorn. Perhaps the wealthiest of Bakshaan's merchants he resides outside the city in a fortified castle, protected by his sorcerer-bodyguard, Theleb K'aarna of Pan Tang, and a private army. It is Elric's doom to slay Nikorn, despite having pledged to leave him unharmed, after seeking vengeance against Theleb K'aarna.

Gorjhan. Too small and too dour to be a true city-state, but often referred to in the same breath as Ilmar and Bakshaan. Gorjhan is close to both Vilmir and the Weeping Waste and influenced by both. The humourless merchants of Rignariom come to Gorjhan to trade with the nomads of the Weeping Waste, and the township's narrow streets are either dust-clogged, water-logged or mud-choked. It is Gorjhan's doom to fall prey to Terarn Gashtek, the Flamebringer, and his horde when they sweep across the Weeping Waste from the Unknown East, murdering all in their path.

Ilmar. Vibrant Ilmar vies with Bakshaan for position and status. Its merchant princes and guilds are every bit as ambitious, but less inclined to fractious jealousy amongst themselves, which lends Ilmar an altogether quieter, safer nature. Ilmar has outgrown its walls twice over the years, such is the rate of expansion in the city, and people regularly flock to its bustling port and huge market, eager to seek their fortune.

Fads in fashion, art and architecture are common; the current vogue is to emulate the style of the Bright Empire, leading to a whole slew of ornate towers to be thrown-up around the Ilmari sky line, and for the city's fashion victims to demand goods from the Dragon Isle, including the kinds of narcotics and wines imbibed by Imrryr's dreaming residents. The result is a rapid increase in madness, suicide and other, more depraved activities as the Ilmari fashionistas struggle to control the intense visions and dreams brought about by their excesses.

Karlaak. Otherwise known as Karlaak-by-the-Weeping-Waste, for short, Karlaak is a beauty on the edge of a desperate landscape. A city of squat towers, wide, tree-lined streets, elegant spires, graceful minarets and beautiful, light-catching domes, it is welcoming and homely. It prospers without the need for Bakshaan's jealousy and avarice, or Ilmar's one-upmanship. Karlaak is confident in and of itself, and therein lies its strength.

Ruled by the benevolent Voashoon family, Karlaak is a place of peace and tranquillity. Some have mistaken it for Tanelorn. It advocates liberal tolerance and allies itself with neither Law nor Chaos, perhaps in emulation of Tanelorn, but more likely from the simple common sense wisdom of Lord Voashoon himself.

In time Elric comes to make Karlaak his home, when he rescues Lord Voashoon's daughter, Zarozinia, from the nearby Forest of Troos, and marries her. He finds peace in Karlaak, and can even closet Stormbringer awhile, but fate interrupts his idyll when Zarozinia is kidnapped and Elric must ride out again on his last, cataclysmic adventure.

Nadsokor, City of Beggars

Easily the most renowned, and by far the least-loved, region of the northern lands is the city of Nadsokor. Once part of Vilmir, this hive of corruption and filth was abandoned by most of its citizens during a plague long ago. Now the rotting hulk of the city is home to the worst scum of the Young Kingdoms, and it is not for nothing that the city earned the name the City of Beggars.

Disease is rampant in the streets here, after-effects of the long-passed plague coupled with the spread of fresh illness and contagion from dirty living and disgusting, squalid

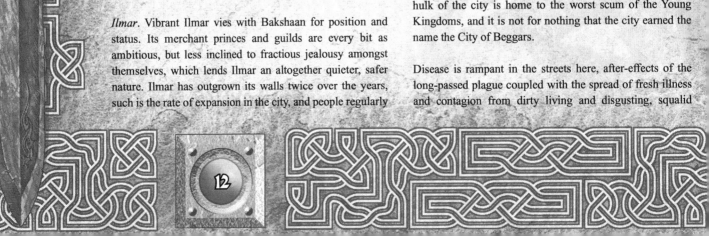

conditions. The buildings are tumbledown, mould covered and decaying where they stand. The city walls are blackened with grime, almost as if they stand only to keep disease in, rather than keep invaders out. No one would lay siege to Nadsokor anyway, of course. There is nothing to win from conquering the Young Kingdoms' greatest, filthiest slum.

Nadsokor supplies beggars as much as it shelters them. They spill from the gates and venture out into other lands, panhandling and pleading for coin on the streets of every town and city in the known world. Most of these souls ultimately consider Nadsokor home, and serve the only true power in the City of Beggars: the black-hearted King Urish the Seven-Fingered. Whilst impoverished and disowned, the beggars are watchers and listeners, gatherers of information that can be fed into the networks controlled by King Urish. With the right methods the beggars' lines of communication can provide knowledge valuable to those who hold subtle agendas. The bureaucrats of Vilmir, despising what the beggars represent, value what they see and hear. So too does the mysterious Mereghn network of the Ilmioran city states, which numbers many beggars amongst its lower orders of informants. Greasing Urish's greedy, mutilated palm with silver puts that knowledge to wider and more sinister uses and has made Urish very rich and drunk with his own, over-inflated sense of power.

Urish dies in the years to come, and Chaos takes root in Nadsokor; Narjhan, a Chaos entity, takes Urish's role as beggar-lord. Out of twisted spite and bitterness, Nadsokor launches ill-fated raids against the city of Tanelorn, seeking to bring down the Eternal City.

The Sighing Desert

Two millennia ago, the sun-blasted region now known as the Sighing Desert was once the grand and presumptuous Quarzhasaat Empire. Due to the miscasting of a spell during Quarzhasaat's war with Melniboné, 2,000 years ago, the

endless seas of sand were spread across the empire, burying it in the desert found today. The invading Melnibonéans left unharmed; the citizens of Quarzhasaat died in their thousands. From that day forward a moaning wind blew across the dunes, giving the Sighing Desert its grim name. Occasionally the wind peels back the topmost layers of the desert revealing the bones of buried armies or the riches of the sand-drowned empire. Many travellers venture north to see such claims for themselves. Most do not return. In the intervening years 14 separate armies have attempted to find and loot Quarzhasaat, only for each one to be lost to the unforgiving sands.

Scimitar-wielding desert-dwellers of the so-called Nomad Nations make their home here, the only human population of

Nadsokor-nurtured beggars are known by their peculiar begging bowls. These shallow, yellowing bowls seem, at first glance, to be made from a rough clay. In some instances they are rune-covered and the owner may claim his bowl is a vessel for powerful magic. This may be true. Nadsokor beggar-bowls are always carved from a human skull.

the region. These silk-clad warriors are atheistic, a curious cultural aspect among the people of the Young Kingdoms, and took to the Sighing Desert after fleeing the oppression of the Bright Empire many centuries ago. They are a meditative, spiritual people, seeking enlightenment on their own terms with no thought for either Law or Chaos. Each year the clans meet at the Silver Flower Oasis, named for the cactus blossoms found there, trading news and information, as well as enjoying each others' company and indulging in old rivalries.

Active in this region are the strange *Dreamthieves*, men and women who, with their crooked staffs, can enter the dream planes that exist close to our own, searching for mysteries, treasures and other powerful secrets. The Dreamthieves claim not be native to the plane of the Young Kingdoms and are said to have some knowledge of both the past and the future. As their name suggests, they are able to steal the fabric of dreams which are bartered in a marketplace within the Dream Realms. Elric himself is guided by the Dreamthief Oone on his quest for the Pearl at the Heart of the World, as desired by Lord Gho of Quarzhasaat.

Hidden in the depths of the Sighing Desert is the lonely mountain stronghold of Mordaga, the Sad Giant, destined to be slain by Moonglum in the quest for the Chaos Shield, a tool Elric uses in the final fight against Chaos. Mordaga is an Earth-bound god, stripped of his place in the divine realms. He lives in fear of his own, foretold death and will do anything to avoid it.

Quarzhasaat

The city of Quarzhasaat is a place of intrigue and decadence. Its streets are wide and triumphantly named, such as the 'Avenue of Military Success' and the 'Boulevard of Ancient Accomplishment', each broad street framed by its beautiful architecture. Run by the Council of Six and One Other (the mysterious 'nameless seventh'), the city operates to a complex system of guilds, sects (the 'sorcerer adventurers') and blood-oaths, all with careless and contemptuous plotting and scheming at their heart. The leaders of the multitude of sects – clans, families and loose affiliations of faith and profession – are intense rivals, each seeking position on the Council of Six and One Other. No trick is too dirty; no connivance too unsubtle, to gain position and prestige. Lord Gho Faazi provides Elric with a 'medicine' that is highly addictive and poisonous to secure his service in obtaining the Pearl at the Heart of the World; he also sends assassins against the Sighing Desert nomads and is responsible for countless other atrocities all committed in the name of

power. His greed for power and the Pearl is satiated when Elric makes him eat it…

The Council of Six and One Other rules Quarzhasaat through a mixture of fear and lies. In its arrogance it has convinced its populace that, far from being an empire in complete decline, Quarzhasaat was victorious in its brief war with Melniboné, causing the Dragon Isle to sink beneath the waves. Doubtless other lies are perpetrated to maintain the pretence of grandeur; and, as is the nature of lies, they are there to be unravelled and exposed.

Quarzhasaat sects are named for birds, plants, animals and many other nature symbols that belie the sect's true nature. The Yellow Sect; the Foxglove Sect; and Gho Faazi's Sparrow Sect. All employ convoluted blood oaths and contracts defining membership, duty and codes of conduct. Few are worth the parchment they are written on.

Even the term 'sorcerer-adventurers' may be a misnomer. Many have been sent in search of the Pearl and all have failed. Their talents are certainly dwarfed by Elric's, but even by the modest standards of human sorcerers, they may be little more than grandly-titled hedge magicians.

Org and the Forest of Troos

The kingdom of Org is home to the squat, malformed Orgians. They dwell in a land rumoured to be haunted by monsters only slightly more frightening than the cultureless, violent and primitive Orgians themselves. It is a realm few ever travel to, and one that rarely sends its native sons beyond its borders. No other realm in the Young Kingdoms wants much of anything to do with the brutish Orgians or their dark forest realm. The sentiment is apparently returned by the inbred and primal Orgians, who remain in their tree-bordered homeland at all times.

The malevolent Forest of Troos, within the tiny, degenerate kingdom of Org, is a relic of the previous cycle of time and its rulers, The Doomed Folk. Whilst the Doomed Folk long-since left this plane, a handful of people remained, closeted in the forest, and founded Org, the forgotten kingdom. Even Melniboné's privations escaped it, and Org remains forgotten.

The forest is a dark, sinister place, twisted by whatever forces The Doomed Folk unleashed in their exodus. Shadows cloak the trees and strange plants and all manner of mutated, pathetic creatures, predators and prey alike, haunt its grim glades. For sorcerers Troos is a treasure garden, overgrown with the rare plants and herbs necessary for sorcery and other magics. Few venture here. The forest does not welcome visitors almost as though it possesses a sentience and a wit to reject them. Those who enter Troos soon leave, making it the perfect cover for The Doomed Folk's descendents, secure in their dark little realm.

When Elric travels away from the Ruby Throne, he comes to the Forest of Troos, Stormbringer in hand. Here he will meet and slay the ruler of the Orgians, King Gutheran, as well as the barbaric monarch's family and ghoulish court, such as it is. Until then, Gutheran and his warriors strengthen the hostile reputation of their muddy, bloody realm by butchering any travellers that come into their lands.

Tanelorn, the Eternal City

It is claimed by certain sages in the matters of the Multiverse that Tanelorn, or a version of it, exists on every plane at once, a haven for those seeking respite from the fractious nature of Law and Chaos, an oasis of peace and enlightenment. Only those who genuinely seek rest can find Tanelorn; many spend their lives searching in vain, either because they want it too much, or because they seek to pervert it or destroy it somehow. In the Young Kingdoms, Tanelorn has been known to appear at the borders of the Sighing Desert, and it appears in this world as a city of flat-roofed homes, beauteous spires, wondrous domes and cobblestone streets, while the air is turned into soft music by gentle birdsong and ululating breezes. Elric himself is destined to one day walk its streets. Indeed, he will be the

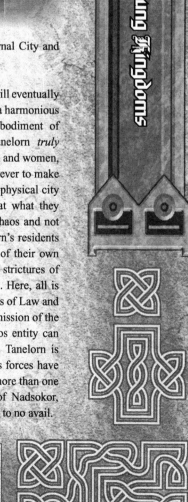

one and only mortal to ever reside in the Eternal City and find no inner peace; such is his curse.

The truth of Tanelorn is a lesson some mortals will eventually learn. The physical city is a shell, representing a harmonious state of mind. Tanelorn is the physical embodiment of equilibrium; the Cosmic Balance itself. Tanelorn *truly* exists within the souls of all mortal men and women, though it seems to be the fate of most never to make that realisation. Those that do, find the physical city and, at the same time, understand that what they seek is freedom from both Law and Chaos and not freedom from one or the other. Tanelorn's residents are those who have sought a way out of their own worlds, to come to a place free of the strictures of gods and the demands of mortal rulers. Here, all is in balance, harmony, and the great Lords of Law and Chaos may never enter without the permission of the citizens. In truth, no Law god or Chaos entity can even find Tanelorn without assistance. Tanelorn is anathema to Chaos in particular and its forces have attempted to seize the Eternal City on more than one occasion. Narjhan, the chaotic ruler of Nadsokor, seeks Tanelorn's destruction repeatedly, to no avail.

Finding Tanelorn

Adventurers might be hired to seek-out Tanelorn on behalf of a patron, or even desire to find it for themselves. Their search will be in vain unless they have a compelling reason – the rejection of Law, Chaos and other unworldly powers – to find it and make it their home. One cannot use Tanelorn as a safe haven or a base of operations. Once inside its walls, an understanding of the harmony of the Balance settles upon its residents and they raise themselves only in the city's defence. Occasionally Tanelorn might dispatch emissaries to seek aid against its enemies and this is perhaps an easier route to finding the Eternal City.

Vilmir

Whilst Ilmar follows a more liberal, enlightened approach to Law, Vilmir takes its doctrines to a logical extreme. A terrible divide exists between the people of Vilmir. The rich live in splendour and the poor are reduced to awful conditions barely above those in the City of Beggars. The whole kingdom is a manifestation of why Law does not necessarily equal good, and Chaos does not equate to evil. The entire realm is strangled and decayed by its allegiance, while at the same time profiting from the advances Law offers that are seen nowhere else in the Young Kingdoms. It is this paradox which separates the people, and it is this paradox which is killing most of them.

Once, Vilmir's land was a forest paradise. Now it stands as grassland, ruined by the slash-and-burn farming of several generations of land-workers, punctuated by the huge, uninspiring, pyramid-walled cities. Rural life is hard here – crops fail in the poor-quality soil and the ruined earth offers up little bounty. Most citizens are peasants, half-starved and working themselves into early graves just to feed themselves on the destroyed land. Levies and taxes claimed by the noble caste and the state-wide Church of Law mean that most peasants have trouble holding onto any food, coin or supplies beyond the bare minimum required to survive.

The wealthy and the high-placed souls of Vilmir claim almost everything for themselves, parasitically sucking life from those who toil hardest and deserve it most. To be a noble, or a priest of Law, in Vilmir is to be exalted above the masses, though it also means one is likely to belong to a bloodline of inbred weaklings and incestuous relationships with xenophobic relatives. The inbreeding takes its toll on the dynasties and bloodlines of the noble caste and each generation creates increasing numbers of fools, deformities and disease-prone weaklings.

To battle the supply crisis facing Vilmir, King Naclon's state-sanctioned raiders and privateers take what the kingdom needs from other nations nearby, which sours any hopes of diplomacy that might otherwise exist between Vilmir and the other Young Kingdoms. The rule of Naclon is not unopposed, however. The thin separation between church and state means that Cardinal of Law, Garrick, has as much (if not more) power than the monarch himself, and in the years to come, after Naclon meets his death in the Sack of the Dreaming City, it is Garrick's choice of puppet-ruler that takes the throne, leaving the cardinal as the true ruler of Vilmir.

This harsh culture is not without its wonders. Clockwork knights – men of metal and ticking gear-joints – stand guard outside the pyramid temples of the Church of Law. Water-driven mills and looms form a burgeoning industry, and the first printing presses are spreading the written word to a barely literate populace. Such marvels are counterweighted by the bland sandstone and uniform appearance of Vilmir's growing cities which are uninspired and uninspiring. Grey is a common colour, from the stone of the buildings, through to the clothes worn by peasant and noble alike.

But there is an exception to this stagnation. A noble by the name of Avan Astran rules over the city of Old Hrolmar. Astran is a beacon of enlightenment amidst the grey and the drab. An explorer who has travelled to the Unknown East, Astran rejects the harsh tenets of the priests and embraces a philosophy akin to that of Ilmar and Bakshaan. In Old Hrolmar he establishes a subculture of those free-spirited artists, philosophers and artisans who turn their backs on the rule of Law and the leadership of Cardinal Garrick. In his final expedition, in search of legendary R'lin K'ren A'a he falls to Elric's blade, and Old Hrolmar cultural rebellion dies with the duke.

The Weeping Waste

On the eastern borders of Ilmar and Vilmir, raised during the war between Grome and Straasha, the Weeping Waste is an immense plateau inhabited by insular nomadic barbarians who believe that their rain-soaked, misty grassland realm is the only true world, and all beyond is a Chaos-touched nightmare. They believe, truly, that outside the plains they call home, Hell stretches out in every direction. The Weeping Waste is so called because of the incessant rainfall that batters a plains land broken by rivers and lakes. This is a remote land without villages or towns. Its people are herders and hunters, following the game-trails across the soaked prairies, eking-out a meagre existence whilst attempting to placate Lord Straasha whose tears rain down upon them.

Wildlife is plentiful in the Weeping Waste, though the animals are often predatory and vicious. Bears, mastodon and smilodon prowl the lands and are easily more than a match for most warriors. It is probably fair to say that the humans of the Waste, and anyone travelling through them, are merely competing for space with the creatures that call the realm home.

The barbarians revere nature spirits and elementals, as well as the shades of their own ancestors. Like many nomadic peoples, they are excellent hunters and crafty at life in the wilderness, though their travels take them on traditional tribal journeys along paths unknown to outsiders. On the backs of their shaggy steppe ponies, the hardy warriors of the wastes are well-known as riders almost without compare. With their ritual tattoos and scars, and armour carved from the wood of stunted trees found only on the Weeping Waste (its secrets of production a closely guarded secret known only to a handful of tribes), the Wastelanders are viewed as fearsome and barbaric. Fearsome, certainly; but their knowledge of the land and their customs based around kinship, respect and the natural order of the world, is as enlightened as any in the Young Kingdoms; and, in many respects, much more enlightened than some who claim to be civilised.

The Southern Continent

The lands of the southern continent were the first to rise up against the Bright Empire. Lormyr, inspired by Earl Aubec of Malador, seized the opportunities presented by the aftermath of the Dharzi War, forcing Melniboné to abandon its lands and retreat to Imrryr. This victory secure, Lormyr moved outwards across the continent, assisting Filkhar and Argimiliar to similar victories. Lormyr then stepped into the power vacuum and established its own, Lawful empire for a time which, whilst never reaching the extremes of Vilmir, resulted in Filkharian and Argimiliaran resentment. Many small wars within this new empire took place, each eroding Lormyr's ambitions further. Now, in Elric's time, that empire has faded entirely and Lormyr has lapsed into a peaceful dormancy whilst its neighbours flourish in their independence.

Lormyr's rise and slow decline are now seen with little bitterness among the people of the southlands. But the remains of the Bright Empire are still very much in evidence with tumbledown ruins and ancient, abandoned monuments scattering the southern realms, each seen as demon-haunted, cursed places by the southerners (and many of them are). Adventurers come south to pick through the bones of the empire's golden years, but many find secrets humans were never meant to know.

Argimiliar

Argimiliar is the current power in the southern continent, having risen to ascendancy at Lormyr's expense. A land of rich agricultural prospects and high profits, with an educated citizenry and a nobility founded on principles of honour and archaic, Lormyrian chivalry. Most of the country is given over to vast herds of livestock and cattle farms, whilst the prosperous northern cities of Cadsandria and The City of the Yellow Coast are always open to travellers from other lands. The University of Cadsandria, in the world-famous capital, welcomes all with a mind to learn more of the sciences and the world around them. In the far south Andlermaign, once a Bright Empire citadel, is now the stronghold of the cattle barons. It relaxes in decadent splendour, taking advantage of the Melnibonéan architecture and some of the Dragon Lords' secrets buried deep in the old crypts.

For all is not well in Argimiliar. The Church of Chaos is growing in the kingdom, flourishing behind the closed doors of Andlermaign and spilling out, eventually reaching the northern settlements. Law prevails, but Chaos is rising, and across the land small, secretive cults worshipping Xiombarg, Slortar and other Lords of Misrule are establishing themselves. The spread of Chaos can be traced to the careless reign of the foppish King Jiku. A vain and foolish man, he seeks to hide his flaws by coveting the attentions and affections of those more learned and creative than he. Such traits are found in those allying with Chaos and Jiku has been semi-seduced, turning a blind-eye to the rising storm. All around him, his court and fellow nobles fall into the hedonistic pursuits offered by the Chaos cults.

This will all change when Jiku is killed in the Sack of Imrryr. The ruler who follows is King Hozel, raised in a Lawful monastery and burning with a zeal to rival anything bred in Vilmir. Where his predecessor was weak, King Hozel, given to fits of madness, the result of generations of incestuous unions, takes the throne and institutes a crusade of bloody purges to stamp out all taints of Chaos within his realm. His method is to engender suspicion and treachery in a bid to root-out even the slightest hint of Chaos allegiance. Children

Hozel swallowed and spoke, his voice trembling. 'I've seen your muttering kind in the market places, Elric. Men who prophecy all kinds of dooms that never take place — mad-eyed men such as you. But we do not let them live in Argimiliar. We flay them slowly, finger by finger, inch by inch until they admit their omens are fallacious! Perhaps we'll have that opportunity, yet!'
– Stormbringer

betray their parents, and parents their children. Sane people are caught in Hozel's blood-lust, accepting the royal shilling to expose Chaos worshippers on the flimsiest of evidence. Eventually even intellectuals, scholars, students and lore masters fall prey to these pogroms, flayed, inch by inch, until they confess to their Chaotic 'crimes', begging for death.

Dorel

Separated from Pikarayd by the bleak, snow-swept peaks of the Dying Hills, Dorel is a vast, unwelcoming moor land, forsaken by the civilised lands. Even Melniboné had little time for Dorel. A few, ardent sorcerers made it their base due to its proximity to the writhing stuff of Chaos that marks the edge of the world, and a few Melnibonéans found beauty and poetry in its grey and petulant landscape. Their fortresses are ruined now, sacked by the barbarian tribes who live here, though they are a superstitious lot and fearful of what lies in the wrecked spires and the labyrinthine caves beneath.

Dorel has always bred wild and hardy folk. Lashed by rain and winds, themselves eddied by the brooding stuff of Chaos further to the south, where the world blurs and is unformed. Dorelite shamans have, in the past, called upon their spirit ancestors to help tame the lands, but their prayers and sacrifices have been in vain. As the world's demise nears, it seems that the turbulence of Chaos grows ever more restless, threatening to unleash half-formed shapes into the moor lands. The Dorelites are thus ever more fearful, ever more watchful and ever more distrusting.

There are countless barbarian tribes scattered across Dorel. They war with each other frequently and for the flimsiest of reasons. Life is hard in these lands and the many wars ensure that the toughest and most uncompromising survive. The weak are despised and treated as slaves or sacrifices to their gods: Lashaar the Air Empress and her consort King Grome Earth Father. Ancestor and hero-cults abound amongst the Dorelites (and becoming a hero is a simple matter of killing lots of enemies and dying bravely, there are no living heroes in Dorel), but Chaos is truly hated and feared. If the Dorelite tribes knew anything of the Lords of Law they might offer worship, but for them, Empress Lashar and Earth Father Grome suffice. If *they* cannot appease Chaos, what chances have any foreign gods?

The Dorel tribes are known for their chariots, drawn by the short, stocky, immensely strong moor land ponies. Favoured chariots are accorded similar worship to heroes with entire clans offering prayers to vehicle and Elemental Lords alike. Chariots and good ponies ensure victory in raiding – either other tribes or the small border settlements of Pikarayd and Argimiliar, where the huge herds of the cattle barons offer rich pickings. Filkhar and Lormyr are left alone. Both nations have led small armies against the tribesmen of western Dorel and the message is clear: raid and you will be destroyed.

All tribes are patriarchal and organised on clan and caste lines. Roughly woven tartans and woad tattoos define clan identity and tribe membership, and it is the goal of every young Dorelite warrior to be taken to the Breaking Stones of his tribe and there initiated into manhood. Women tend the ponies, forage for herbs and tend the hearth of the tented settlements. Men hunt for boar, marsh deer, terns and herds of wild cattle escaped from the ranches of Argimiliar; and, of course, to raid and fight wars. Once a man is too old to keep up with the raiding parties, or a woman too frail to keep up with the travelling clan, they are treated to the final rite of Cairn Sleep, whereby the wise-women prepare a sleeping draft from the roots of the silver gorse bush and the old and frail drink of it willingly, commending their souls to Grome Earth Father. Then, the sleeping bodies are laid in a shallow grave and a cairn of stones is built atop, marking the place of final rest.

Dorel is littered with these cairns and, often, half-buried in the heavy stones that have crushed them, the broken skeletons of awakened sleepers who tried to claw their way out.

Filkhar

Smaller than either Lormyr to the west or Argimiliar to the east, Filkhar is prosperous and booming, claiming a rivalry to Ilmiora (which it closely resembles culturally). The deep water port of Raschil is a thriving hub of trade on the southern continent, outstripping nearby Trepasaz and challenging Cadsandria. The rest of the Young Kingdoms, particularly the Island of Purple Towns, are awakening to Filkhar's markets and their merchants flock to Raschil's wide, welcoming streets.

Once a series of Lormyrian counties, Filkhar was united under Earl Rasch three hundred years ago at the height of the Lormyrian empire. Tired of Lormyr's administrative fickleness and the constant skirmishes with Argimiliar, the counties made a declaration of independence and ceded from Lormyrian control. It was not without struggle. Lormyr's knights fought many battles with Earl Rasch and his irregulars along the borders of Filkhar suffering defeat after humiliating defeat. Eventually Lormyr withdrew its opposition and Filkhar was born, Raschil, named for Filkhar's father, being its capital. Lormyr's dominance of the southern continent was over, and the slow decline still evident today began.

In the time of Elric, Filkhar and Lormyr enjoy a steady alliance. The same is not always true of its relationship with Argimiliar which, likewise, rebelled against Lormyr. Argimiliar had intended to absorb Filkhar into its own borders, not see a separate kingdom arise. It gazes still at the lush countryside of Filkhar with greedy, avaricious eyes, particularly the cattle barons of Andlermaign who have secret plans (it is said) for Filkhar's southern grasslands.

Filkhar is not densely populated with much of the populace living in Raschil and the ever-growing satellite towns radiating south from it. Moving south the land is a lush garden with rolling pastures, many lakes and deep, fine rivers, good soils and acres of free grazing. Consequently it boasts substantial wealth from vast herds of healthy livestock, excellent fishing and shellfish prospects, as well as vineyards and orchards across the country. Filkhar has a reputation for gourmet food and fine wines, and cookery is considered a fine art here. Chief amongst these and with a reputation as both lover and chef, is Konrad of Raschil, chef to Jerned, the gourmand King. Rumours of Konrad working his way through the women of the court are rife in Raschil and Konrad, ever the consummate performer, confirms (or denies) nothing. There has certainly been a spate of pregnancies in the capital but

Konrad, when challenged, merely claimed the quality of Raschil Bay's oysters as the probable reason.

Raschil is famed also for its storytellers, especially in the inns and taverns of the harbour district. Fiercely competitive performers, they strive to outdo each other with increasingly taller tales, more lurid descriptions and unreliable recounts of myth. Most celebrated is the drunkard Ranyart Finn, who seems to improve with the quantity of wine imbibed.

As a result of their wealth, many Filkharians are proud (and often vain) along with their riches. Fashion is a matter of extreme importance in almost all levels of Filkhar's society, with the King, Jerned, and his courtiers leading the way in deciding what stands as elegant couture each season. All tiers of Filkhar's population live well by the standards of other nations, and despite the kingdom's modest size the people count themselves as among the most urbane and civilised in the world. It is a land of courts and courtiers, with political intrigue and hedonistic excess all masked behind a façade of respectability.

Lormyr

Lormyr's story begins with Aubec. Five hundred years ago, Lormyr was a collection of many small kingdoms and Aubec was an Earl of Malador in the province of Klant. A hero of the Lormyrian kingdoms and an ardent Champion of Law, Aubec helped spread Lormyr's own rule across the south in the wake of Melniboné's retreat from the southern lands, uniting the disparate kingdoms into the single country that now exists.

Lormyr's key cities follow the mighty Zaphra-Trepek River which winds its way from the icy southern wastes of the country, eventually bifurcating into the Zaphra and Trepek rivers. The capital, Iosaz, is the seat of King Montan, a cautious, uneasy ruler who mourns Lormyr's lost glories and envies the ascendancy of neighbouring Filkhar. His emissary, the merchant prince Fadan, promises a new Golden Age for Lormyr, and convinces Montan to take part in the sacking of Imrryr, but when Fadan dies in that ill-fated expedition, so do Montan's dreams of a new, Lormyrian empire.

The worship of Law and its respective deities is the legal religion of Lormyr, though it has none of Vilmir's zealousness. The faith of Lormyr is not Law unrestrained, but Law as a necessary opposition to Chaos, which grows ever stronger in the world and this philosophy is partly to blame for King Montan's gloomy outlook. Montan's outlook

The Young Kingdoms

makes Lormyr's eventual betrayal that much bitterer, for, when the Pan Tangians make their war upon the world and Chaos threatens all existence, King Montan spinelessly allies with the theocrat, Jagreen Lern.

This defection is instrumental in the fall of the south and the ultimate defeat of Elric's alliance, which stuns the forces of Law, who have always recognised the nobility of Lormyr as chivalrous and honourable. Chivalry is a notion much-prized in Lormyr's upper classes, and has been for generations. Chivalry and honour were traditions established by Earl Aubec and the Knights of Malador still guard Lormyr from its enemies, occasionally venturing into the relics and ruins of the Bright Empire, in search of Earl Aubec's legendary sword (little realising that the weapon, which still exists, is now an heirloom of Melniboné, and has been wielded by Elric himself).

Waterborne trade is Lormyr's lifeblood. Barges and merchant vessels ply the Zaphra-Trepek between Alorasaz, the frozen, southern-most city, through Iosaz, Stegasaz, and thence to the major ports of Ramasaz (straddling the Zaphra estuary) and Trepasaz, hugging the Trepek delta. Similar vessels are found on the Schlan, a tributary of the Zaphra-Trepek, which eventually becomes thick with white-water rapids and waterfalls as it nears Stegasaz and cargoes must transfer to land before rejoining the Zaphra-Trepek, destined for the coastal cities.

Beyond the river, Lormyr is picturesque and cultured, with pleasant farmsteads, well-nurtured fields and pasturelands, vineyards, famed for their ice-wines, and wide, peaceful forests that turn a burnished gold in the autumn months.

Men of Schlan

Ruddy-featured and noted for their wide, curling moustaches (of which there is much pride and competition), the river-men of Schlan fish the deep, plentiful waters, act as navigators for barges and merchant cogs and as guides for land-bound caravans. The people of the Schlan River are lovers of news and gossip, sharing it with any pausing to listen. They favour heavily embroidered smocks of linen and thigh-length leather boots. In times past, they were staunch defenders of Lormyr, ready to lay-down their nets and lines and take up arms on behalf of their country.

King Montan's gloom is in stark contrast to the natural beauty of his realm; on the contrary, his people are happy and well-fed, content with everything Lormyr offers.

Alorasaz, the most southerly city, is a place of graceful towers, made from finely carved wood, and beautiful, welcoming timber houses and lodges. It is the up-river nexus for fur trappers, miners, timber merchants and craftsmen who work the lush pine forests of the steep hills overlooking the city. The streets are lit and heated by huge braziers, tended night and day by citizens employed to do nothing else but keep the home fires burning. The people of Alorasaz, like most Lormyrians, are open and welcoming. Honest folk in a frozen landscape.

The Empress of the Dawn

In the centre of this room was a bed, draped in ermine, with a canopy of white silk.
And on the bed lay a young woman.
Her hair was black and it shone. Her gown was of the deepest scarlet. Her limbs were like rose-tinted ivory and her face was very fair, the lips slightly parted as she breathed.
She was asleep.
Elric took two steps towards the woman on the bed and then he stopped suddenly. He was shuddering. He turned away. Moonglum was alarmed. He saw bright tears in Elric's crimson eyes.'
– The Vanishing Tower

Farther south than Alorasaz, standing almost at the edge of the world, is Castle Kaneloon, refuge of one of the greatest Champions of Law, Myshella, Empress of the Dawn. Perhaps immortal, Myshella occupied Kaneloon even when Earl Aubec was alive, and it was she who took him as a lover (as she has taken so many heroes over the centuries) directing him to carve-out new lands from the seething stuff of Chaos at the world's edge. More than anyone, save Elric, it is Myshella who holds absolute Chaos at bay.

Searching for Theleb K'aarna, Elric is brought to Kaneloon by Oonai summoned by Myshella, finding her placed in a sorcerous sleep of Theleb K'aarna's devising. Later, in Alorasaz, she comes to Elric as a vision, instructing him to help her against the Pan Tangian, who has allied himself with Prince Umbda and the Kelmain Host, a vicious army serving Chaos from a nearby plane and seeking domination of the entire southern continent. Riding Myshella's fabulously jewelled mechanical bird across the Boiling Sea, Elric travels to another of Myshella's strongholds, Ashaneloon, and confronts one of Theleb K'aarna's demons, slaying it and taking its heart – a precious nanorian stone – the only thing that can break the spell holding Myshella in slumber. Elric also returns with a cloth of gold bag containing a pinkish dust, a component in the hideous spell known as the Noose of Flesh, which Myshella uses to destroy Prince Umbda's army.

Castle Kaneloon, should Myshella wish it, can reflect the deepest desires of those who walk its halls. This is how the Empress of the Dawn seduced Aubec and how she has seduced countless other lovers and heroes. In the time of Elric of Melniboné Myshella's needs are frequent and it is entirely possible for itinerant adventurers to be summoned to Kaneloon to serve her needs.

Oin & Yu

Separated by the Ar River, but joined at the hip in the shared capital of Dhoz-Kam, Oin and Yu are considered one by a unity of barbarism and poverty. Prince Yyrkoon, Elric's cousin, fleeing the wrath of the Bright Emperor Elric, seeks refuge in Dhoz-Kam for a time, before claiming the Ruby Throne when Elric decides to wander the Young Kingdoms for a year.

Oin, the more civilised portion of the joint kingdom, is blanketed by an almost tropical rainforest, the result of the warm currents from the nearby Boiling Sea, and the locals claim the forests are plagued by demons and evil spirits. Those who have ventured into the jungles would confirm this and the dark depths echo with the howls, cries and moans of whatever creatures suffer within. Yu is arid and almost lifeless, bleached by hot winds from the Boiling Ocean that laps at its coasts, the soil baked dry in the summer and lashed into vast tracts of mud by the hot rains of the winter.

The primitive folk of Oin and Yu live in dirty, squat cities along the habitable portions of the coast with architecture only barely worthy of the name. The faith of these barbarians is mainly focused around nature spirits and the Elemental Rulers, particularly Kakatal and Straasha, whose eternal war, they believe, creates the Boiling Sea. Dhoz-Kam is the only city of note. With little hope of working the soil for sustenance, the only industry here is fishing from the great bay next to the city, and even this is more a means of survival than one of mercantile enterprise. Dhoz-Kam is flat-roofed and ugly, consisting of little more than shacks, huts and small buildings each no more than a single storey. The people

are destitute and the few visitors to the city are essentially nobility by local standards, though there is precious little to enjoy even with such relative wealth. The largest building, destined to be inhabited by the renegade Prince Yyrkoon, is a remnant of the Lormyrian empire, and stands a 'mighty' three-storeys high.

Pikarayd

Impoverished Pikarayd mirrors its eastern neighbour, Dorel, far more than enlightened Argimiliar in the west. With the exceptions of Ryfel and Chalal (both small and uncultured as southern cities go) the country is a harsh expanse of inhospitable marshes, moors, bogs and swamps, punctuated by rocky stretches of hills and snow-wracked forests. The people dwelling here are unfriendly to outsiders, but that is hardly surprising given that the clans of Pikarayd's wilderness also loathe each other, with battles occurring frequently, be they over new territory or grudges as ancient as the land itself. Although large towns do exist, claimed by the clans, they are small affairs dominated by unease and hatred with a casual attitude to violence and a disregard for life.

Leaders of these barbarian regions offer up hostages to the king of Pikarayd as assurances of goodwill, though they war among each other often enough, sometimes using mercenary armies and with hired generals from more cultured and educated lands. Pan Tang, in particular, has sent many mercenaries to Pikarayd, considering it an excellent training ground for its warriors. At one point Elric's closest friend and companion, Moonglum, is a commander in Pikarayd, working as a mercenary general for one petty clan-noble against another.

King Marvos rules Pikarayd now, from his sprawling, dark-stoned castle overlooking Chalal. His worship of Chaos is open and unsubtle, and he is known as Marvos the Bloodthirsty, with the title already finding its way into tomes of lore and history. He has openly courted the attention of sorcerers from Pan Tang, and their presence might account in some way for the growing cults of Chaos in Argimiliar.

The people still offer reverence to Grome and Straasha, though these traditionalist ways are being supplanted with new gods: Mabelode, Chardros and Xiombarg dominate in the tribal lands, their worship spreading and led by a figurehead called only the *Hierophant*. This mysterious figure claims as much power as the tyrant Marvos, and has amassed it through much less bloodshed.

Marvos and the Hierophant are not slain with most of the other Young Kingdoms rulers in Elric's treacherous assault on the Dreaming City. Instead, Marvos abstains from the conflict, and is usurped several years later by his son, the Balance-worshipping Kolthak. The new king institutes a rule of wisdom and prosperity, dragging his people from the dark age they endured under his father. Although a prophet rises to aid Pikarayd in its era of returning to the ways of Balance, all is for naught when Jagreen Lern's Chaos host sweeps the world bare of human life and the flame of hope in Pikarayd gutters and dies.

The Western Lands

Compared with the eastern and southern continents the western lands are insular realms lacking the general vibrancy of the Young Kingdoms. The blame for this lies with Pan Tang which controls the seas separating the west from the lucrative markets of eastern and southern continents. Pan Tangian privateers and pirates regularly attack the ships braving the Straits of the Chaos and northern reaches of the Oldest Ocean, seizing cargos for Hwamgaarl's stores and the crews for its slave pits. As a result the west is a muted place, fearful of Pan Tang's growing power and that of its vassal, Dharijor. It is only two centuries since most of the western lands finally rejected Melnibonéan dominance. Freedom and independence from the Dragon Lords is still a relatively new concept to the peoples of the west, and the Melnibonéans are regarded with particular loathing in most of the western lands.

Yet the western continent is not uncultured. Elric resides here for a while, mainly during his dalliance as a lover with Yishana of Jharkor. As with the other land masses, the western continent boasts its fair share of cultured nations with prosperous cities, and hostile, primitive realms, where inhuman beasts prowl the wild lands away from the lights and sounds of civilised men.

Dharijor

Dharijor is the most powerful of the kingdoms on the western continent, having exchanged one form of slavery for another. In casting off Melnibonéan oppression, Dharijor seemingly welcomed the iron-clad rule of Pan Tang. The kingdom is thoroughly subservient and allied to the priesthood of the City of Screaming Statues, rather than the sorcerers of the Dragon Isle. King Sarosto, a descendent of Atarn the City Builder, Dharijor's legendary founder, is the latest in a long line of monarchs relishing the patronage of Jagreen Lern and the sorcerer-priests of Pan Tang. Ruling from his heavily fortified palace in Lashmar Sarosto binds the scattered provinces together through his legions, enforcing his rule while being supported (and controlled) by the adherents to Chaos. The populace, having little option, follow Sarosto's lead. Sarosto's court is choked with Pan Tangian advisors who ensure that Jagreen Lern's will, no matter how opposed to true Dharijorian interests, is enforced.

In truth the people of Dharijor are not exactly unwilling victims of Pan Tang's ambitions. They were ever a bloodthirsty and warlike people, travelling from the populated coastal regions of their land in order to raid neighbouring realms for profit and amusement. Both Jharkor and Tarkesh are victims of Dharijor's expansionist ambitions, the former having ceded much territory to Dharijor's incursions. Sarosto's privateers continually raid the Tarkesh coast disrupting trade and feeding Sarosto's swollen coffers.

The warrior is greatly respected in Dharijor and the warrior cults of Chaos – Chardros, Mabelode and Xiombarg – dominate. Gladiatorial contests can be found in all the major cities and Gromoorva boasts the largest coliseum outside of Hwamgaarl. Thousands flock to the amphitheatres to watch the act of bloodletting, the best fighters being greatly admired by all who witness a skilled warrior slaying his foes.

Life is quieter beyond the cities, but tainted with avarice and suspicion. The land is not blessed with fertility, as it is in Jharkor and Tarkesh, and the small towns scratch by on poor quality crops. Sarosto's legions ensure the populace stays quiet and the priests of the Chaos cults harangue the masses regularly, declaiming Dharijor's glory and its destiny to rule the world (with Pan Tang, of course). People are kept in order by the occasional distribution of plunder from privateer raids, but the corrupt local rulers and nobles are allowed to treat the peasantry almost as slaves.

Despite their ferocity and renown for casual cruelty, the armies of Dharijor, are disorganized and corrupt. Whilst answering to King Sarosto local generals, who delight in the pomp and finery of their superior armour and weapons, are as corrupt as the land barons and petty nobles. Discipline is lax in the legions, but this will not prevent them from eventually marching alongside the hordes of Chaos at the end of the world, armoured in iron plate, darkened to black and intimidating even in its blandness.

Jharkor

Larger than Dharijor, enjoying a balmy climate and fine, wide countryside suited to all types of agriculture, Jharkor is the breadbasket of the west, governed soundly by the much respected (though young) king, Dharmit. A vast fleet answers the monarch's orders and a merchant fleet, even larger still, spreads the name and wealth of Jharkor across the seas of the Young Kingdoms, despite Pan Tang's and Dharijor's predations. In Elric's time Jharkor's power is rising to match that of Ilmiora and the Island of Purple Towns Yishana will take the throne in time, after Dharmit, her brother, is slain in the Sack of Imrryr. Until then, King Dharmit rules with a moderate hand and an unopposed authority over his people.

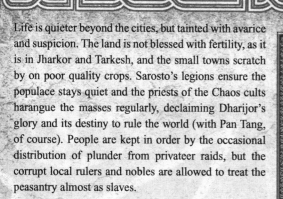

The intrigues that grip Dharmit's court tend to focus on Yishana and her notorious enjoyment of strong, young men, mischief, and the occasional dabbling with the proponents of Chaos. Yishana is neither young nor conventionally beautiful; but she is an arch manipulator and derives great satisfaction from having people – men especially – in her thrall whilst Dharmit administers the country. This is how she came to be involved with Theleb K'aarna, an emissary from Dharijor who becomes besotted with the princess and later utterly obsessed with her. Yishana, relishing the attention of a sorcerer, and ignoring the warning of her brother, develops the liaison with Theleb K'aarna and in so doing cultivates the jealousy that is eventually his undoing.

The capital, Dhakos, the City of Spires, boasts a colossal harbour the envy of many of the Young Kingdoms. This city is the beautiful and exotic capital of Jharkor, a place of countless graceful spires emulating those of Imrryr, tree-lined avenues, and the vast central market place that is always thronged with traders. Overlooking the city is the royal palace, where the monarch is guarded at all times by a legion of elite royal warriors, the *White Leopards*, clad in the skins of these rare creatures, native to the dense forests of the Western Marches, skirting Jharkor's most westerly border. Jharkor pays lip-service to the Lords of Law but in truth its people follow no single religion and are sometimes sceptical of the supposed fight between Law and Chaos. This scepticism is fundamentally challenged when Pan Tang and its Chaos hordes sweep in from Dharijor and Jharkor's golden-armoured soldiers are forced to march north to meet them in the decisive battle for the west.

Myyrrhn

Hidden far to the west of Jharkor, amongst the western mountains and beyond even the Vale of Xanyaw, is the kingdom of Myyrrhn. The Myyrrhn, also called the Winged Folk, are believed to be the descendents – created through magic – of the winged ape-beasts called Clakars. In the realm of Myyrrhn both races exist in miniscule numbers, rarely chancing upon each other, but inevitably shedding blood on the rare occasions they do meet.

Little formal society exists among the Winged Folk, who dwell in their mountaintop aeries and care nothing for the world outside of their ancestral lands. The only notable traditions of the Myyrrhn are their complicated and stunning aerial ceremonies for worshipping the Elemental Ruler Laasa (as she is known to the Myyrrhn) and their pictographic language – also called Myyrrhn – which decorates the walls of mountaintop caves.

Ostensibly near-human in appearance, the Myyrrhn differ by virtue of the great feathered wings extending from their shoulder blades. The race of Winged Folk is delicately-boned in order to aid their flight, and all are muscular and deep-chested. Modesty rarely concerns the Myyrrhn, who wear naught but loincloths when among their own kind. The small family-based communities of the Winged Folk survive in solitude by hunting small game and foraging in the mountain forests for nuts, mosses, fruits and berries. The females go through pregnancies of much shorter duration than human women, and do not, as some scholars have insisted, lay eggs.

The only real hostile creature in Myyrrhn is the race called Clakars, who still take savage joy in butchering their evolved cousins. An ancient ancestral enemy of the Winged Folk were a race of giant white owls, though these are now thought to be extinct since a great aerial war played out many centuries ago.

The Karasim

The green-skinned Karasim, hailing from the abyss of the same name, were, during Melniboné's early days, a threat to the Dragon Isle. Taking hostages from Myyrrhn the Karasim sundered the alliance with the Mernii and launched several vicious attacks from their sylph-powered flying longships. In one such raid they seized the prince of the Mernii, Silverskin. Casting the prince overboard, Silverskin was saved by the Winged Folk who took him to live in their lands for a time. Eventually escaping, with the aid of a rescue party led by his father, King Elrik, the Mernii destroyed many of the Karasim's longships and were pursued deep into The Silent Lands and the Melmane Marshes (now known as the Marshes of the Mist). The Karasim, if they still survive, have not been seen in the Young Kingdoms for a hundred centuries, but this is not to presume they do not wait beyond the edges of their abyss, plotting.

Shazar

Quiet Shazar dreams in Jharkor's shadow. It has few aspirations as a nation and is curiously unmoved by the incursions of Pan Tang and Dharijor into its northern neighbour. As the southernmost nation of the west Shazar is rarely troubled by the reavers of the north, and it takes care to trouble no one. It is a peaceful realm of plains and grassland often buried in the loose mists born from over the great Marshes of the Mist to the south. Along Shazar's

The Marshes of the Mist

South of Shazar these stinking, mist-shrouded bogs teem with life, all of it unpleasant. Swamp bears, marsh serpents and moaning, half-dead spirits number amongst the foul beings resident here, but the most terrifying is the creature known as Bellbane, the Mist Giant. Perhaps Bellbane is the last of its kind, a ghoul of the swamps, feeding on both souls and blood. Bellbane was understood to haunt regions much further to the west, but Elric and Shaarilla (a wingless woman of the Myyrrhn who befriends Elric in Aflitain), encounter the monster as they search for the Dead God's Book. Bellbane is ghoulish, but not unintelligent. It recognises, and fears, the list of names, ('Balaan! Marthrim! Aesma! Alastor! Saebos!... Haborym of the Fires Which Destroy!') sorcerers and minors dukes of Hell perhaps, Elric screams at it before engaging it in a duel to Bellbane's death.

What brings Bellbane to the Marshes can only be guessed at: is there some treasure or great prize hidden somewhere amongst the quicksands and bottomless reed-beds?

southern coast is a range of vicious crags called the Serpent's Teeth, which are difficult to navigate in the alarming coastal winds and responsible for shipwrecks of countless sailors, unable to cope with the treacherous waters.

Shazar is renowned for the quality of its horses, and the inland plains are home to great wild herds that have a mercurial temperament, but are the finest stock in the Young Kingdoms. Thoroughbreds from Shazar are prized throughout the world, and while most Shazarian folk tend to be skilled riders, the cavalry warriors of this kingdom are exceptional in battle. These bronze-armoured fighters, the Knights of Aflitain and Dioperda, are regarded as among the finest mounted warriors in the world, clever and well-disciplined. The Knights come to Jharkor's aid at the final battle for the west, and whilst that battle is fought in vain, Shazar's knights fight valiantly.

The Silent Lands

Past the Marshes of the Mist are The Silent Lands, where practically no human ever treads. If the legends are true, the hostile marsh was created specifically by Grome's earth magic in order to repel any conquest of the Silent Land by the armies of Melniboné. The truth may never be known, as the folk of the Silent Land have no interest in relaying the facts of the matter.

Ten thousand years ago The Silent Lands were home to the diminutive, but courageous, Pukwadji barbarians, venerators of Grome Earth King. They opposed the Mernii when their king refused to return the Black Blade guarded by Grome; in response they threatened to destroy the Mernii's ships which they relied upon for trade. The hero, White Crow, went in search of the fabled Actorios stone in a bid to make the king relent and return the Black Blade to Lord Grome. His success earned the Pukwadji's trust and sealed the pact with Lord of the Earth that Elric, a hundred centuries later, still invokes from time to time.

The realm itself is comprised mainly of black mountains that remain forever under dark skies that emit no storms but always seem moments from thunderous rainfall. It is within these black mountains that the last remnants of the Doomed Folk dwell, crawling around in the utter blackness and hating all those who walk the world in this current, hated cycle. Like the despised kingdom of Org these refugees from the previous cycle of time are rumoured to be half-dead cannibals with foul rites and even fouler gods.

Tarkesh

Most northerly of the Young Kingdoms, Tarkesh is a divided land. The fierce northerners are longship-sailing, axe-bearing raiders, living off stunted crop yields, poor soil and hunting in their mountainous homeland. They regard the southern city-dwellers of Banarva, and rural farmers of the hinterland, as soft and weak, engaged in too close a relationship with sick Dharijor. The cultured people of the south regard the northerners as ignorant barbarians, fur-clad reavers with little learning or culture beyond the lurid decorations that cover their boats.

Despite the divide, both northerners and southerners worship the elemental rulers above all other faiths, particularly Pozz-Mann-Llyrr, their god of the sea (and either a kinsman of Straasha, or a guise Straasha assumes for his dealings with the folk of Tarkesh). They have little love for Law, but reserve their true hatred for the Chaotic Lord of the Depths, Pyaray, Tentacled Whisperer of Impossible Secrets, who feasts upon the souls of drowned sailors.

If one thing could unite Tarkesh, then it is their quality, craftsmanship, and skill with boats. Both north and south acknowledge each other's talent for creating fine vessels from the dense, pure woodlands that blanket the country. Whether longship raider or coastal bireme, merchant cog or masted clipper, Tarkeshite ships are highly prized by the sailors of the Young Kingdoms and many are wary of trusting their lives to any other kind of vessel.

Young King Yaris is the last ruler to preside over the bitter north-south rivalry, which he tolerates because he has no inkling of how it could, or if it even should, be settled. It is in his reign as monarch that civil war erupts between the north and the south, with skirmishes and outright battles breaking out along the ill-defined borders. Before the world's end, however, Tarkesh is fated for a short peace. King Yaris dies with so many other Young Kingdoms rulers in the Sack of Imrryr, and his cousin Hilran takes the throne. When Chaos sweeps over the world, Tarkesh is a unified nation, and is ultimately destroyed in this unity by Jagreen Lern.

The Chasm of Nihrain

Older than even Melniboné and once its allies, the chasm-city of Nihrain is unknown to most mortals and forgotten by even the Dragon Isle. Built within a fissure that splits the earth of the western mountains, this strange city-kingdom is home to the black-skinned immortals under the command of

Sepiriz, a being who will one day ally again with Melniboné when Elric comes seeking answers in the final days of the world. Sepiriz and the Nihrain are avowed servants of the Cosmic Balance, and they rest in a stasis within a volcano not far from the chasm-city they call home, awaiting the doom of the Young Kingdoms, and anticipating the next cycle of Time.

The city of Nihrain is built within the vast caverns of the chasm, a realm of carved statues, twisting spires, spiral staircases and homes made from immense rock formations. Here the almost-human servants of the Nihrain tend to their masters and their unique steeds, which exist in at least two dimensions simultaneously. The steeds of Nihrain are tireless beasts that do not heed the laws of the Young Kingdoms, capable of galloping across earth and sea at great speeds.

R'lin K'ren A'a

Not a part of the western continent as such, but located in unexplored lands in the south west of the Young Kingdoms, R'lin K'ren A'a is a city that occupies the steaming jungles and could be the ancestral city of the Mernii predating their migration to the Dragon Isle. In Elric's time R'lin K'ren A'a is nothing but a legend, even amongst Melnibonéans, and Elric doubts its existence – until Duke Avan Astran shows the albino a map claiming its whereabouts and enlists his help in finding the place.

R'lin K'ren A'a received its name after the lords of the Higher worlds chose it as a place to meet and discuss the rules of the cosmic struggle that have shaped their actions ever since. Their arrival signalled the exodus of the Mernii, save for one, who remained behind to spy on their conference. He was discovered and doomed to eternal life, carrying the terrible knowledge of their meeting forever more. The city's inhabitants, these legends say, crossed the sea to Sorcerers' Isle and then further north, to an island inhabited by dragons: Melniboné.

Avan Astran is drawn to seek R'lin K'ren A'a for more practical reasons than ancient history. The tale recounts how the inhabitants left behind a colossal statue of Arioch, carved from jade, with huge gems for eyes. Astran seeks this treasure, which he believes can reveal the secrets of the higher beings. R'lin K'ren A'a proves to be a reality, as does the statue, but it also proves to be Astran's downfall.

The city is reached by a winding river penetrating deep into the lush, insect-swarmed jungle. It is protected by the olab, reptilian beings with feathered crests and neck wattles but essentially human faces. They move on stork-like legs, towering above the jungle waters, and assail strangers with great clubs which are used to hurl razor-sharp crystalline discs. Beyond them, R'lin K'ren A'a still stands, its walls and buildings broken as though brought down by an earthquake. The place is untouched by weeds or other trappings of the forest, and there, at the city's heart, and the only thing still standing, is the jade statue Astran seeks.

Still living amongst the ruined buildings and ghosts of the Mernii, J'osui C'rein Reyr, the creature doomed to live, is flesh and blood. The knowledge he holds has driven him beyond madness and despair. He wants rid of the curse, which may only be removed by Arioch, and only if the jade statue is animated and recovers its eyes so that it may see to leave the city. Elric summons the duke of Hell, and is forced into taking Astran's life in the process. Arioch heeds the summons but warns Elric that in obeying his command, a course of events the albino may not desire will be set in motion.

There, in the ruins of an ancient, forgotten city, surrounded by death and one who could not die, Elric determines the doom of the Young Kingdoms.

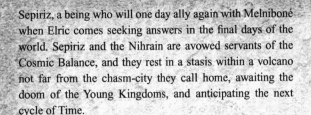

The Islands of the Young Kingdoms

Four principal islands are detailed in the Elric saga: Melniboné, the Isle of Purple Towns, Pan Tang and Sorcerers' Isle. With the exception of Sorcerers' Isle, all are major powers. Melniboné's place in the scheme of the Young Kingdoms is now established, and at the time of the Young Kingdoms the Isle of the Purple Towns is one of the foremost nations, a land of merchant princes and explorers, such as Smiorgan Baldhead. Pan Tang broods in the northern seas, plotting and pillaging, building its reserves of magic and chaotic allegiance, ready to assume an empire of its own – mightier than Melniboné – and institute a reign of Chaos upon the Earth.

A fifth, smaller island is also mentioned: Ashaneloon, one of Myshella's fortresses, hidden in the Boiling Sea.

Ashaneloon

Ashaneloon is the name of the palace situated there, rather than the island itself, but the distinction is moot: Ashaneloon appears on no maps or charts of the Young Kingdoms and

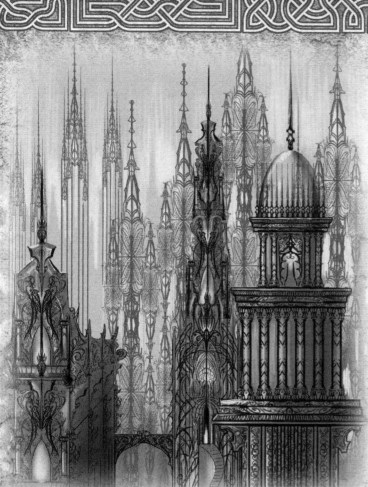

Melniboné: the Dragon Isle

Dreadful, dreaming and doomed, Melniboné is the centre of the Bright Empire, home to dragons and the strange, amoral descendents of a Balance-worshipping race that settled legendary R'lin K'ren A'a more than 10,000 years ago. When the lords of the higher worlds demanded R'lin K'ren A'a as their meeting place, its people fled; first to Sorcerers' Isle and then to the group of four islands they occupy today. Along the way they developed a pact with Arioch and so began their inexorable climb to cruel greatness: they became Melnibonéans.

Dragons occupied the island long before it became Melniboné. The Phoorn had built a great city of rock and ash before and had lived there for thousands of years before the Mernii arrived. The Mernii learned to communicate with the Phoorn and eventually developed bonds of kinship, sharing their city before establishing their own. Later, as Chaos-aligned Melniboné, the dragons would help forge the Bright Empire, seemingly oblivious or carefree of the changing religious affiliations of their kinsmen.

it is a place of importance to only one person: Myshella, Empress of the Dawn.

Myshella divides her time between Kaneloon in southern Lormyr, and Ashaneloon, a small island hidden in the Boiling Sea. It is here that Elric is sent to fetch the component for the Noose of Flesh. Here, too, he encounters a guardian demon of Theleb K'aarna's devising which has at its heart a Nanorian stone.

The island is small and rocky – easily overlooked, for nothing sails in the Boiling Sea. The palace of Ashaneloon is described as being of slender towers, turrets and domes. The eastern tower holds what Elric looks for – perhaps it holds other Lawful charms too – but he does not have the chance to explore the palace thoroughly. It may be that Ashaneloon and Kaneloon are identical – twin buildings in separate locations. It could also be that they are very different and hold different wonders reflecting Myshella's moods and whims. Does Ashaneloon have its walls draped in the standards and colours of her dead lovers?

Chaos came to the Mernii in the shape of Lord Arioch who, having been inadvertently invited to this realm by Prince Silverskin, seduced the Mernii with promises and visions of power. The Mernii divided: the Melnibonéans chose Chaos and the Menastrai chose the Balance. The Menastrai retreated to A'sha'hiian, the first city of the Mernii, while the Chaos-worshipper built a new city, Imrryr, which eclipsed all other cities in beauty and grace. War followed, known in Melnibonéan legend as *The Chaos Wars*, and A'sha'hiian was bombarded with demon magic and dragon flame. The Menastrai, fled, leaving the entire island to Imrryr and Chaos. The ruins of A'sha'hiian still stand at the southern tip of the main island, overrun with weeds and barely visible; but there is still no denying its beauty and grace. Before making its pacts with Chaos, the people of Melniboné were a calm, detached race not given to acts of casual violence and disdainful cruelty. A'sha'hiian symbolises the ruination of Chaos; what might have the people of Melniboné become if they had continued along the original path of the Mernii?

The smaller islands have been abandoned by the Melnibonéans, although deserted castles of wondrous, impossible architecture still stand, and in Elric's time the empire is centred on the main island and Imrryr, the Dreaming City. It is the main island that bears the name of Melniboné and it is formed of a range of steep, wooded hills along its spine, separating Imrryr from the vast Meadows of Lassitude and the Intangible Forest that covers the eastern stretches of the island. To the north, the Isolated Fells hold the Lake of the Moon, a lake of liquid silver amidst the gorse and rocky outcrops. Melniboné's coastline is ragged and treacherous, with wild currents and buried reefs. Only one safe landing place is available; the deep bay where Imrryr stands. It is almost impossible for boats to harbour safely along any of the other coasts, making invasion almost impossible. If any warship could anchor safely, its troops would find their progress across country eventually halted by the steep, sharp hills that divide the island and protect Imrryr. As a result, none have tried.

Imrryr is a huge accretion of spires, towers, domes, minarets and weirdly carved battlements. It is built from a cascade of colours, some sorcerously achieved, and it rises, glittering, above the huge harbour maze that protects the city from unwanted guests. Imrryr was not always known by this name. When the people first arrived it was called H'hui'shan and was a simple staging post that rose to grandeur. It was destroyed in The Chaos Wars and the Menastrai who built it retreated to A'sha'hiian. The city was raised again by a mixture of slave labour and sorcery and renamed Imrryr. The harbour maze was built at the same time, and only specially trained pilots know the safest routes through it, and into the harbour itself.

Imrryr is indeed a wonder. The most beautiful city of the Young Kingdoms and the cruellest, it is decadent and amoral, like its inhabitants. The broad avenues and jade towers mask terrible activities and depravities, for the people of Imrryr seek the most extreme and dangerous of pleasures. Drugged slaves, some human, others almost-human and most altered in slight mystical ways, form the overwhelming majority of Imrryr's population. With their obedience enforced by endless drugging and sorcerous compulsion, the nobles of the Dreaming City are free to live their race's last days in the blind ignorance of the truly decadent. The Melnibonéans themselves spend most of their time in gentle drugged hazes or at court, dancing to the songs of tortured chorus-slaves or scheming to advance their own status before the eyes of their peers.

Despite its beauty and secrets people still flock to Imrryr. Its markets in the Foreigners' Quarter are the greatest in the Young Kingdoms, filled with riches from across the Young Kingdoms and beyond. Melnibonéans rarely tread this quarter's streets, instead sending slaves to conduct commerce on their behalf. Most who visit Imrryr will never

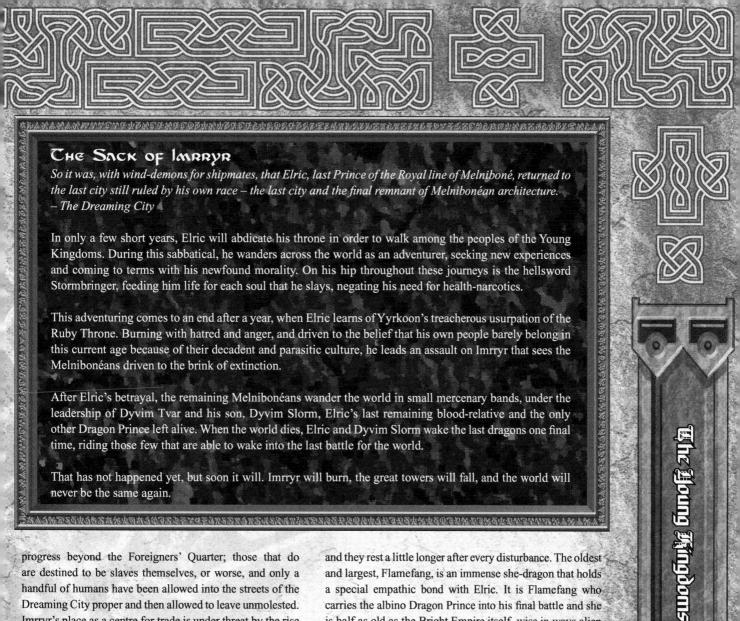

The Sack of Imrryr

So it was, with wind-demons for shipmates, that Elric, last Prince of the Royal line of Melniboné, returned to the last city still ruled by his own race – the last city and the final remnant of Melnibonéan architecture.
– The Dreaming City

In only a few short years, Elric will abdicate his throne in order to walk among the peoples of the Young Kingdoms. During this sabbatical, he wanders across the world as an adventurer, seeking new experiences and coming to terms with his newfound morality. On his hip throughout these journeys is the hellsword Stormbringer, feeding him life for each soul that he slays, negating his need for health-narcotics.

This adventuring comes to an end after a year, when Elric learns of Yyrkoon's treacherous usurpation of the Ruby Throne. Burning with hatred and anger, and driven to the belief that his own people barely belong in this current age because of their decadent and parasitic culture, he leads an assault on Imrryr that sees the Melnibonéans driven to the brink of extinction.

After Elric's betrayal, the remaining Melnibonéans wander the world in small mercenary bands, under the leadership of Dyvim Tvar and his son, Dyvim Slorm, Elric's last remaining blood-relative and the only other Dragon Prince left alive. When the world dies, Elric and Dyvim Slorm wake the last dragons one final time, riding those few that are able to wake into the last battle for the world.

That has not happened yet, but soon it will. Imrryr will burn, the great towers will fall, and the world will never be the same again.

progress beyond the Foreigners' Quarter; those that do are destined to be slaves themselves, or worse, and only a handful of humans have been allowed into the streets of the Dreaming City proper and then allowed to leave unmolested. Imrryr's place as a centre for trade is under threat by the rise of the Isle of the Purple Towns and the markets of Dhakos and Raschil. Merchants have tired of the illogical, resented fact that Melnibonéans must guide each and every vessel that seeks to trade through the sea maze. The Melnibonéans are oblivious to this decline, but one, Emperor Elric, 428th Bright Emperor, is sensitive to what threatens Melniboné. His strategy is to gain greater understanding of the Young Kingdoms, and perhaps relax Imrryr's dealings with humans. The strategy is not popular. Elric's cousin, Prince Yyrkoon, rejects such notions and would see Melniboné assert itself once again with dragons and battlebarges.

Beneath Melniboné, accessible only by those accorded the rank of Dragon Prince, are the dragon caves. These vast subterranean lairs are where Melniboné's wyrms slumber, dreaming of things unknowable by mortals. The dragons symbolise Melniboné's power and their sleep reflects the empire's decline. It takes great effort to rouse the dragons

and they rest a little longer after every disturbance. The oldest and largest, Flamefang, is an immense she-dragon that holds a special empathic bond with Elric. It is Flamefang who carries the albino Dragon Prince into his final battle and she is half as old as the Bright Empire itself, wise in ways alien to mortals, but curiously understandable to Elric.

Just as the dragons slumber, so do most Melnibonéans. Dream couches hold sleeping forms, helping their occupants to project their consciousness across the Million Spheres in search of new challenges and pleasures. The dream couches were devised as a tool to train each Bright Emperor, enabling the dreamer to experience many lifetimes in the space of a few nights' sleep. In this way the emperors of Melniboné gained the knowledge and experience for both sorcerous training and the skills necessary to administer, single-handedly, an empire spanning the known world. Now, in these final years of the Bright Empire, the dream couches are used solely for pleasure, their effects enhanced by the powerful narcotics the residents of Imrryr prefer. Not all succumb to the lure of the dream couches, but the damage is done. Imrryr is impotent and on the verge of extinction. Its time has passed, fading into half-memory like a dawn-chased dream.

Isle of Purple Towns

Named for the colour of its buildings, made from a purple stone found only on the island, the Isle of Purple Towns is more notable for what the Melnibonéans regard as its 'impudence'. It has dared to expand and grow into the secondary (and soon, primary) trade hub of the Young Kingdoms, eclipsing Melniboné due to its industrious sailors, wise merchants, ideal location and its money-hungry, ambitious and smart leaders. Traders from the Purple Towns spread throughout the Young Kingdoms, acting as brokers and aides when not delivering their own sea-borne cargoes and raising themselves up as merchant-princes. The ports of the other Young Kingdoms bustle with Purple Town vessels and sailors, and trade routes are established to and from all nations, with old agreements honoured and expanded, and new fortunes made on fresh promises and profits.

The powerful nobles and newly-risen merchant-princes of the Purple Towns are a separate lot, comprising traditionalist feudal lords with slipping fortunes and new money merchants with immense caches of coin invested and stored as they see fit. Menii is the port capital of the island; a trade hub that rivals, and will soon dwarf, that of Imrryr. Kariss is a northern city preferred by the traditional nobility, leaving them largely ignored by most of the island.

Once, the religion of the island was based around the elemental rulers Straasha and Lassa. Now however, as trade booms, a golden pyramid-temple of Law has arisen in Menii, and the people are content with their new faith.

Count Smiorgan Baldhead, destined to be a companion (and eventually betrayed) by Elric, is a noble-born ruler who has made a vast fortune by working alongside and among the new merchant caste. When he is killed in the Sack of Imrryr, the Isle of the Purple Towns suffers a brief destabilisation, even going to war with Lormyr, a nation that has long held a grudge against the ascending nation while it itself dwindles.

The last battle of the Isle of the Purple Towns fleet occurs during the doom of the world. Abandoned by most of their allies and without a hope of victory, the Purple Towners sail against the Theocrat of Pan Tang's fleet, facing death with bravery and honour rather than await it on their island.

Pan Tang

A thousand years ago, a race of humans called the Mabden came to this plane of existence for reasons they never shared with others. They made their home on the barren, inhospitable island in the centre of the Pale Sea and named it Pan Tang. The Mabden are a tenacious people, passionate, creative, and bearers of grudges. Perhaps this is why they turned to Chaos. As Melniboné began its inexorable decline as an empire, the Mabden saw the possibilities of Chaos and how the Melnibonéans had let their control of it slip. They would raise their own empire, this time in concert with the Lords of Chaos and not in defiance of them. New pacts were made, temples built and sacrifices offered. Over the steady course of the millennium Pan Tang honed its skills as practitioners of magic, unearthing knowledge carefully hidden by Melniboné, refining their dark arts.

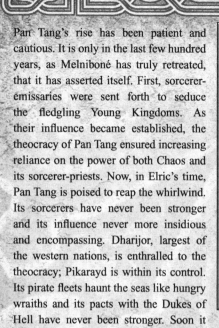

Pan Tang's rise has been patient and cautious. It is only in the last few hundred years, as Melniboné has truly retreated, that it has asserted itself. First, sorcerer-emissaries were sent forth to seduce the fledgling Young Kingdoms. As their influence became established, the theocracy of Pan Tang ensured increasing reliance on the power of both Chaos and its sorcerer-priests. Now, in Elric's time, Pan Tang is poised to reap the whirlwind. Its sorcerers have never been stronger and its influence never more insidious and encompassing. Dharijor, largest of the western nations, is enthralled to the theocracy; Pikarayd is within its control. Its pirate fleets haunt the seas like hungry wraiths and its pacts with the Dukes of Hell have never been stronger. Soon it will initiate war against the Young Kingdoms in a bid for their complete conquest, the Pan Tangian armies swollen with hell-spawned troops.

Pan Tang has but a single city: Hwamgaarl, city of screaming statues, so named because its enemies and dissidents are transformed into the huge, shrieking sculptures lining the city walls, their soul-wracking cries of pain and insanity echoing across the isle. Hwamgaarl's streets are disordered and maze-like, with buildings leaning inwards at impossible angles, creating deep pools of shadow that even the brightest sunlight cannot dispel. The harbour is thronged with ships, but these are not the trading vessels of Raschil, Menii and Dhakos; these are pirate boats, slavers and war-galleys. Cargo is not traded but stolen, and captured vessels are stripped of their trappings and daubed in the colours of Pan Tang: deep green and black, emblazoned with the merman crest of the theocracy.

Dominating it all, overlooking the harbour, is the imposing and menacing palace of the theocrat. The current incumbent of that exalted position is Jagreen Lern, a cruel and depraved individual, utterly insane, and bent on taking his island to conquest. He would seek to emulate Melniboné's cruelty and decadence but he lacks the aesthetic sensibilities marking Melnibonéans from humans. He is a parody of Melniboné's emperors; thin-faced, dark-eyed, but bearing the swarthiness of his Mabden ancestors. His crest is the merman, scores of which inhabit the deep waters surrounding the island, and he flies this device from every flag of every vessel under Pan Tangian control.

Tigers & Devil Lizards

Pan Tang's elite troops are the Tyger Guard. They fight side-by-side with trained smilodon, captured from the Weeping Waste or bred in captivity. Guard and sabre-tooth share an empathic bond and fight as one. The warriors of the Tyger Guard are as ferocious as their pets, and before any battle the animals are starved to ensure maximum aggression.

The cavalry of Pan Tang does not ride horses. Instead they ride huge, six-limbed reptilian beasts of appalling viciousness, bred by sorcery. Their riders carry long, curve-bladed sabres, ideal for slashing and beheading, and they ride into the fray surrounded by prowling tigers, and their grim-faced handlers, intent on the carnage to follow.

The church of Chaos rules all in Pan Tang. Its priests are warriors and sorcerers, all devotees of one or more Lords of Chaos. The patron demon is Chardros the Reaper, grim lord of chaotic death. Others are worshipped: Maluk the stitch-lipped; Hiornhurn the executioner; Pyaray the tentacled whisperer, admiral of the Chaos fleet; Xiombarg the faceless, Queen of the Swords. Temples to these twisted deities abound throughout Hwamgaarl, the chants, shouts and screams of priests, worshippers and victims echoing around the rough-hewn granite walls. The elementals are given lip-service, but true worship is reserved for the Lords of Chaos, and the warrior-priests of Pan Tang are masters of their secrets.

Pan Tang is feared and loathed, not respected, by the other Young Kingdoms. When the armies of Jagreen Lern rise up to claim the world for Chaos, all who still live will see the influence of the Pan Tangians firsthand. These are the people who doom the world, twisting it with their hatred and their sorcery. They follow Chaos for the power it offers through evil, rather than the natural aspects that serve the Balance. The Chaos Gods, slavering for a chance to claim this world, are eager patrons for the theocrat's armies, and keen generals serving at his side.

Sorcerers' Isle

Magic winds had caught the Filkharian trader as she crossed the unnamed water between the Vilmirian peninsula and the Isle of Melniboné She had been borne into the Dragon Sea and thence to The Sorcerer's Isle, so called because that barren place had once been the home of Cran Liret,

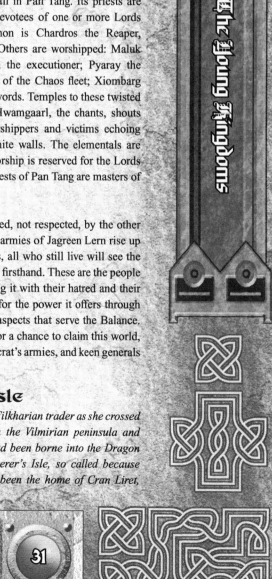

The Rise & Demise of the Spell Thief

The semi-immortal Cran Liret rose to prominence under the rule of Emperor Yrysool IX, known also as the Shining Emperor. Always an exceptional scholar of sorcery, Cran Liret's talents were recognised and indulged early-on by Yrysool, and Cran Liret rose quickly to become the chief architect of the Shining Emperor's plans for the Bright Empire.

A dutiful student of Chaos, and devout disciple of Slortar the Old, Cran Liret's abiding interest was in the nature of the Multiverse itself and his studies led him to discover the fabric of the Million Spheres, perfecting several ways of traversing the Moonbeam Roads. In order to develop his discoveries, Cran Liret retired to Sorcerers' Isle – long a home to scholars of Chaos, but derelict for centuries, and there began the construction of his Chaos Engines. Yrysool, his emperor and patron, visited often, bringing with him those he wanted punished. Cran Liret built two machines, *Forge and Sculptor* solely to please Yrysool. Forge was designed to rend souls from their bodies; and Sculptor to redesign them into new shapes. The Shining Emperor was so pleased with these new means of torture that he granted Cran Liret free rein in his experiments.

Through his discoveries of the secrets of the Multiverse, Cran Liret learned how to steal spells. He stole from many of his contemporaries and this angered the sorcerers of Melniboné, who had an unspoken pledge not to plunder each other's secrets. Yrysool turned a blind eye to Cran Liret's thievery, but his enemies decided to bide their time. When Yrysool was eventually assassinated by his half-brother, Saber, and the Ruby Throne passed into Saber's hands, Cran Liret was immediately declared an enemy of Melniboné and sentenced to death. Even Duke Arioch endorsed the sorcerer's fate, so angered was he to learn that Cran Liret considered himself the equal of the nobles of Chaos.

Saber sent four battlebarges and awoke five dragons to destroy Cran Liret. The Spell Thief, for once unprepared, was taken by surprise and his home on Sorcerers' Isle was quickly reduced to its current rubble by the venom of the Phoorn dragons that made the attack. The battlebarges and their warriors made an assault on the island, destroying Cran Liret's followers (of which he had many), but found the Spell Thief's shattered body collapsed beside Forge. Dyvim Vlass, commander of the assault force, was prepared to wreck these machines, but Emperor Saber stayed his hand, believing the machines would prove useful at some time in the future. But Cran Liret protected his inventions too well, and their secrets of operation could not be unlocked. Forge and Sculptor remained inert and were, in time, forgotten. Forgotten too was Cran Liret's soul, still locked in Forge. The Spell Thief knew that, if taken alive, his torture would be beyond compare. Fooling Melniboné into believing he was dead was the only course of action open to him.

So, trapped in one of his own infernal machines, Cran Liret craves a suitable host for his huge, hideous intellect. The krettii are simply unworthy; their brains are not developed enough to accommodate the weight of his knowledge and power. A few souls over the centuries have been tested and have failed. But Cran Liret is patient, his conscience still active, and it sends forth messages, carried as dreams, to lure the perfect, unwitting body, to Sorcerers' Isle.

the Thief of Spells, a wizard infamous for his borrowings, who had, at length, been dispatched by those he sought to rival. But much residual magic had been left behind. Certain spells had come into the keeping of the krettii, a tribe of near-brutes who had migrated to the island from the region of The Silent Land less than fifty years before.'
– Elric at the End of Time

Sorcerers' Isle looms from the dense mists surrounding it. A spiky, almost bare crown of land surrounded by jagged cliffs of granite appearing through the grey smudge clinging to the sea. The water is strangely calm around the isle – as though entranced into a slumber.

This misty, mysterious island lies south east of the Shazarian coast and due west of Melniboné. For millennia it was the haunt of powerful magicians, hence its name, and legend has it that the hellswords Stormbringer and Mournblade were forged there by the Doomed Folk. Sorcerers' Isle was also the first port of call for Elric's ancestors when they fled R'lin K'ren A'a, before they reached the isle now called Melniboné. How long they remained is unknown, but clearly Sorcerers' Isle remained on their charts, because Melniboné's sorcerers used it many times over the course of the Bright Empire's reign.

Its last resident was Cran Liret, the Spell Thief, although the fortress he occupied was destroyed by Melniboné many years ago. Cran Liret stole one spell too many from his Dragon Lord comrades, and they took their revenge with dragon venom and battlebarge, razing his castle and putting his foul practices to an end.

Sorcerers' Isle is still occupied. The krettii, a race of stunted, bestial creatures, migrated here from the swamps of Shazaar several centuries ago and made Sorcerers' Isle their home. The krettii have changed little in their habits or appearance. Their intellect is still limited, and their skills confined to subsistence farming, hunting and, when times are hard, cannibalism.

Yet they are not alone. Cran Liret's Chaos Engines – the devices he used to steal spells – still exist within the island. And so too do his ultimate creations, the Spells That Live, still wandering aimlessly. The krettii fear these remnants but worship their power as others worship the Lords of Law and Chaos.

The Unknown East

Far to the east of the Sighing Desert and the Weeping Waste, hidden by the mountain range known to the barbarians as The Ragged Pillars, are the unmapped kingdoms of the Unknown East. Elric travels there, aiding the Countess Guyë of Anakhazan to defeat the Haghan'iin Host, before riding through the lands of the Valederian Directorates, across the Teeth of Shenkh, and to Eshmir, home of his comrade, Moonglum. Several nations of the Unknown East are mentioned in the saga, but none described in any detail: Nishvalni-Oss; Bas'lk; Maidahk; Phum, home of warrior-priests, of which Rackhir the Red Archer was once a member; and Okara and Changshai.

Only Eshmir is given much in the way of description, and its capital city, Elwher, is said to be a place where men worship the stars and have no faith in the powers of Law and Chaos. The Flamebringer, Terarn Gashtek, originates from Okara. His tame sorcerer, Drinij Bara, commands a form of sorcery even Elric is unfamiliar with, his soul hidden in the body a small, dark cat.

But adventurers from the Unknown East find their way into the Young Kingdoms, as demonstrated by Moonglum and Rackhir. Duke Avan Astran has travelled there, so, although these lands are beyond the scope of this book, *Elric of Melniboné* adventurers can originate from these unknown kingdoms.

The Young Kingdoms

CHARACTER CREATION

Adventurers are the players' gateway to participating in the Elric saga, acting as their alter-egos in the Young Kingdoms. Following the information on the world, this chapter focuses on its people and how players create *Elric of Melniboné* adventurers.

Characteristics

All adventurers and most creatures have seven Characteristics.

Strength (STR): A character's brute force, Strength affects the amount of damage he deals, what weapons he can wield effectively, how much he can lift and so on.

Constitution (CON): A measure of the adventurer's health, Constitution affects how much damage he can sustain in combat, as well as his general resistance to disease and other illnesses.

Dexterity (DEX): A character's agility, co-ordination and speed, Dexterity aids him in many physical actions, including combat.

Size (SIZ): This is an indication of the adventurer's mass and, like Strength and Constitution, can affect the amount of damage a character can deal and how well he can absorb damage. Unlike most other Characteristics, a high score in Size is not always an advantage. While a large adventurer can take more damage, a small adventurer will have a much easier time when sneaking around in the shadows.

Intelligence (INT): An adventurer's ability to think around problems, analyse information and memorise instructions. It is a very useful Characteristic for adventurers interested in becoming accomplished scholars or sorcerers.

Power (POW): Perhaps the most abstract Characteristic, Power is a measure of the adventurer's life force – *his soul* – and his personal force of will. POW is an essential component of most sorcery skills and is used in determining the adventurer's available Magic Points.

Charisma (CHA): This quantifies both an adventurer's attractiveness and leadership qualities. It is also a measure of the adventurer's strength of personality and force of character. Some creatures do not have a CHA Characteristic listed in their description because it is simply inapplicable in human terms.

Determining Characteristics

Players will need a number of six-sided dice to generate their adventurers' Characteristics. To generate the values for STR, CON, DEX, POW and CHA, roll 4D6, drop the lowest die and total the remaining dice, generating a number between 3 and 18. INT and SIZ are given a higher base number reflecting the reasoning and mental capacity of humans. For these two Characteristics, roll 2D6 and total the dice. Add 6 to the result.

The Games Master may also allow players to assign their rolls to specific Characteristics, so that a player who wants to play a burly warrior can swap a rolled 15 from CHA to STR, for example. Players should not be allowed to move rolls from INT or SIZ to any of the other five Characteristics.

Adventurer Race

Whilst the vast majority of adventurers will be human, there are three other racial types permissible, with Games Master approval, as adventurers: half Melnibonéan, Melnibonéan and Myyrrhn. Each race is outlined below along with the differences in determining Characteristics.

Half-Melnibonéan

Despite being disdainful of humans, Melnibonéans frequently breed with them – either slaves or those they find intriguing and/or useful in some way. The offspring, half-Melnibonéans, combine the physical and mental superiority of their Melnibonéan parent with the softer,

worldlier emotions of their human side. Half-Melnibonéans exhibit most Melnibonéan physical attributes; tall, elfin-faced and with narrow, slanted eyes tapering towards the skull, but are heavier of frame and darker in complexion. As half-breeds they can never be treated as true-blooded Melnibonéans, and many remain as slaves, but those who are cunning, clever and ambitious can achieve a certain position in Melnibonéan society, often being used as emissaries to the Young Kingdoms – a task deemed too lowly for someone of pure Imrryric blood. After the sacking of the Dreaming City, many

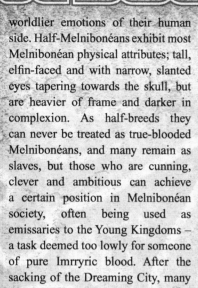

Playing a Melnibonéan

* Treat most humans as slaves, potential slaves or, at best, uncultured simpletons.
* Adopt a sneer in the voice and a condescending manner.
* Use archaic language including lots of 'thees' and 'thous'.
* Never admit to mistakes. Melnibonéans are incapable of making them.
* Survey everywhere as though you own it. After all, you probably *did*, once.
* Do not shirk from displays of casual cruelty.
* Take offence easily and exact a drawn-out, stone-cold revenge.
* Love deeply and passionately, but never display a single ounce of remorse.

of the city's survivors are half-Melnibonéan mercenaries serving under the command of Dyvim Tvar, Dyvim Slorm or other Melnibonéan generals. Some leave behind their semi kinsmen and become adventurers-at-large.

STR, CON, DEX and CHA, roll 3D8, drop the lowest die, and add 2 to the result. For SIZ, INT and POW, roll 3D8, drop the lowest die, and add 4 to the result. Half-Melnibonéans have a Movement of 4m.

Melnibonéan

Elegant, aloof and evidently inhuman, Melnibonéans are generally tall, regal-looking, arrogant and almost cat-like in their mannerisms and habits. The skull is narrow and tapered, the eyes slanted and watchful, their ears tapering to a fine point. The skin is invariably pale in complexion and, to humans, every Melnibonéan is never less than striking and otherworldly.

They are an emotional people but restrained in their demonstration of feelings; they are, without fault, self-centred and unconcerned with the welfare of others – especially humans. Notions such as kindness and cruelty are alien concepts that they find, at best mildly amusing, but are usually considered an irritation. The pursuit of pleasure is foremost in the Melnibonéan mind and they are unrestrained in how that is achieved. Torture, sexual deviancy and the abundant use of narcotics that would drive humans instantly insane are indulged daily, with no thought for the consequences. Many spend their days in a drug-induced slumber, reclined on dream couches where they travel to distant realms beyond the Young Kingdoms plane, indulging in activities known only to them.

All Melnibonéans have the capacity to be sorcerers and at the Bright Empire's height, many of them were. These days, sorcery is considered too time consuming and complicated to pursue, although most know a few conjurations and how to manipulate them. It is only the most ardent students, such as Princes Elric and Yyrkoon, who have the diligence to study the magical arts and become true practitioners of sorcery.

STR and CON, roll 3D8, drop the lowest die, and add 2 to the result. For SIZ and DEX, roll 3D8, drop the lowest die, and add 4 to the result. For INT, POW and CHA, roll 3D8, drop the lowest die, and add 8 to the result. Melnibonéans have a Movement of 5m.

Myyrrhn

The winged folk of Myyrrhn are human-like but not human and predate even Melniboné. Their ancestors and mortal foes are the ape-like clakars. Myyrrhn, though, have developed a higher, more cultured form and, whilst very rare as adventurers, are sometimes found abroad in the Young Kingdoms.

Myyrrhn are slender, tall and very light of frame. Their chests are deep, with improved lung capacity, and their shoulders are a complex assembly of wing joints, tendons and musculature; they are naturally agile and move with a distinct grace. Not all Myyrrhn are winged. Shaarilla, who befriends Elric, was born without them, exhibiting just stumps where her wings should be. It is the Games Master's decision whether a Myyrrhn adventurer is winged or not. As creatures of the air, they worship Lassa and their natures reflect this compact. They have

short attention spans, sometimes speaking in fragmented sentences, failing to finish one point before moving to the next. They are observant, but prone to lapses of concentration. Clothes, which interfere with flight, are shunned, and a simple loin cloth is usually the only apparel. If frequenting human areas, light clothing or simple robes are worn, but the Winged Folk *never* wear armour.

STR, CON, INT and POW, roll 3D8, drop the lowest die, and add 2 to the result. For DEX, roll 3D8, drop the lowest die, and add 4 to the result. For SIZ, roll 3D8, drop the lowest die, and add 8 to the result, *if the adventurer is winged. If not, add 2*. For CHA, roll 3D8, drop the lowest die, and add 3 to the result. Myyrrhns have a Movement of 5m, 10m when flying.

Attributes

These are a set of secondary scores that define exactly what the adventurer is capable of.

Combat Actions (CA): This is the number of actions an adventurer can perform in each Combat Round.

Combat Actions

DEX	Number of Combat Actions
6 or less	1
7–12	2
13–18	3
19 or more	4

Damage Modifier (DM): The Damage Modifier applies whenever the adventurer uses a melee or thrown weapon. It is calculated by adding together STR and SIZ and consulting the following table.

Damage Modifier

Total of STR and SIZ	Damage Modifier
1–5	–1D8
6–10	–1D6
11–15	–1D4
16–20	–1D2
21–25	+0
26–30	+1D2
31–35	+1D4
36–40	+1D6
41–45	+1D8
46–50	+1D10
51–60	+1D12
61–70	+2D6
71–80	+2D8
81–90	+2D10
91–100	+2D12
101–120	+3D10
121–140	+3D12
141–160	+4D10
161–180	+4D12
181–200	+5D10

Hit Points (HP): These determine how much damage the adventurer can sustain before reaching unconsciousness or death. Hit points are located in certain areas of the adventurer's body, representing exactly how much damage he can sustain.

Magic Points (MP): Magic Points are used to activate Sorcery. Starting Magic Points are equal to the POW Characteristic. However, if an adventurer dedicates a portion of his POW to a deity (which is necessary when making a Pact), the dedicated POW is *not* available to calculate the Magic Point total. Thus, a sorcerer with a POW of 16 begins with 16 Magic Points. If he dedicates

Hit Points

	Total of SIZ and CON							
Location	1–5	6–10	11–15	16–20	21–25	26–30	31–35	36–40	+5
Each Leg	1	2	3	4	5	6	7	8	+1
Abdomen	2	3	4	5	6	7	8	9	+1
Chest	3	4	5	6	7	8	9	10	+1
Each Arm	1	1	2	3	4	5	6	7	+1
Head	1	2	3	4	5	6	7	8	+1

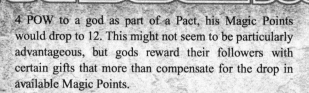

4 POW to a god as part of a Pact, his Magic Points would drop to 12. This might not seem to be particularly advantageous, but gods reward their followers with certain gifts that more than compensate for the drop in available Magic Points.

Strike Rank (SR): This determines how quickly the adventurer acts in combat. Strike Rank is determined by adding together the adventurer's INT and DEX, halving the result and rounding up.

Hero Points

What separates adventurers from the rank and file of the Young Kingdoms are Hero Points. These are the marks of true heroes, allowing them to survive in a dangerous world, for they are obviously destined for greatness. Every adventurer starts with a fixed number of Hero Points that are used throughout his adventures. See page 127 for information on gaining Hero Points. Every Young Kingdoms adventurer begins with *3 Hero Points*, reflecting the harsh nature of their world and the desperate times they live in. If the adventurer is a sorcerer (see page 108), he begins with only *1 Hero Point*, reflecting the bartering sorcerers have had to do to attain their knowledge.

Age

Adventurers can be of any age between 15 and 30, and the adventurer creation system is geared towards producing adventurers with skills reflecting this degree of life experience.

Appearance

The adventurers of the Elric saga tend to have highly distinctive features of personality and appearance. Regional clothing, favoured types of dress or a unique item, scars, moodiness, care-worn demeanours; all are apt elements for a Young Kingdoms adventurer. Think about the tough times they live in, and what might have happened to them in the years before.

Basic Skills

Every adventurer has a range of Basic skills that allow him to perform a variety of actions with varying degrees of expertise. Each Basic skill is set by the total of one or more Characteristics. Some skills will also suffer a penalty from other Characteristics. The Basic Skills table

on page 48 of the Skills chapter lists all the Basic skills every adventurer possesses and the Characteristics used to determine the skill's base score.

Previous Experience

There are three stages involved in determining the adventurer's previous experience. First the player must pick the adventurer's cultural background. This provides certain starting skill bonuses that reflect this upbringing. Second, the player must pick a profession and gain further associated skills with that profession. Thirdly, the player spends the adventurer's free skill points.

Cultural Backgrounds

The regions of the Young Kingdoms available for adventurers are listed below, along with the cultural backgrounds and, where applicable, races noted. The previous chapter offers more detail on each region. The player is free to choose the background the adventurer comes from (with Games Master approval), which then determines skill bonuses, starting money and which Advanced skills are available. The backgrounds available are as follows.

Barbarian

The barbarians of the Young Kingdoms tend to be confined to the northern and southern extremities, and this background recognises their hardiness, tenacity and understanding of their environment. Barbarians are not uncultured; their societies and traditions are every bit as complex as those of the refined Ilmiorans or Lormyrians. Extended family groups based on clans and tribes are common. They are uneducated by civilised Young Kingdoms standards and have cultures based on superstition, taboo and oral tradition, but these are rich in emotion, myth and social ethics – elements sometimes lacking in so-called civilised societies. The folk of the Weeping Waste have no written form of their language, Mong, for instance; whilst the barbarians of northern Tarkesh have complex sagas and legends that, whilst written, are designed to be sung or told as stories around the group hearth.

Regions

Dorel, Pikarayd, Sighing Desert, Tarkesh, Weeping Waste.

Skills

Basic: Athletics +10%, Perception +5%, Resilience +10%, Stealth +5%. *Pick Two (at +5%)* from Boating, Lore (Animal), Lore (Plant), Riding. *Pick Three (at +10%)* from 1H Axe, 1H Hammer, 2H Axe, 2H Hammer, Blowgun, Bow, Dagger, Shield, Sling, Spear, Staff, Throwing, Unarmed.

Advanced: Language (Native) +50%, Lore (Regional), Survival. *Pick One* from Craft, Dance, Lore, Play Instrument, Tracking.

Available Professions: Acrobat, Animal Trainer, Barbarian, Bard, Blacksmith, Craftsman, Explorer, Farmer, Fisherman, Herdsman, Healer, Hunter, Mercenary, Ranger, Soldier, Thief.

Starting Money: 4D6 x100 bronze pieces.

Civilised

There are scores of great cities in the Young Kingdoms and many adventurers were born and raised in the streets of Ilmar, Bakshaan or Karlaak. Standards of education are growing, though few can read more than their own name and perhaps a few words on a goods tariff or prayer sheet. Some older civilised cultures, such as Lormyr and Vilmir, have excellent education for their populace, although this is not to say that all remain in education as hoped for (or forced to, in the case of oppressive Vilmir). The civilised cultures of the Young Kingdoms always have a sense of their own purpose and history, twisted, naturally, to exaggerate their own place in it.

Regions

Argimiliar, Dharijor, Eshmir, Filkhar, Ilmiora, Isle of Purple Towns, Jharkor, Lormyr, Melniboné, Myyrrhn, Pan Tang, Quarzhasaat, Shazar, Tarkesh, Vilmir.

Skills

Basic: Evaluate +15%, Influence +15%, Lore (World) +10%. *Pick One (at +10%)* from: 1H Sword, Bow, Crossbow, Shield.

Advanced: Courtesy, Language (Native) +50%, Lore (Regional). *Pick Three* from: Artistic Expression, Craft, Dance, Language, Lore, Mechanisms, Play Instrument, Seduction, Streetwise.

Available Professions: Alchemist, Bard, Blacksmith, Courtier, Courtesan, Craftsman, Diplomat, Explorer, Knight, Lord, Merchant, Physician, Sailor, Scholar, Soldier, Spy.

Starting Money: 4D6 x300 bronze pieces.

Mariner

Maritime traditions are strong in the Young Kingdoms. Almost all the major cities of the Young Kingdoms are on the coasts, and they breed excellent sailors with sea travel being commonplace. In Lormyr this culture encompasses the bargees who work the Zaphra-Trepek River for they have water-borne skills and traditions every bit as powerful as the sea-going merchants. Mariners have the sea in their blood. They know the tides, how the moon affects them, local currents and rips, where to find the best fishing and how to avoid the obstacles of their own harbour.

Regions

Argimiliar, Dharijor, Filkhar, Ilmiora, Isle of Purple Towns, Jharkor, Lormyr, Melniboné, Pan Tang, Shazar, Tarkesh, Vilmir.

Skills

Basic: Acrobatics +5%, Athletics +10%, Boating +15%, Dodge +5%, Lore (Animal) +5%, Lore (World) +10%, Sing +5%, Throwing +5%. *Pick Two (at +10%)* from: 1H Hammer, 1H Sword, Dagger, Unarmed.

Advanced: Language (Native) +50%, Lore (Regional). *Pick One* from: Craft, Language, Lore (Seas of the Young Kingdoms), Shiphandling.

Available Professions: Craftsman, Explorer, Fisherman, Mercenary, Merchant, Pirate, Sailor.

Starting Money: 4D6 x125 bronze.

Noble

Young Kingdoms nobles are not always the result of privileged dynastic families. It is entirely possible, through hard work, tenacity and business acumen, to work one's way into a noble title, as is the case with the Isle of Purple Towns. Its merchant-princes are from self-made families who have worked and schemed for their positions.

But, in most cases, nobles are the result of family and breeding. They are used to power (though not forced to exercise it wisely), and are likely to own both land and workers (though they do not always care for the welfare of either). In the case of Melniboné, the nobility has withdrawn completely from everyday life, spending their time on the dream couches in a hazy stupor. Elsewhere, nobles are only slightly richer than those below them: Pikarayd, and Oin and Yu, for example. And in some cities, such as Hwamgaarl and Jadmar, nobility is equated with rank in the church, and is therefore a question of faith and the direct exercise of power, more than it is money.

In choosing this cultural background players should consider what *type* of nobility they hail from.

Regions

Argimiliar, Dharijor, Eshmir, Filkhar, Ilmiora, Isle of Purple Towns, Jharkor, Lormyr, Myyrrhn, Melniboné, Pan Tang, Pikarayd, Quarzhasaat, Shazar, Tarkesh, Vilmir.

Skills

Basic: Influence +10%, Lore (World) +10%, Persistence +10%. *Pick Two (at +15%)* from: Evaluate, Dodge, Perception, Riding. *Pick Two (+15%)* from: 1H Sword, 2H Sword, Dagger, Rapier, Shield.

Advanced: Language (Native) +50%, Lore (Regional). *Pick Two* from: Craft, Dance, Language, Lore (Seas of the Young Kingdoms), Play Instrument, Shiphandling.

Available Professions: Diplomat, Explorer, Knight, Lord, Merchant (may refer to himself as Merchant Prince).

Starting Money: 4D6 x1,000 bronze.

Nomad

The nomadic cultures follow the seasons and the sources of food. Like the barbarian cultures, they should not be considered simple or uncultured; their way of life simply has no need for surfaced roads and buildings of stone. Their towns and cities are tents and awnings; their roads the ancestral hunting trails and pastures. Nomads know their terrain intimately and how to survive in it. They worship the Elemental Lords because their effects can be seen daily: when Lassa is pleased she sends cool breezes on hot days. When Straasha is displeased he weeps the monsoon and Lassa consoles him by sending the Wind Brothers to berate Lord Grome. Nomads read their terrain with the Elemental Lords in mind and see omens, foul and fair, in anything that veers from the expected. There are two distinct nomadic types: desert and temperate, reflecting the climate of the region.

Regions

Dorel (temperate), Myyrrhn (temperate), Oin and Yu (temperate), Pikarayd (temperate), Quarzhasaat (desert), Sighing Desert (desert), Weeping Waste (temperate).

Skills

Desert Nomad

Basic: Athletics +5%, Lore (World) +5%, Perception +5%, Resilience +10%, Riding +10%, Stealth +5%. *Pick Two (at +15%)* from: 1H Axe, 1H Spear, 1H Sword, Bow, Dagger, Shield.

Advanced: Language (Native) +50%, Lore (Regional), Survival. *Pick One from:* Craft, Lore, Tracking.

Temperate Nomad

Basic: Athletics +10%, Lore (Animal) +5%, Lore (Plant)

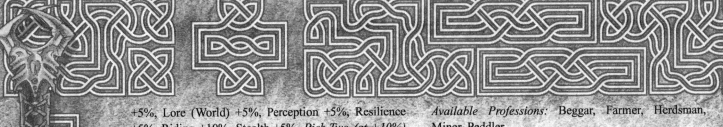

+5%, Lore (World) +5%, Perception +5%, Resilience +5%, Riding +10%, Stealth +5%. *Pick Two (at +10%)* from: 1H Axe, 1H Hammer, Bow Dagger, Shield, Sling.

Advanced: Language (Native) +50%, Lore (Regional), Survival. *Pick One from:* Craft, Languages, Lore, Tracking.

Available Professions (both Nomad types): Animal Trainer, Craftsman, Explorer, Herdsman, Hunter, Ranger.

Starting Money: 4D6 x20 bronze.

Serf

Serfs work the land but do not own it. Education is based on fields, crops, seasons and hardship, but not reading, writing or numeracy. Their income, whether in produce or coin, is generally tithed to either a local noble or to the church. In return, the serf is meant to be protected and cared for, but he notes with irony that such protection often means joining the fyrd or militia when his landlord demands it. Serfs are slightly higher than slaves. They can own property if they can afford it (they generally cannot), and they are supposedly free men but shackled to their ploughs, scythes and grindstones. Some have heard that the slaves of Melniboné live like noblemen and, in some cases, better than the nobles who own the land worked by the serfs. They wonder frequently why they must toil to be free when the enslaved enjoy such privilege, but little knowing that, in Imrryr or Hwamgaarl's spires, slaves can be slaughtered on a whim and for no reason other than it gives their masters pleasure.

Regions

Argimiliar, Dharijor, Filkhar, Ilmiora, Isle of Purple Towns, Jharkor, Lormyr, Myyrrhn, Nadsokor, Pan Tang, Pikarayd, Shazar, Tarkesh, Vilmir.

Skills

Basic: Athletics +5%, Lore (Animal) +10%, Lore (Plant) +10%, Resilience +5%. *Pick Four (at +10%)* from: Boating, Dodge, Driving, First Aid, Persistence, 1H Axe, 1H Flail, 1H Hammer, 2H Axe, Dagger, Sling, Spear, Staff, Unarmed.

Advanced: Language (Native) +50%, Lore (Regional). *Pick Two from:* Craft, Dance, Lore, Play Instrument, Survival.

Available Professions: Beggar, Farmer, Herdsman, Miner, Peddler.

Starting Money: 4D6 x25 bronze.

Slave

Slavery is commonplace in the Young Kingdoms. Melniboné's culture depends on them to function; Pan Tang's is similar, but their slaves endure shorter and less privileged lives than those of the Dragon Isle. Slavers ply the sea lanes, either transporting captives for sale or looking for new ones. Criminals, dissidents and those deemed superfluous to society find themselves indentured to slavery without hesitation. Slaves are frequently used in the galleys, triremes and biremes of the fleets of Pan Tang, Dharijor and Melniboné's battlebarges. Conditions vary considerably. Melnibonéan slaves might occupy a status that far outranks some of the nobility of the Young Kingdoms. Tanglebones, Elric's tutor, is himself a slave, but trusted with parts of Elric's education and possessing a fierce loyalty towards his master. In Pan Tang and Dharijor, slavery is perhaps worse than death. Appalling treatment is commonplace, with casual brutality, rape and mutilation an all-too frequent occurrence. Some become gladiators and earn freedom and respect; most do not.

For adventurers, this background represents someone who has spent most of their life in slavery, learning skills through service and hard labour. Some slaves are granted their freedom by a benevolent owner, whilst others escape; if so, they might be hunted by a vengeful master.

Regions

Dorel, Melniboné (human or half-Melnibonéan slave), Nadsokor, Pan Tang, Pikarayd.

Skills

Basic: Athletics +10%, Persistence +10%, Resilience +10%. *Pick Four (at +10%)* from: Boating, Dodge, Driving, First Aid, Lore (Animal), Lore (Plant), 1H Axe, Dagger, Sling, Spear, Staff, 1H Sword, Unarmed.

Advanced: Language (Native) +50%, Lore (Regional). *Pick Two from:* Craft, Courtesy, Dance, Play Instrument, Seduction, Survival.

Available Professions: Animal Trainer, Bard, Beggar, Courtesan, Craftsman, Farmer, Fisherman, Healer, Spy.

Starting Money: 4D6 x20 bronze.

PROFESSIONS

An adventurer's profession defines his expertise in a variety of skills and reflects the way he has made his living up until becoming an adventurer. It also reflects his family background; it is traditional for sons to follow in the footsteps of their father. Of course, many adventurers continue with their profession, but as the adventuring life takes over they will inevitably learn new skills and perhaps pursue a new way of life shaped by the circumstances of their adventures.

Each profession has a certain number of Basic and Advanced skills, plus their bonuses, listed. If a profession has no entry for Advanced skills, then none are available for that profession.

Acrobat

Basic: Acrobatics +10%, Athletics +10%, Dodge +10%, Throwing +10%, Sleight +10%,

Alchemist

Basic: Evaluate +10%, First Aid +10%, Lore (Plant) +10%
Advanced: Engineering, Lore (Alchemy)

Animal Trainer

Basic: Driving +5%, First Aid +5%, Lore (Animal) +20%, Persistence +10%, Resilience +5%, Riding +5%

Bard

Basic: Influence +10%, Lore (World) +10%, Perception +5%, Sing +10%, Sleight +5%
Advanced: Pick One: Artistic Expression, Courtesy, Dance, Language, Lore, Oratory, Play Instrument

Beggar

Basic: Evaluate +10%, Influence +10%, Perception +10%, *Pick Two at* +10% from: 1H Sword, Club, Dagger, Resilience, Sleight, Stealth, Unarmed

Blacksmith

Basic: 1H Hammer +10%, Craft (Blacksmith) +10%, Evaluate +5%, Lore (Mineral), Resilience +5%
Advanced: Pick One: Craft (Armourer), Craft (Weaponsmith), Engineering, Mechanisms

Courtesan

Basic: Evaluate +5%, Influence +10%, Perception +10%, Persistence +5%, Resilience +5%, Stealth +5%

Advanced: Pick One: Artistic Expression, Courtesy, Dance, Seduction, Streetwise

Courtier

Basic: Influence +15%, Lore (World) +5%, Perception +5%, Sleight +5%
Advanced: Courtesy. *Pick One from:* Artistic Expression, Dance, Lore (Art), Lore (Heraldry), Lore (Philosophy), Lore (Regional), Oratory, Play Instrument

Craftsman

Basic: Evaluate +20%, Influence +5%, Persistence +5%
Advanced: Craft. *Pick One from:* Artistic Expression, Craft (other), Engineering, Mechanisms

Diplomat

Basic: Influence +20%, Perception +10%, Lore (World) +10%
Advanced: Pick One from: Artistic Expression, Courtesy, Dance, Language, Lore, Oratory, Play Instrument

Explorer

Basic: Lore (World) +20%, Perception +5%, Resilience +5%,
Advanced: Pick Two from: Language, Lore (Astronomy), Lore (Geography), Shiphandling, Survival

Farmer

Basic: Athletics +5%, Driving +5%, Lore (Animal) +15%, Lore (Plant) +15%, Resilience +10%,

Fisherman

Basic: Athletics +5%, Boating +20%, Lore (Animal) +5%, Resilience +10%, Throwing +10%

Herdsman

Basic: First Aid +5%, Lore (Animal) +20%, Resilience +5%, Sling +10%, Survival

Healer

Basic: First Aid +20%, Lore (Animal) +10%, Lore (Plant) +10%
Advanced: Healing

Hunter

Basic: Bow +5%, Lore (Animal) +10%, Spear +5%, Stealth +10%
Advanced: Survival, Tracking

Character Creation

Knight

Basic: Athletics +5%, Influence +5%, Riding +10%.
Pick Two (at +10%) from: 1H Sword, 2H Sword, Shield, Spear
Advanced: Pick One: Courtesy, Dance, Oratory, Play Instrument

Lord

Basic: Influence +10%, Persistence +10%, Riding +10%
Advanced: Courtesy +10%, Oratory

A lord owns a minor castle and controls an area of land equal in square kilometres to his CHA+INT+10 from which he derives an annual income of 1D100 x 500 bronze per year.

Mercenary

Basic: Lore (World) +10%. *Pick Two (at +15%) from:* 1H Axe, 1H Flail, 1H Hammer, 1H Sword, 2H Axe, 2H Flail, 2H Hammer, 2H Sword, Bow, Crossbow, Polearm, Shield. *Pick Two (at +5%) from:* Athletics, Dagger, Dodge, Driving, Evaluate, Resilience, Riding, Unarmed

Merchant

Basic: Evaluate +20%, Influence +10%, Lore (World) +10%
Advanced: Pick One from: Language, Lore (Commerce), Shiphandling

Militiaman

Basic: 1H Axe +5%, Athletics +10%, Dodge +5%, Resilience +5%, Shield +10%, Spear +10%, Unarmed +5%

Miner

Basic: 1H Axe +10%, 2H Axe +10%, Athletics +10%, Resilience +10%,
Advanced: Lore (Mineral)

Peddler

Basic: Driving +5%, Evaluate +10%, Influence +10%, Lore (World) +10%. *Pick One (at +5%) from:* 1H Hammer, Crossbow, Staff, Unarmed
Advanced: Pick One: Language, Lore, Streetwise, Survival

Physician

Basic: Evaluate +5%, First Aid +20%, Lore (Plant) +10%, Perception +5%
Advanced: Healing

Pirate

Basic: 1H Sword +10%, Athletics +10%, Dodge +10%, Resilience +10%
Advanced: Shiphandling

Ranger

Basic: 1H Sword +5%, Perception +5%, Lore (World) +10%
Advanced: Lore (Regional), Survival, Tracking

Sailor

Basic: Acrobatics +10%, Athletics +10%, Boating +10%, Lore (World) +5%, Resilience +5%
Advanced: Shiphandling

Scholar

Basic: Evaluate +5%, Lore (World) +10%, Persistence +5%
Advanced: Lore (any). *Pick Two from:* Artistic Expression, Engineering, Healing, Language, Mechanisms

Soldier

Basic: Dodge +5%, Lore (World) +5%, Resilience +5%, Unarmed +5%. *Pick Three at +10% from:* 1H Axe, 1H Flail, 1H Hammer, 1H Sword, 2H Axe, 2H Flail, 2H Hammer, 2H Sword, Athletics, Bow, Crossbow, Dagger, Driving, Polearm, Riding, Shield, Sling, Spear

Spy

Basic: Acrobatics +5%, Dodge +5%, Lore (World) +5%, Influence +5%, Perception +5%, Persistence +5%, Sleight +5%, Stealth +5%
Advanced: Pick One: Disguise, Language, Tracking

Ilmioran Spies are part of the highly secretive Mereghn organisation, centred on Bakshaan.

Thief

Basic: Acrobatics +5%, Evaluate +5%, Perception +10%, Sleight +10%, Stealth +10%
Advanced: Pick One: Disguise, Mechanisms, Streetwise

Free Skill Points

Every adventurer receives 100 additional skill points. The player can add these free skill points to his skills in the following ways:

✱ Add to a Basic or Weapon skill score.
✱ Add to an Advanced skill score, as long as the adventurer already possesses the skill.
✱ Purchase an Advanced skill. This costs 10 free skill points and the Advanced skill starts at its basic Characteristic-derived score.

Important Note: No single skill can benefit from more than 30 free skill points.

Starting With Experienced Adventurers

Most of the characters and adventurers portrayed in the Elric saga are not fresh-faced youths engaging in their first forays into the wide and dangerous world of the Young Kingdoms. Moonglum is a wandering mercenary and veteran of several large battles; Smiorgan Baldhead is an established merchant-prince of the Purple Towns; Rackhir the Red Archer has trained as, and is tired of being, a warrior-priest of Chaos. Elric himself outstrips most mortals in terms of his fighting, sorcerous and even mundane skills – a result of the training received on Melniboné's dream couches. It is only natural for *Elric of Melniboné* players to want to create adventurers that match these heroes, or begin play with an adventurer that has already seen something of the world and is ready for more challenging and heroic deeds. The system below provides Games Masters with an optional mechanism for generating more experienced adventurers.

There are several starting points for *Elric of Melniboné* adventurers. Ideally, all Player Characters in a given campaign should start at the same power level. Given the dangerous nature of the Young Kingdoms, Games Masters and players may find that an *Elric of Melniboné* campaign is more rewarding if started at the *Seasoned* or *Veteran* levels.

Seasoned

Seasoned adventurers have survived their first few adventures, but are still relatively unexceptional.

✱ **Free Skill Points:** 150 skill points; individual skills may benefit from a maximum of 50 free skill points.
✱ **Money:** Double normal for their background.
✱ **Characteristics:** 1D3 additional Characteristic points, split between Characteristics as desired.
✱ **Status:** Seasoned adventurers may hold minor military ranks or cult positions, but are otherwise unexceptional.

Veteran

Veteran adventurers have seen a great deal of combat, but have not yet distinguished themselves – either they have never had the opportunity for true heroism, or they lack that spark that distinguished the victory from the hero.

Playing Sorcerers

None of the professions available to adventurers include any automatic sorcerous training or magical abilities. Sorcery is both rare and feared; few wish to have anything to do with it.

The subject of sorcery is discussed at length in *The Silver Grimoire* beginning on page 107. However, players who want to play a sorcerer can create an adventurer with sorcerous abilities under the following conditions.

* The Games Master *must* approve. Sorcery is *powerful*, can be dangerous, and requires full Games Master consent before any adventurer can begin the game with sorcerous knowledge.
* The player must provide a plausible explanation and background for how his adventurer came by his sorcerous skills.
* To become a sorcerer the adventurer must have Language (High Speech) as one of his skills. If this language has not been taken as one of the skills offered by nationality, culture or profession, it must be bought as one of the skill choices using the adventurer's free skill points.
* Next, the player must choose a higher power to nominally serve: Chaos, Law or one of the elements. To learn sorcery one must be a member of a cult. See *Lords of the Million Spheres* beginning on page 83 for more details on the higher powers and the cults available in the Young Kingdoms.
* Learning magic from a cult is only possible at initiate level and greater. Becoming an initiate requires making a Pact with the god, or one of the gods, worshipped by the cult. See page 91 for more on how Pacts work. Forming a Pact does not cost any of the adventurers free skill points, but it *does* require a dedication of POW.
* The adventurer can now buy sorcerous skills using his remaining free skill points. See page 54 for details on the sorcerous skills available. Note what summonings are taught by the cult and buy only those skills that are appropriate. Each Summoning spell is treated as an Advanced skill, and must be purchased as such by starting sorcerer characters.
* Note that the Summoning and Command skills *cannot* exceed the High Speech percentage. If the basic level of any of these skills would be higher than the High Speech level, then the skill's level is equal to that of High Speech.

* **Free Skill Points:** 200 skill points; individual skills may benefit from a maximum of 70 free skill points.
* **Money:** Five times normal for their background.
* **Characteristics:** 1D4+1 additional Characteristic points, split between Characteristics as desired.
* **Status:** Veteran adventurers are often captains or knights, such as Lormyr's Knights of Malador or Jharkor's White Leopards; or they are adventuring initiates of a cult; guild members or respected citizens in a town.

Master

Master adventurers have demonstrated great skill and determination, to attain true mastery in their chosen field.

* **Free Skill Points:** 300 skill points; individual skills may benefit from a maximum of 90 free skill points.
* **Money:** Ten times normal for their background.
* **Characteristics:** 1D6+2 additional Characteristic points, split between Characteristics as desired.
* **Status:** Master adventurers are knights, lords, high-ranking members of cults and so forth.

Hero

Hero adventurers are legends, whose deeds will be remembered for centuries.

* **Free Skill Points:** 500 skill points; individual skills may benefit from a maximum of 90 free skill points.

- **Money:** Twenty times normal for their background.
- **Characteristics:** 1D8+4 additional Characteristic points, split between Characteristics as desired.
- **Status:** Heroes are always hugely influential – if they seek political power, they are lords and dukes. If they are military leaders, then they command armies. If they are sorcerers or cult members then they champions of their order.
- **Legendary Abilities:** Any two Legendary Abilities provided either by the adventurer's cult, or chosen from the list on page 129 of *The Seventh Dark* chapter.

Farric of Raschil – Example of a Young Kingdoms Adventurer

Pete is about to create his first *Elric of Melniboné* adventurer. Being a fan of the books he has in mind a reasonably experienced mercenary who has no particular allegiance to Law or Chaos at the moment, but has seen the power of Chaos at work in some of his character's previous escapades and is terrified of what the Lords of Entropy can do. With the Games Master's guidance he decides to create a Filkharian mercenary, and the Games Master allows Pete to use the benefits accorded to a 'Seasoned' adventurer, using the Experienced Adventurer rules.

Pete rolls for his characteristics, using 4D6, dropping the lowest score from each roll. For SIZ and INT he rolls 2D6 and adds 6 to the result. Pete gets the following results: STR 15, CON 12, DEX 14, SIZ 9, INT 13, POW 9, CHA 13. Pete's character is small, fast and strong for his size. He has 5 hit points in each leg, 6 for his abdomen, 7 for his chest, 4 for each arm and 5 for his head. Because he is 'Seasoned' he gains an additional 1D3 characteristic points to distribute as he wishes. Pete rolls a 5, halved to a 3. He puts all three points into DEX, raising it to 17. He decides his adventurer will be good humoured but deeply superstitious, especially of Pikaraydians, where his character spent some time in one of the armies commanded by Moonglum of Elwher. Pete names his adventurer Farric of Raschil.

From these characteristics Farric has the following attributes: Damage Modifier +0, 3 Combat Actions, and a Strike Rank of +15. Like all adventurers, Farric starts with 3 Hero Points.

Next is Farric's background and skills. As a Filkharian from Raschil, Pete chooses the 'Civilised' background and the Mercenary profession. He decides Farric was most likely a pikeman. Referring to the Cultural Background and Profession tables, Pete allocates Farric's skills as follows: Cultural Skills: Evaluate +15% (28%), Influence +15% (28%), Lore (World) +10% (23%); 1H Sword +10% (39%); Courtesy (27%), Language (Common) +50% (63%), Lore (Filkharian) (13%). For his Mercenary skills: Lore (World) +10% (23%), Polearm +15% (Filkharian Pike 43%), Shield +15% (43%), Dodge +5% (20%), Resilience +5% (26%), Engineering (13%), Survival (22%).

As a Seasoned adventurer, Pete now has 150 free skill points to distribute amongst his skills, with no single skill benefiting from more than 50 points. Pete reckons Farric has spent a lot of time skirmishing, so he decides for: 1H Sword +50%, Polearm +50%, Dodge +30% and Shield +20%. His skills are now: Evaluate 28%, Influence 28%, Lore (World) 23%; 1H Sword 89%; Courtesy 27%, Language (Common) 63%, Lore (Filkharian) 13%, Polearm (Filkharian Pike) 93%, Shield 63%, Dodge 50%, Resilience 26%, Engineering 13%, Survival 22%.

Farric is therefore a highly competent warrior, and Pete decides he has picked up several nasty scars and a few Pikaraydian Honour Tattoos during his time in the tribal wars. He has a total of 2,100 Bronze pieces to his name (a roll of 13 on 4D6 for Farric's Civilised background, multiplied by 75, and then doubled for his Seasoned status). Farric has left Pikarayd well-paid and as part of his starting equipment he has his pike, but pretty much just the clothes he stands in. Pete decides Farric will spend a hundred bronze on a passage back to Raschil, via the City of the Yellow Coast, and spend his earnings in the taverns and markets, intending to buy some new armour, perhaps a new longsword (Pete decides Farric's broke in a skirmish with a Pikaraydian axeman), and perhaps the attentions of one of Raschil's excellent courtesans.

The Games Master begins the game. As Farric is preparing to board the merchant cog bound for Raschil, he is hailed by none-other than Moonglum of Elwher, his old commander. Moonglum, it seems, is sailing for Raschil too, and has heard that one of the wealthy merchants there is in need of a pair of bodyguards for a forthcoming trip to Dhakos. Farric agrees to team up with the cocky Eshmirian and the stage is set for great adventures in Filkhar, on the high seas, and later in Jharkor…

Character Creation

SKILLS

Adventurers are defined more by their skills than anything else. A skill measures learning, experience and expertise and suggests a great deal about the character's background and upbringing. Skills define what an adventurer is capable of doing in a given situation and define what he can potentially achieve given time and the right resources. This section describes the skills used in *Elric of Melniboné* and how they are used during play.

Skill Tests

An adventurer's skills measure how proficient he is at a particular task. Under most circumstances, there is no need to make a skill test – a character with only a few percent in Riding can ride a horse from one village to another without problems, and there is no need to make a Language test when reading an ordinary book or talking to a friend. Tests should only be made in especially important or dangerous situations, when the adventurer is pressed for time, when the task is difficult or dramatic, or when the margin of success is important.

Roll D100 and compare this to the relevant skill's score. If the dice roll is equal to or less than the skill's score, the attempt is successful. If the total is greater than the skill's score, then it has failed.

Difficulty & Haste

Any modifiers are temporarily applied to the skill for the duration of the test only. A penalty will make the test harder while a bonus makes it easier. Where several modifiers can be applied to the same test, they will all have an effect, 'stacking' to make one final bonus or penalty.

Critical Successes

If the dice roll in a test is equal to or less than 10% of the modified skill, then a critical success has been achieved. The actual result of a critical success during a test is largely up to the Games Master. It normally achieves one of the following results:

✳ The task is completed sooner.
✳ The task is completed to a higher degree of expertise than normal.
✳ The task is completed with élan and style, generally impressing witnesses.
✳ The adventurer gains additional information or insight into the task thanks to their brilliance.

Fumbles

Whenever a skill test results in a roll of 00, the adventurer is assumed to have fumbled the roll.

The actual result of a fumble is largely up to the Games Master to decide. It normally results in one of the following mishaps:

✳ The task takes twice as long to finish and is still a failure.
✳ The task produces a useless result, that actually makes further actions more difficult.
✳ The task is failed spectacularly, opening the adventurer up to derision and scorn from witnesses.
✳ The adventurer becomes impeded or even harmed by his failure.

Automatic Success & Failure

✳ Any test result of 01 to 05 is an automatic success.
✳ Any test result of 96 to 00 is an automatic failure (and, in the case of 00, a fumble).

Difficulty & Haste Modifiers

Difficulty	Time Taken	Test Modifier
Very Easy	Ten times normal time	+60%
Easy	Five times normal time	+40%
Simple	Double normal time	+20%
Normal	Normal time	+0%
Difficult	—	–20%
Hard	Half normal time	–40%
Very Hard	—	–60%
Nearly Impossible	Almost instantly	–80%

Opposed Tests

Opposed tests are made by both characters attempting the relevant skill test. Both characters make the test as normal, rolling 1D100 and attempting to roll equal to or under their skill.

One Character Succeeds

If one character succeeds their test and the other fails, the successful character has won the opposed test.

Both Characters Succeed

Whoever rolled the highest in their skill test wins the opposed test.

Both Characters Fail

Re-roll until one or both character succeeds.

One Character Rolls a Critical Success

A critical success (10% of the modified skill or less) always beats a normal, highest-rolled success.

If both participants roll a critical, the higher roll wins the opposed test.

Example: Farric is arm wrestling with Moonglum. This calls for an Athletics (Brute Force) opposed skill test. Farric's Athletics (Brute Force) is 24% and Moonglum's is 95%. The dice are rolled and Moonglum scores 94 – a very good roll since it is a high roll and less than his skill percentage. Farric's roll is 02 – a critical success, and this beats Moonglum's standard success. Farric's lucky burst of strength clearly overwhelmed Moonglum's technique. Had Farric rolled between 03 and 24, Moonglum would have won because whilst both characters succeeded, Moonglum's was the higher roll whilst still being a success.

Very High Skills

Very High Skills and Automatic Failure

It is not uncommon for adventurers to attain scores in excess of 100% in Basic and Advanced skills. For normal skill tests, this means that the adventurer simply has only a very small chance of failing in their specialised skill (the usual 96 to 00 chance of failure, with 00 being a fumble). However, once an adventurer's skill score reaches 200% in a particular skill, they only suffer a failure on 97 to 00 when rolling tests with that skill, with 00 still being a fumble. Once an adventurer reaches

300%, the failure chance reduces to 98 to 00. At 400%, the chance is reduced to 99 to 00. Finally, at 500%, the adventurer will only fail on a roll of 00 and this is not considered a fumble.

Very High Skills and Opposed Tests

To make an opposed test when one or more of the opponents has a skill exceeding 100%, follow this process:

1. Apply all relevant test modifiers to both skills.
2. Halve both skills.
3. If one skill still exceeds 100%, halve both skills again. Repeat until both skills are below 100%
4. Resolve the test normally.

Every time that both scores are halved in this process, the chance of an automatic success (by rolling 01 to 05) is reduced by one.

Group Tests

With a group test, the Games Master may make a single percentile roll to determine the success of a group of individuals all performing the same task.

Team Tests

In a team test, success is cooperative; everyone reaps the benefit from a single success. If the roll is a failure, everybody fails.

Sorting Tests

In a sorting test, success is individual and some participants will succeed or fail depending on whether their skill score is above or below the result rolled.

Large Groups & Percentile Success

From time to time, the Games Master may need to determine the success of a large group of people performing the same task, in a situation in which there is no room for error. In this case, he may simply take the skill or Characteristic being employed and use that as the percentage of success.

Assistance

Adventurers will often have the opportunity to help one another during various tests. Every assisting character adds his critical score (10% of his skill) to the primary adventurer's skill.

Basic Skill Descriptions

Acrobatics (DEX)

This allows a character to perform a variety of gymnastic and balancing tasks, such as tumbling, walking a tightrope or keeping balance on a narrow or unstable ledge. The adventurer can move at half his normal speed across an unstable surface without penalty. To move at a normal rate requires an Acrobatics test. A successful Acrobatics test will also halve the damage suffered from falling.

Athletics (STR+DEX)

This broad skill covers a range of athletic activities useful to adventuring characters, including climbing, jumping and swimming.

Brute Force: Brute force is a particular application of Athletics that relies purely on power, with no finesse involved. Brute force basically involves pushing, lifting or dragging. Rather than the normal Characteristics, brute force Athletics tests rely on STR+SIZ rather than STR+DEX.

Climbing: Given enough hand and footholds, an adventurer can climb any surface given enough time without the need for a test. Under normal circumstances, an adventurer can climb or descend one quarter of their Movement as a Combat Action. An adventurer can double the rate of his climb or descent by taking a –20% penalty on his Athletics test.

Jumping: In general, a successful Athletics test allows an adventurer to jump up to twice his own height horizontally or up to half his own height vertically, if he has at least five metres to run first. If he is making a standing jump, these distances are halved.

Penalties for jumping Athletics tests can be accrued by trying to jump further. A cumulative –20% penalty is bestowed for every extra metre the adventurer is trying to jump.

Swimming: Adventurers normally swim at half their usual Movement. Athletics tests are only required when conditions are less than ideal – swimming while heavily encumbered or in strong currents, for example.

Basic Skills

Skill	Base Characteristic(s)
Acrobatics	DEX
Athletics	STR+DEX
Boating	STR
Dodge	10+DEX–SIZ
Driving	10+POW
Evaluate	INT
First Aid	INT
Influence	10+CHA
Lore (Animal)	INT
Lore (Plant)	INT
Lore (World)	INT
Perception	INT+POW
Persistence	30+CHA+POW
Resilience	30+CON+POW
Riding	DEX+POW
Sing	CHA
Sleight	DEX
Stealth	10+DEX–SIZ
Throwing	DEX
Unarmed	STR

Boating (STR)

This covers small waterborne craft propelled manually by oars or sometimes paddles. Travelling across calm water does not usually require a test but adverse conditions such as currents and weather can bestow penalties.

Dodge (10+DEX–SIZ)

The Dodge skill is used to avoid incoming objects that are swung or thrown at the adventurer. The Dodge skill is normally used when using either the dodge or dive Reactions is combat.

Driving (10+POW)

If an adventurer is driving a wagon, chariot or similar vehicle at not more than a walking pace across flat terrain, a Driving test will never be required. Tests become required when an adventurer wants to do something out of the ordinary with a vehicle – traverse treacherous terrain, jump obstacles and so on.

Evaluate (INT)

The Evaluate skill enables the adventurer to determine the value placed on something by others, assessing or guessing its market value. Particularly common, or obscure, objects might give a bonus or penalty to the test but success allows an adventurer to guess the average monetary value of the object (normally guessing accurately to within 10% of its actual value)..

First Aid (INT)

First Aid is always applied to a specific location. An adventurer may apply First Aid to himself, though there is a –10% penalty.

First Aid Actions

Injury or Ailment	Treatment
Impalement	A successful First Aid test removes the impaling item without causing more damage to the victim.
Unconsciousness	A successful First Aid test can revive an adventurer from unconsciousness, though drugged patients may inflict a penalty on the First Aid test.
Injured location	A successful First Aid test on an injured location (but not one below 0 hit points) will heal 1D3 hit points to that location.
Serious Injury	A successful First Aid test on a location suffering from a Serious Injury will restore the location's hit points to 0. A limb is no longer considered useless and an Abdomen, Chest or Head location will no longer require tests to stay conscious.
Major Injury	A successful First Aid test on a location suffering from a Major Injury will not restore the location's hit points. This First Aid merely stabilises the patient enough so that they will not die of blood loss.

It normally takes at least 1D4+1 Combat Actions to administer First Aid. Both adventurers must remain stationary and may not use Combat Actions or Reactions while this occurs.

A location that has had any variation of First Aid administered to it may not benefit from First Aid again until it has fully healed (is restored to maximum hit points once more). The use of First Aid requires suitable medical equipment such as bandages or salves.

Influence (10+CHA)

Influence tests are normally opposed by the Perception, Persistence or another's Influence skill and are modified by how much an adventurer is trying to change an opponent's mind.

Lore (INT)

The Lore skill is actually several different skills, each of which must be improved separately. The skills of Lore (Animal), Lore (Plant) and Lore (World) are all Basic skills. All other Lore skills are Advanced skills.

Each Lore skill defines an area of knowledge for the adventurer and tests are made whenever a player wants to see if his adventurer knows something about the subject at hand.

Lore (Animal)

This covers the ability to recognise an animal, know its feeding habits, breeding cycle, habitats and so on. An adventurer with a Lore (Animal) skill of at least 50% may try to domesticate a wild animal, making a test after every full week of training. If the adventurer also has a Riding skill of at least 50% and the animal is capable of being ridden, he may train the animal to ride during this period. The adventurer may later train the animal not to panic in battle and to strike at his enemies. This takes a further period of training, with the adventurer making a test at the end of each week to succeed.

Lore (Plant)

An adventurer well versed in Lore (Plant) can identify plants in the wild, discover good places to grow crops, decide which plants are edible and what unusual properties they may possess.

Lore (World)

This Lore skill is used to define the adventurer's knowledge of the world he lives in. This includes history, politics, weather cycles, geography, superstitions and information on public organisations.

Perception (INT+POW)

The Perception skill is used to represent the senses of the adventurer when detecting objects or other characters. It also has a further use: gaining a brief insight into the behaviour and motives of a character, or their current state of mind. When using Perception in this way the CHA of

Skills

the character being studied is used as a negative penalty to the Perception skill.

Persistence (30+CHA+POW)

Persistence is used whenever an adventurer has his mental willpower called into question.

Resilience (30+CON+POW)

The higher an adventurer's Resilience, the more likely he is to handle adverse physical conditions, such as weathering a vicious sandstorm, surviving in a drought or overcoming the effects of poison or disease.

Riding (DEX+POW)

If a character is riding a creature with the help of saddle and stirrups, at not more than a walking pace across flat terrain, a Riding test will never be required. Tests become required when a character wants to do something out of the ordinary with a mount – traverse treacherous terrain, jump obstacles, ride bareback and so on.

Sing (CHA)

A successful test with this skill will result in the audience being pleased by the character's performance.

Sleight (DEX)

This skill is used to hide or take objects, without drawing undue attention. It is usually opposed by a Perception test if trying to avoid getting caught.

Stealth (10+DEX-SIZ)

The Stealth skill is used whenever a character attempts to personally evade detection by another character. This usually happens when a character either tries to move quietly past an enemy, hide from one or performs a combination of both. Stealth tests are opposed by the Perception skill and are modified according to the situation.

Throwing (DEX)

The Throwing skill is usually used to judge the accuracy of the adventurer when throwing improvised objects, from small stones to bar stools. Weapons that are thrown can either use their own specific skill, such as Spear for javelins, or the Throwing skill, at the adventurer's preference.

A thrown object will have a maximum range of one metre for every point the adventurer's STR exceeds its SIZ. The Throwing test measures the adventurer's accuracy during the throw and the Games Master may choose to treat this as a ranged combat attack.

Unarmed (STR)

The Unarmed skill covers all untrained unarmed combat from simple brawling to grapples to rude fisticuffs. Punches, kicks, head-butts and all other Unarmed attacks do 1D3 points of damage. Unarmed parries may only parry other Unarmed attacks and have an AP value of 2.

Advanced Skills
Artistic Expression (POW+CHA)

This skill allows an adventurer to create works of art. Like the Lore and Craft skills, it is actually a large number of skills grouped together under one heading.

Courtesy (INT+CHA)

With this skill, the adventurer knows how to navigate the murky and treacherous waters of life amongst the nobility. He understands the subtleties and extravagances of courtly behaviour, and can use them to his own advantage.

Craft (INT)

The Craft skill is actually several separate skills grouped under a single heading. Craft (Armourer), Craft (Carpenter) and Craft (Potter) are all individual skills. The following list is by no means exhaustive:

Armourer, baker, basketweaver, blacksmith, bowyer, brewer, butcher, candlemaker, carpenter, cartographer, cobbler, cooper, fletcher, joiner, leatherworker, mason, painter, potter, sculptor, smith, tailor, weaponsmith, weaver.

Using Craft Skills

Most Craft skills require raw material as well as a facility in which to Craft them. Generally speaking, an object's raw materials cost 25% of the item's purchase price.

Time

Craft time on any item can be determined by looking at the item's base cost. An individual's proficiency with the appropriate Craft skill has only minimal bearing on the length of time needed to make an item.

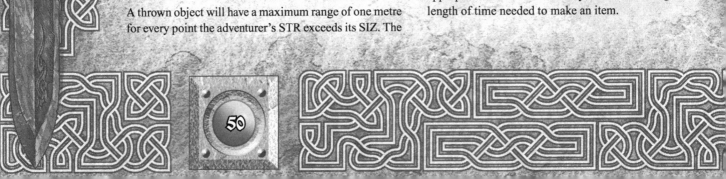

Advanced Skills

Skill	Base Characteristic(s)
Artistic Expression	POW+CHA
Courtesy	INT+CHA
Craft	INT
Dance	DEX
Disguise	CHA
Engineering	INT
Healing	INT+POW
Language	INT
Lore	INT
Martial Arts	DEX
Mechanisms	DEX+INT
Oratory	POW+CHA
Pact (Specific Deity)	Dedicated POW+CHA
Play Instrument	CHA
Seduction	INT+CHA
Shiphandling	INT
Streetwise	POW+CHA
Survival	INT+POW
Tracking	INT

The time required by a skilled craftsman to create a perfectly ordinary, unremarkable item is equal to the item's cost divided by five, in hours. So long as the craftsman has a Craft skill of 50% or greater, he can create the item in question in this time without needing to make a Craft skill test. He is assumed to be good enough at his job to create an ordinary item with some assurance of success. If the craftsman has a skill below 50%, he must make a skill test even when creating a mundane item.

If a craftsman is in a hurry, he may attempt to speed the process along. In this case, the time required to create a perfectly ordinary, unremarkable item is equal to the item's cost divided by ten in hours. To speed up production like this, the craftsman must succeed in a Difficult (–20%) skill test to create the item.

Dance (DEX)

A successful test with this skill will result in the audience or partner being pleased by the character's performance.

Disguise (CHA)

This skill is used to change a character's appearance and adopt a different outward persona. It is usually opposed by a Perception test if trying to avoid being identified.

Engineering (INT)

This skill is used to design, build, activate, repair, sabotage or disassemble large mechanisms or constructs such as siege machines, city gates and drawbridges, mineshafts, sailing ships and so forth.

Healing (INT+POW)

Use of this skill will always require a healer's kit. Each use of the Healing skill generally takes 1d4+1 minutes to perform

Curing Diseases: A successful Healing test allows a patient under the effect of a disease to add a bonus to his next opposed Resilience versus Potency test to resist the disease equal to the healer's Healing divided by 10 (the critical success range).

Curing Poisons: A successful Healing test allows a patient under the effect of a poison to attempt a second opposed Resilience versus Potency test, with the patient gaining a bonus to his Resilience test equal to the healer's Healing divided by 10 (the critical success range).

Surgery: Surgery is the only way, other than magical healing, that an adventurer may recover from a Major Wound. Once a successful First Aid test has been made to quench the bleeding of a Major Wound, a successful Healing test can attempt to set broken bones, stitch together rent flesh and restore the location so that it is on the road to recovery. As long as the Healing test is a success, the stricken location gains one hit point and will begin to heal as normal for a location at its hit point level.

Language (INT)

The Language skill is actually several separate skills grouped under a single heading. Language (*Low Melnibonéan*), Language (*Mong*) and Language (*Opish*) for example, would each be treated as individual skills.

Every adventurer with a Language skill of 50% or more is fluent in that language, though they will likely bear an accent if it is not their native language.

A score in a Language skill of 80% or more will mean the adventurer can also read and write in that language.

Two languages in particular require more attention: the High and Low speech of Melniboné.

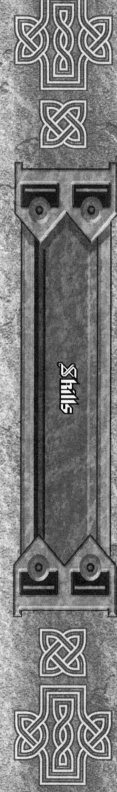

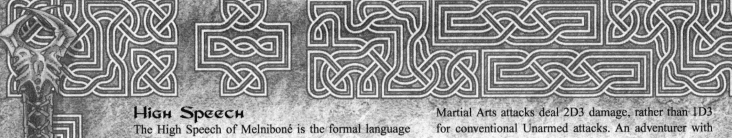

High Speech

The High Speech of Melniboné is the formal language of the Dragon Isle and also the language of sorcery; sorcery simply cannot be worked without its knowledge. It is a complex tongue, blending screams, tortuous contortions of the throat, moans, song, gesture and a particular emotional state relevant either to what is being communicated or the magic being worked.

Low Speech

The Low Speech of Melniboné is used by Melnibonéans as an everyday tongue and was once the common tongue of the Bright Empire. The Common in use throughout the Young Kingdoms is derived from Low Speech and certain words, phrases and pronunciations are common to both languages. Low Speech is still used in some legal documents, trade contracts and in all dealings with the Dragon Isle.

Lore (INT)

This skill is used in the same way as the basic Lore skill. The Advanced range of possibilities for this skill is limited only by a player's imagination but a list of potential areas of Lore study are listed here:

Alchemy, art, astronomy, gambling, geography, heraldry, law, logistics, military tactics, mineral, philosophy, poisons, regional, theology.

One further Lore skill also requires particular attention.

Million Spheres

The Multiverse consists of an infinite number of parallel realms, some are variations of each other, but most are utterly unique. Sorcerers and cult members begin to learn something of this vast reality through study and conversation, but most people of the Young Kingdoms are ignorant of the true nature of reality. They care only for the Young Kingdoms and their own, daily struggle. This Lore skill measures an adventurer's knowledge of the Multiverse, how it might work, and what forces control it. A successful Million Spheres test might let a sorcerer identify the home plane for a particular creature, or recognise the ruling power of a parallel plane he is visiting.

Martial Arts (DEX)

The Martial Arts skill is used in place of the Unarmed skill.

Martial Arts attacks deal 2D3 damage, rather than 1D3 for conventional Unarmed attacks. An adventurer with Martial Arts also counts as possessing natural weaponry. Martial Arts parries may only parry natural weapons or Unarmed attacks and have an AP value of 3.

Mechanisms (DEX+INT)

Picking a lock or disassembling a trap usually takes at least one minute (12 Combat Rounds) to perform, while larger devices will take longer.

Usually, an adventurer will simply make a Mechanisms test in order to succeed at assembling or disassembling a device, with appropriate bonuses or penalties decided upon by the Games Master. If a device has been designed to specifically resist attempts at disassembly, the Mechanisms test becomes opposed by the Mechanisms skill of the adventurer who created it.

Oratory (POW+CHA)

This skill is used when addressing large groups of people, such as a priest addressing the faithful or a general exhorting his troops to victory on the eve of a battle. In effect, it is much like Influence, save that it relies more upon emotional appeal than intellectual stimulation and is used for larger groups of people.

Pact (Specific Deity) (Dedicated POW+CHA)

Pacts are established with the Lords of Law, Chaos, Elements and Beasts. A Pact is a permanent contract in which the adventurer agrees to serve the appropriate Lord in return for supernatural knowledge, aid and power. The rating in this skill reflects the intensity of the pact but does not guarantee that a Lord of Law or Chaos will ever keep their side of the bargain.

Forming a Pact requires the worshipper to *sacrifice* one or more points of their POW Characteristic. The POW is not lost, per se, but it represents the portion of their soul permanently dedicated to their patron, in return for certain gifts, skills and powers, as explained in the *Lords of the Millions Spheres* chapter. Higher sacrifices of POW result in the availability of more or greater gifts from the patron god.

The Pact skill does not increase solely by the methods described on pages 126-127. Players may certainly develop

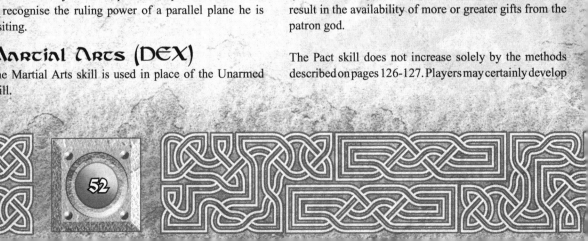

the Pact using improvement rolls and through practice and research, but Pacts also improve *automatically* – see page 92 in *Lords of the Million Spheres* for further details on how Pacts work and advance.

Play Instrument (CHA)

The Play Instrument skill is actually several separate skills grouped under a single heading. For example, Play Instrument (Dulcimer), Play Instrument (Flute) and Play Instrument (Organ Grinder) are all individual skills. A successful test with this skill will result in the audience being pleased by the adventurer's performance.

Seduction (INT+CHA)

Seduction combines charm, flirtatiousness, tenacity and cunning. This skill allows the adventurer to completely win over the target of the seduction attempt using overt romantic or sexual signals, leading to the target becoming deeply enthralled to the adventurer and willing to perform one suggested service or command. The target may try to resist a seduction attempt with an opposed Persistence test.

Shiphandling (INT)

This skill is used in the same way as Boating but is instead applied to waterborne craft that are driven by sail or rows of oars.

Streetwise (POW+CHA)

Streetwise allows a character to find fences for stolen goods, black markets and general information. Such uses of Streetwise normally require a minimum of 1D4 hours.

Survival (INT+POW)

One Survival test will be required every day that a character lacks either food, water or a safe place to sleep. Success indicates the adventurer manages to find whatever he is lacking – failure means he will go without which, over several days, could result in very serious consequences. Survival tests are not used when the adventurer is in a city or town.

Tracking (INT)

With this skill an adventurer can locate the tracks of a specific creature and follow them. A test must be made to locate the trail and then again once every ten minutes they are being followed.

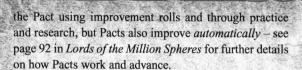

Weapon Skills

All close combat weapon skills are based on DEX+STR (with the exceptions of Unarmed and Martial Arts).

Close Combat Weapons

Skill	Base Characteristic(s)	Weapons Covered
1H Axe	DEX+STR	Battleaxe, hatchet
1H Flail	DEX+STR	Ball & chain, grain flail
1H Hammer	DEX+STR	Warhammer, club, heavy mace, light mace
1H Sword	DEX+STR	Bastard sword, war sword, shortsword, scimitar
2H Axe	DEX+STR	Battleaxe, great axe, halberd
2H Flail	DEX+STR	Military flail
2H Hammer	DEX+STR	Great hammer, heavy mace, war maul
2H Sword	DEX+STR	Bastard sword, great sword
Dagger	DEX+STR	Dagger, knife
Martial Arts	DEX	Fist, foot
Polearm	DEX+STR	Bill, glaive, halberd
Rapier	DEX+STR	Rapier
Shield	DEX+STR	Buckler, kite shield, target shield
Spear	DEX+STR	Javelin, lance, longspear, shortspear
Staff	DEX+STR	Quarterstaff
Unarmed	STR	Fist, foot

Ranged Weapons

Skill	Base Characteristic(s)	Weapons Covered
Blowgun	DEX	Blowgun
Bow	DEX	Longbow, nomad bow, shortbow
Crossbow	DEX	Heavy crossbow, light crossbow
Sling	DEX	Sling, staff sling

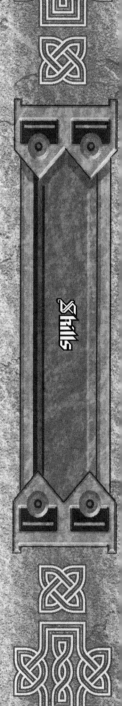

Sorcery Skills

All sorcery skills are Advanced skills. In most cases these are taught either by another sorcerer or within the remit of cult education. It is rare for them to be learned as part of one's general education and training. Also, whilst these are termed *skills*, it is more accurate to think of them as abilities essential to the working of magic.

The specific applications of these skills are discussed in more detail in *The Silver Grimoire* starting on page 107.

Skill	Base Characteristic(s)
Command	POW+CHA
Summoning Ritual	POW
Witch Sight	POW

Command (POW+CHA)

A combination of magical compulsion, negotiation and willpower, the Command skill is used to direct the actions of a summoned magical entity. A Command test is always opposed by the summoned creature's Persistence. If the sorcerer is successful, the creature is compelled to carry out a *single* task in line with its nature and abilities. An air elemental can be commanded to carry the sorcerer over a ravine, for instance, but could not be commanded to provide permanent flight. The task must be worded specifically and carefully by the sorcerer, and the creature will carry out the instruction to the letter. For example, ordering a demon of combat just to fight is too vague; it requires a specific foe ('fight that warrior with the poleaxe and bronze helm'). However, a command such as 'protect me from being attacked' is acceptable, although there is no explicit foe mentioned. Every command must contain a subject and a verb. Issuing a command costs 1 Magic Point.

If the creature successfully resists the Command, it refuses to perform the action. The sorcerer can repeat the Command, but at a cost of 1 Magic Point for each attempt. If the opposed test is fumbled by the sorcerer or he runs out of Magic Points, the sorcerer's control is broken and the creature may act as it pleases. Elementals usually return to their respective plane, but demons and other creatures may behave differently, perhaps becoming troublesome, malicious or violent, but this depends on the demon's type and requires Games Master adjudication.

Note: The percentage of the Command skill can never exceed the sorcerer's High Speech skill.

Summoning Ritual (Specific Creature/Demon) (POW)

Summoning Rituals are different for each creature or demon being summoned. They can be complex and time consuming to prepare, requiring seclusion, privacy and utter concentration. A summoning is a mixture of the written, the aromatic, the aesthetic and the meditative disciplines. Whilst the detail varies according to the summoning, the process is broadly similar: the sorcerer spends 1D8 hours preparing the area with the runes, scents and sacrifices prescribed in the ritual, all the while placing his mind into a semi-trance. Once the area is ready the sorcerer commences the summoning, chanting the creature's name repeatedly until the barriers between the planes of the Multiverse shift, separate and allow the creature through.

The percentage of the Summoning Ritual skill can never exceed the sorcerer's High Speech skill.

Witch Sight (POW)

This is the ability to perceive and read sorcerous powers and emanations. It is the ability to shift the perspective of one's mind to peer between the planes of existence, gaining a glimpse of how magical power has been caused to manifest. A Witch Sight practitioner can learn if a sorcerer is more, or less, powerful than himself by using his Witch Sight to bend his perception to view the aura surrounding the target. When used this way the sorcerer can only tell in *general terms* what the power of the opponent is ('more powerful', 'much more powerful', 'a pathetic fool'); it is impossible to discover anything more precise. Witch Sight can also be used to see the emanations of magical and chaotic creatures and to detect signs of their passing. For every 8 *full* points of Witch Sight the sorcerer can detect a magical trail or aura 1 day in age, and in a 1 metre area. So, for example, a sorcerer with Witch Sight of 35% would be able to sense any magical residue up to 4 days old, anywhere within a 4 metre radius of the sorcerer's position.

EQUIPMENT

The equipment found in the Young Kingdoms is akin to that found in the late medieval period of Europe. It is functional, locally-made (although trade thrives, so goods from far-off lands are found across the key markets of the world), and varies in quality and price. A general guide to equipment is provided herein along with details of currencies, commerce and trade.

Currency & Trade

The standard unit of currency is the bronze piece, known simply as a bronze. Silver and gold pieces are known, but reserved for high denominations and are rarely encountered in everyday transactions. Outside towns and cities, barter is the most common way of doing business with hard currency incurring outright distrust. Gems and jewels are also acceptable currency, again, for prestigious transactions. Melniboné deals exclusively in silver and gold, although the currency of the Dragon Isle is often mistrusted by simple traders. It is very common for coins to be clipped, cut or altered to lower their value in some way. Quarter bronze are typically known as pennies whilst half coins are known as farthings.

The rate of exchange is 10 bronze to a silver and 10 silvers to a gold. A Melnibonéan Gold Wheel has no calculable equivalent owing to their rarity, beauty and quality.

Coinage in the Young Kingdoms

Most countries mint their own coins, stamped with the likeness of the current ruler or his seal or device. Whilst the Bronze piece is ubiquitous, names vary.

* Argimiliar: Shilling.
* Dharijor: Tiger.
* Eshmir: Rhand.
* Filkhar: Crown.
* Ilmiora: Royal (although there is great rivalry between the city states. Depending on relations, different Royals may or may not be accepted in other cities).
* Island of the Purple Towns: Gilder.
* Jharkor: Dharmit (after King Dharmit, Jharkor's beloved ruler).
* Lormyr: Shilling.

* Melniboné: Dragon (silver), Imperial (gold) and Wheel (gold again). Melnibonéan gold wheels are incredibly rare and valuable with only one Wheel existing for each Emperor. These fabulous coins, the size of a man's palm, are intricately carved and more works of precious art than currency.
* Pan Tang: Tiger. All Pan Tangian coins are octagonal and, like Melnibonéan coinage, often distrusted in the wider markets.
* Quarzhasaat: Seventh – named for the unnamed seventh member of the Quarzhasaat ruling council.
* Shazar: Crown.
* Tarkesh: Gilder.
* Vilmir: Shilling. All Vilmirian coins are triangular, in veneration of Arkyn.
* Oin and Yu: Yuro – although this rather worthless currency (a vastly debased mixture of tin, copper and bronze) is found only in Dhoz-Kam. Elsewhere the standard units are the pebble, hen, cockerel, goat, pig, cow, bull and horse, in that order. None are of particularly high quality.

Merchant trade booms in the Young Kingdoms. Markets are vibrant places and the best attract traders from every continent. Sea traders run the gauntlet of pirates and privateers whilst land caravans brave the predations of bandits and hostile communities who somehow see the rise of the towns and cities as a threat. Because merchants run such risks, bodyguards and scouts are essential; lucrative work for adventurers and fortune seekers.

Renowned goods range from the finest spices and silks from distant Eshmir, Filkhar's superb fruits, grains and wines, Tarkesh ale and pork, Ilmioran leather, pottery and ceramics, Lormyrian ice wines, and Jharkorian game (particularly its boar and venison from the royal hunting forests of King Dharmit). Vilmir, despite its austerity, is known for its sweetmeats and breads.

Close Combat Weapons

Dangerous times call for dangerous tools and, at the very least, everyone carries a knife or dagger. Close combat weapons are thus the norm; all self-respecting adventurers carry a sword, even if it is for decoration more

than duelling. Armour, too, is a necessity. Leather body armour, perhaps a breastplate too, is not an uncommon sight in the towns and cities of the Young Kingdoms, although etiquette often dictates that most citizens will not wander around dressed ready for battle.

Each close combat weapon is characterised by the following qualities:

Skill: The skill used to wield the weapon. If multiple skills are listed, any of the listed skills may be used. However, some of the weapon's characteristics may change, dependant on its style of use.

Damage Dice: The damage the weapon deals on a successful attack.

STR/DEX: The minimum STR and DEX scores needed to easily wield this weapon. For every point a Characteristic is below these minimums, a −5% penalty is applied to a character's skill when attacking and parrying with this weapon.

ENC: The weight and bulk of the weapon. See page 80 for more details on Encumbrance and its effects on adventurers.

AP/HP: The armour points and hit points possessed by the weapon. When hit points reach 0, the weapon is broken and useless.

Cost: The average cost in bronze pieces to purchase this weapon.

Ball & Chain: A heavy metal ball attached to a short length of chain. Notoriously difficult to parry, this weapon imposes a −10% penalty on an opponent's parry roll. However, the wielder also suffers a −10% penalty to parry with this weapon.

Bastard Sword: A versatile sword with an elongated grip, allowing it to be used with either one hand or two. It is often called a 'longsword', to distinguish it from the shorter war sword.

Battleaxe: A single-bladed weapon with a sturdy haft, the battleaxe may be used with one or two hands, depending on the wielder's preference.

Bill: A polearm with a hooked blade, descended from (and often recycled from) a common agricultural implement. A mounted defender does not get the standard +20% parry bonus against a bill.

Buckler: A small, round shield designed to be worn on the forearm. Shields suffer a −10% penalty when used to attack.

Club: Perhaps the simplest of all weapons and almost certainly the oldest. The club is simply a long, stout piece of wood used to bludgeon others.

Dagger: Essentially a large knife, the dagger is often carried as a backup weapon or a parrying weapon. It is usually well-balanced enough to throw effectively.

Eshmirian Falchion: A short, curve-bladed sword designed for parrying in two-weapon combat. These weapons are used by Eshmirian mercenaries and are not found extensively in the Young Kingdoms

Filkharian Pike: Almost three metres in length, this long-bladed pike is typically used by the pike militia of Filkhar's army. Effective against charging opponents and mounted knights, it is very limited in effectiveness at close quarters. The length of this weapon gives a +5 bonus to Strike Rank. Mounted opponents must make a Riding test at −40% if charging a pike-armed enemy. A pike can be used to attack an enemy at up to 3 metres distance but at a penalty of −40%.

Glaive: A chopping blade mounted on a polearm shaft.

Great Axe: Dwarfing the battleaxe in size, the great axe may be either single or double-bladed and must be used with both hands. The wielder suffers a −10% penalty to parry with this weapon.

Great Hammer: An enormous weapon that deals impressive bludgeoning damage but is too clumsy to make an effective parrying weapon. The wielder suffers a −10% penalty to parry with this weapon. Great hammers may be used on inanimate objects without being destroyed.

Great Sword: This massive blade is as much as two metres in length. Part of the blade is unsharpened, allowing the wielder to grip it for more effective parries.

Close Combat Weapons

Weapon	Skill	Damage Dice	STR/DEX	ENC	AP/HP	Cost
Ball & chain	1H Flail	1D6+1	9/11	2	4/8	250 bronze
Bastard sword	1H Sword	1D8	13/9	2	4/12	250 bronze
	2H Sword	1D8+1	9/9			
Battleaxe	1H Axe	1D6+1	11/9	1	3/8	100 bronze
	2H Axe	1D6+2	9/9			
Bill	Polearm[2]	1D6+1	7/9	2	2/8	50 bronze
Buckler	Shield	1D4	–/5	1	5/8	50 bronze
Club	1H Hammer	1D6	7/	1	2/4	5 bronze
Dagger	Dagger[4]	1D4+1	–/–	—	4/6	30 bronze
Eshmirian Falchion	1H Sword	1D6+1	8/8	1	6/8	200 bronze
Filkharian Pike	Polearm[1]	2D6	11/7	2	2/12	80 bronze
Glaive	Polearm[2]	1D8+1	7/9	3	2/10	100 bronze
Great axe	2H Axe	2D6+2	13/9	2	3/10	125 bronze
Great hammer	2H Hammer	1D10+3	11/9	3	3/10	250 bronze
Great sword	2H Sword	2D8	13/11	4	4/12	300 bronze
Halberd	2H Axe	1D8+2	13/7	4	3/10	250 bronze
	Polearm[2]	1D8+1	9/9			
	Spear[1,2]	1D8	7/7			
Hatchet	1H Axe[4]	1D6	–/9	1	3/6	25 bronze
Heavy mace	1H Hammer	1D8	11/7	3	3/10	200 bronze
	2H Hammer	1D8+1	9/7			
Improvised	Unarmed	1D6–1	–/–	—	–/–	—
Kite shield	Shield[3]	1D6	13/–	3	10/18	300 bronze
Knife	Dagger	1D3	–/–	—	4/4	10 bronze
Lance	Spear[1,2]	1D10+2	9/9	3	2/10	150 bronze
Light mace	1H Hammer	1D6	7/7	1	3/6	100 bronze
Longspear	Spear[1,2]	1D10	5/5	2	2/10	30 bronze
Lormyrian Axe	1H Axe	1D8+1	12/10	2	3/9	120 bronze
	2H Axe	1D8+2	10/10			
Melnibonéan Lance	Spear[1,2]	1D10+4	9/10	2	4/10	600 bronze
Military flail	2H Flail	1D10+2	13/11	3	3/10	250 bronze
Military pick	1H Hammer	1D6+1	11/5	3	3/10	180 bronze
Natural weaponry	—	As noted	–/–	—	—	—
Pan Tang Sabre	1H Sword	1D8+1	12/10	1	4/12	250 bronze
Quarterstaff	Staff	1D8	7/7	2	3/8	20 bronze
Rapier	Rapier[1]	1D8	7/13	1	3/8	100 bronze
Scimitar	1H Sword	1D6+1	7/11	2	4/10	200 bronze
Shortspear	Spear[1,2,4]	1D8	5/5	2	2/5	20 bronze
Shortsword	1H Sword[1]	1D6	5/7	1	3/8	100 bronze
Target shield	Shield[3]	1D6	9/–	2	8/12	150 bronze
Unarmed	Unarmed	1D3	–/–	—	–/–	—
War maul	2H Hammer	2D6	13/7	3	3/12	150 bronze
War hammer	1H Hammer	1D8+1	11/9	2	3/8	150 bronze
War sword	1H Sword	1D8	9/7	2	4/10	175 bronze
Young Kingdoms Longsword	1H Sword[1]	1D10	11/10	2	4/10	200 bronze
	2H Sword[1]	1D10+1	10/10			

[1] This weapon will impale an opponent upon a critical hit. [2] This weapon may be set against a charge.
[3] This weapon may parry ranged weapons. [4] This weapon suffers no penalty when thrown.

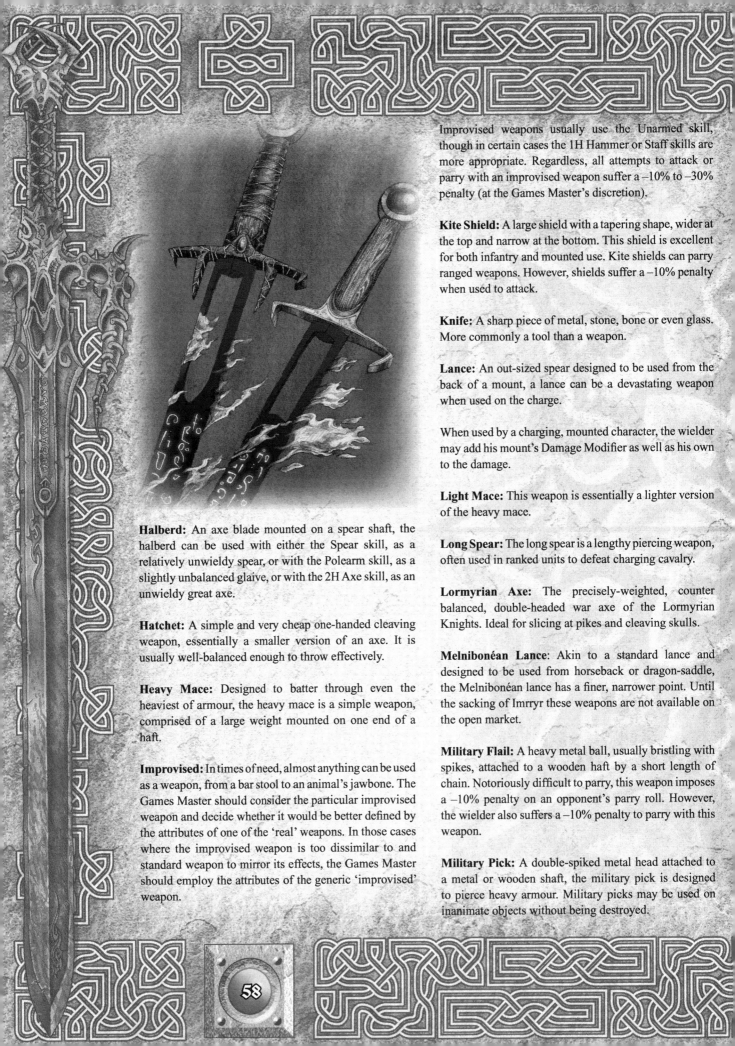

Halberd: An axe blade mounted on a spear shaft, the halberd can be used with either the Spear skill, as a relatively unwieldy spear, or with the Polearm skill, as a slightly unbalanced glaive, or with the 2H Axe skill, as an unwieldy great axe.

Hatchet: A simple and very cheap one-handed cleaving weapon, essentially a smaller version of an axe. It is usually well-balanced enough to throw effectively.

Heavy Mace: Designed to batter through even the heaviest of armour, the heavy mace is a simple weapon, comprised of a large weight mounted on one end of a haft.

Improvised: In times of need, almost anything can be used as a weapon, from a bar stool to an animal's jawbone. The Games Master should consider the particular improvised weapon and decide whether it would be better defined by the attributes of one of the 'real' weapons. In those cases where the improvised weapon is too dissimilar to and standard weapon to mirror its effects, the Games Master should employ the attributes of the generic 'improvised' weapon.

Improvised weapons usually use the Unarmed skill, though in certain cases the 1H Hammer or Staff skills are more appropriate. Regardless, all attempts to attack or parry with an improvised weapon suffer a −10% to −30% penalty (at the Games Master's discretion).

Kite Shield: A large shield with a tapering shape, wider at the top and narrow at the bottom. This shield is excellent for both infantry and mounted use. Kite shields can parry ranged weapons. However, shields suffer a −10% penalty when used to attack.

Knife: A sharp piece of metal, stone, bone or even glass. More commonly a tool than a weapon.

Lance: An out-sized spear designed to be used from the back of a mount, a lance can be a devastating weapon when used on the charge.

When used by a charging, mounted character, the wielder may add his mount's Damage Modifier as well as his own to the damage.

Light Mace: This weapon is essentially a lighter version of the heavy mace.

Long Spear: The long spear is a lengthy piercing weapon, often used in ranked units to defeat charging cavalry.

Lormyrian Axe: The precisely-weighted, counter balanced, double-headed war axe of the Lormyrian Knights. Ideal for slicing at pikes and cleaving skulls.

Melnibonéan Lance: Akin to a standard lance and designed to be used from horseback or dragon-saddle, the Melnibonéan lance has a finer, narrower point. Until the sacking of Imrryr these weapons are not available on the open market.

Military Flail: A heavy metal ball, usually bristling with spikes, attached to a wooden haft by a short length of chain. Notoriously difficult to parry, this weapon imposes a −10% penalty on an opponent's parry roll. However, the wielder also suffers a −10% penalty to parry with this weapon.

Military Pick: A double-spiked metal head attached to a metal or wooden shaft, the military pick is designed to pierce heavy armour. Military picks may be used on inanimate objects without being destroyed.

Pan Tang Sabre: The long, slender sabre used by the Pan Tangian Devil Riders to slash at heads from their six-legged devil mounts.

Quarterstaff: Often unappreciated, the quarterstaff is one of the finest weapons in existence. In the hands of a skilled user, it is a fast and effective weapon for both offence and defence. The wielder gains a +10% bonus to parry with this weapon.

Rapier: Fast and light, the rapier is unlike any other one-handed sword, requiring its own specialised skill. Its narrow blade is intended for thrusting attacks rather than slashing attacks.

Scimitar: A sword with a long, dramatically curved blade, designed for cutting and slashing.

Shortspear: Heftier than a mere javelin, a shortspear is commonly used in conjunction with a phalanx of shields. The shortspear has been proved time and again as one of the most versatile weapons in existence, though not necessarily the most powerful.

Shortsword: A straight, broad-bladed sword designed for thrusting.

Target Shield: A large, round shield that makes an effective weapon and an excellent means of parrying. Target shields can parry ranged weapons. However, shields suffer a –10% penalty when used to attack.

War Maul: Originally meant as a tool for splitting wood, the maul has a long history of use in warfare by peasants conscripted into service. It is a large hammer with a wooden head, usually bound in iron bands. War mauls may be used on inanimate objects without being destroyed.

War Hammer: A weapon approximately the same size as a mace, tipped with a hammer head and a metal spike.

War Sword: Designed for slashing and cutting in battlefield combat, the war sword is one of the most common sword types available. Generally slightly less than a metre in length, it is an effective weapon for both attacking and parrying.

Young Kingdoms Longsword: Shorter than a great sword, and more slender than a bastard sword, the Young Kingdoms longsword is used all across the Young Kingdoms by soldiers and mercenaries.

Throwing Close Combat Weapons

If thrown, a close combat weapon has a range of 8m and suffers a penalty to the attack equal to its ENC x 10. Either the usual Weapon skill or the Throwing skill may be used.

Setting Weapons against Charges

Setting a weapon against a charge occurs at the same time the character decides to delay in combat. In this case, the circumstance the character is waiting for is for someone in front of him to charge his position. As long as the charge occurs, the character gains a +20% bonus to the opposed skill test to determine who strikes first.

Ranged Weapons

Weapons that are thrown or propel a missile, such as a bow or sling. The Young Kingdoms does not appear to have developed the crossbow in any shape or form; certainly they are not mentioned in the course of the Elric saga.

Skill: The skill used to fire or throw the weapon.

Damage Dice: The damage the weapon deals on a successful attack.

Range: This is the effective range of the weapon. The maximum range a weapon can be fired or thrown is twice this score.

Load: This shows how many Combat Actions are required to load or reload the weapon.

STR/DEX: The minimum STR and DEX scores needed to easily wield this weapon. For every point a Characteristic is below these minimums, a –5% penalty is applied to a character's skill when attacking with this weapon.

ENC: The weight and bulk of the weapon.

AP/HP: The armour points and hit points possessed by the weapon. When hit points reach 0, the weapon is broken and useless.

Equipment

Cost: The cost in bronze pieces to purchase this weapon.

Blowgun: A hollow tube, usually made of wood, that is used to expel a dart by blowing on one end. As the dart itself does little damage, blowguns are seldom used without some kind of poison. A character's Damage Modifier is never applied when using a blowgun.

Dart: A dart resembles an arrow with a longer head and shorter shaft (usually slightly less than half a metre in length).

Javelin: A light spear designed to be thrown.

Long Bow: A bow with a shaft as much as two metres in length, designed to be fired on foot. A long bow cannot be used from horseback.

Melnibonéan Bone Bow: A recurved composite bow of wood, bone and sprung steel, it is immensely powerful and utterly deadly in the hands of Melniboné's warriors and slave-archers. Melnibonéan bone bows find their way into Young Kingdoms circulation after the sacking of Imrryr.

Nomad Bow: A shorter bow than the long bow, the nomad bow sacrifices some range and power in exchange for portability.

Short Bow: Designed to be fired from horseback, the short bow is equally useful as a foot soldier's weapon.

Sling: A long strip of cloth or leather used to fling a stone or bullet at a target.

Staff Sling: A sling mounted on the end of a wooden haft, which generates greater force in throwing.

Throwing Star: A light piece of metal with four to six sharp points.

Using Ranged Weapons in Close Combat

If used in close combat some ranged weapons, such as bows, are treated as improvised weapons. Usually, the 1H Hammer skill or the Staff skill may be used as applicable.

Ranged Weapons

Weapon	Skill	Damage	Range	Load	STR/DEX	ENC	AP/HP	Cost
Blowgun	Blowgun	1D2	15m	1	–/9	—	1/4	30 bronze
Dagger[2]	Dagger or Throwing	1D6	10m	—	–/9	—	4/6	30 bronze
Dart[1]	Throwing	1D4	20m	—	–/9	—	1/1	10 bronze
Hatchet[2]	1H Axe or Throwing	1D8	10m	—	7/11	1	3/6	25 bronze
Javelin[1]	Spear or Throwing	1D6	40m	—	5/9	1	1/8	20 bronze
Long bow[1]	Bow	2D8	175m	1	13/11	1	2/7	200 bronze
Melnibonéan Bone Bow	Bow	2D8	200m	1	13/12	1	2/9	800 bronze
Nomad bow[1]	Bow	1D10	120m	1	11/11	1	2/5	150 bronze
Rock/improvised	Throwing	1D4	10m	—	5/9	1	3/5	—
Short bow[1]	Bow	1D8	60m	1	9/11	1	2/4	75 bronze
Shortspear[1,2]	Spear or Throwing	1D8	25m	—	5/9	2	2/5	20 bronze
Sling	Sling	1D6	50m	1	–/11	—	1/2	5 bronze
Staff sling	Sling	1D8	60m	2	–/11	2	2/6	20 bronze
Throwing star	Throwing	1D4	15m	—	–/13	—	4/1	15 bronze

[1] This weapon will impale an opponent upon a critical hit.
[2] This weapon suffers no penalty when used in close combat.

Armour

Each piece of armour is characterised by the following qualities:

AP: How many armour points are given to each location covered by this armour. If a character is wearing multiple pieces of armour on a location, only the highest armour point score is used.

ENC: The weight and bulk of the armour.

Locations: Which hit locations this type of armour covers.

Skill Penalty: Add together the AP of all the armour the character is wearing – this is the character's Skill Penalty. If a character is wearing multiple pieces of armour on a location, only add the highest armour point score.

The Skill Penalty applies to tests with most skills that use the DEX Characteristic to calculate their base scores, plus some other skills. Skills included in this list are: Acrobatics, Athletics, Craft, Dance, Dodge, Martial Arts, Mechanisms, Riding, Sorcery, Stealth, Throwing and all Weapon skills.

Cost: The cost in bronze pieces to purchase this armour.

Effects of SIZ on Armour

Armour made for a character of SIZ 1 to 5 will have its cost and ENC halved from that shown on the Armour table. Characters of SIZ 21 or higher will double the cost and ENC for armour made for them.

Chainmail Coif: A hat made of chainmail, covering the top, back and sides of the head. It is lined with soft leather.

Chainmail Shirt: Heavy but effective protection, a chainmail shirt hangs from the shoulders to just below the groin, covering the chest, arms and abdomen. It is lined with soft leather.

Chainmail Skirt: Hanging to the knees, a chainmail skirt allows for maximum freedom of movement without sacrificing protection. It is lined with soft leather.

Chainmail Trews: Essentially a pair of pants crafted from chainmail, these trews offer the same protection as a chainmail skirt but are slightly more cumbersome. It is lined with soft leather.

Full Helm: A rigid helmet covering the entire head, except for eye holes and a vent for breathing.

Armour

Armour	AP	ENC	Locations	Cost	Total Skill Penalty
Chainmail coif	5	1	Head	500 bronze	−5%
Chainmail shirt	5	4	Abdomen, Arms, Chest	1,250 bronze	−20%
Chainmail trews	5	3	Legs	1,000 bronze	−10%
Full helm	6	1	Head	1,000 bronze	−6%
Heavy leather hauberk	2	1	Abdomen, Chest	350 bronze	−4%
Heavy leather cap	2	1	Head	75 bronze	−2%
Helmet	5	1	Head	300 bronze	−5%
Leather hauberk	2	1	Abdomen, Chest	150 bronze	−4%
Leather shirt	1	1	Abdomen, Arms, Chest	150 bronze	−4%
Leather trews	1	1	Legs	100 bronze	−2%
Melnibonéan Plate[1]	7	1	All	20,000 bronze	−14%
Plate (breast and back)	6	4	Abdomen, Chest	4,500 bronze	−12%
Plate leggings	6	4	Legs	3,000 bronze	−12%
Plate (suit)	6	12	All	9,000 bronze	−42%
Plate vambraces	6	3	Arms	2,000 bronze	−12%
Weeping Waste Armour	3	3	Abdomen, Arms, Chest	1,000 bronze	−12%

[1] Melnibonéan Plate must be made specifically for the wearer.

Heavy Leather Hauberk: Fashioned of thick and stiff boiled leather, this hauberk is a sleeveless garment that falls from the shoulders to just below the groin.

Heavy Leather Cap: A cap of stiff leather, protecting the top, back and sides of the head.

Helmet: A rigid metal helmet, covering the top, back and sides of the head. These helmets usually have a nose guard as well.

Leather Hauberk: One step above normal clothing, this piece of armour is essentially a weaker and more flexible version of the heavy leather hauberk.

Leather Shirt: A leather shirt hangs from the shoulders to just below the groin, covering the chest, arms and abdomen.

Leather Trews: A pair of pants crafted of thick leather, protecting the wearer's legs.

Melnibonéan Plate: The ornate, finely-crafted, strong, exceptionally light plate mail worn by all Melnibonéan warriors. Helmets are often crafted into the likeness of a dragon, or bear dragonish designs on the breastplate,

vambraces and greaves. Samples of Melnibonéan plate find their way onto the Young Kingdoms markets after the sacking of Imrryr.

Plate Armour: The best and heaviest form of armour available on the Continent, plate armour is the province of the richest nobles and most successful knights.

Weeping Waste Armour: Carved from wood, lacquered, and inscribed with tribal designs, Weeping Waste armour is light, strong and buoyant. It is carved to fit the wearer precisely and will only fit another person with the same SIZ as the original owner.

General Items

Backpack (Cost: 5 bronze): A standard piece of adventuring equipment, held to the back with two shoulder straps. It can hold 20 ENC of equipment.

Block & Tackle (Cost: 1 bronze): Useful for constructing traps, hauling up stubborn logs and so forth. Adds +10% to Mechanisms tests to make or disarm large traps and makes Engineering tests possible in some circumstances. It requires at least 10m of rope to function.

Candle, 1 Hour (Cost: Quarter bronze): A small, stubby candle that will burn for one hour before exhausting its fuel. Originally used by miners to mark the passage of time while they were underground, many adventurers have adopted them for the same purpose. A candle illuminates a one metre radius. Any wind stronger than a slight breeze will extinguish a candle.

Climbing Kit (Cost: 25 bronze): Consisting of a leather harness, several short lengths of rope, pitons and sundry other tools, a climbing kit provides a bonus of 20% to any Athletics skill tests made to climb.

Craft Tools (Cost: 75 bronze): This is a small satchel containing portable tools appropriate to a particular craft. These tools are the bare minimum required to practise the craft without a skill penalty. A set of craft tools is useful for only one craft – a character must buy more sets of tools for any additional crafts.

Crowbar (Cost: 25 bronze): Adds +10% to brute force Athletics tests to lever open doors, casket lids and the like. If used as a weapon, it is considered a club (wielded with a –10% penalty).

Grappling Hook (Cost: 5 bronze): Tied to a rope, it can be lofted onto a battlement with a Throwing test. It will support the weight of 50 ENC or 50 SIZ, or any combination thereof.

Healer's Kit (Cost: 150 bronze): Stocked with bandages, mortar and pestle, poultices, barber's tools, basic surgical equipment and everything else a healer needs to practise his trade on the road, a healer's kit is necessary for a character to use the Healing skill.

Lantern (Cost: 10 bronze): A lantern provides clear illumination out to a three metre radius. It will burn for two hours on a flask of oil.

Lock Picks (Cost: 75 bronze): An item no self-respecting thief would ever be without, lock picks allow a character to use his Mechanisms skill to pick a lock. The Games Master may assign penalties or bonuses to this test based upon the specific circumstances.

Oil, Flask (Cost: 1 bronze): A flask of oil is enough to fuel a lantern for two hours, or, if broken on the ground and ignited, enough to sustain a small fire for one minute.

First Aid Kit (Cost: 25 bronze): A first aid kit is made up primarily of bandages, tourniquets and herbal compresses. It allows the owner to use the First Aid skill without penalty. A first aid kit is good for five uses (whether the skill test succeeds or fails) before it is used up.

Fish Hook (Cost: Quarter bronze per 20): A small metal hook used to catch fish. This item allows a character to use his Survival skill to catch a fish without suffering a penalty on the test.

Quiver (Cost: 2 bronze): Quivers can generally hold up to 30 arrows or crossbow bolts.

Rope, 10 Metres (Cost: 10 bronze): An essential piece of equipment for an adventurer, a standard rope can support the weight of 50 ENC or 50 SIZ, or any combination thereof.

Sack, Large (Cost: 1 bronze): A wide sack of leather or canvas, able to hold 10 ENC of equipment.

Sack, Small (Cost: Quarter bronze): A small sack can hold 5 ENC of equipment.

Waterskin (Cost: Half bronze): A waterskin can hold enough water to sustain an adventurer for two days.

Food & Lodging

Item	Cost
Lodging, poor	½ bronze
Lodging, average	1 bronze
Lodging, superior	5 bronze
Food & drink, poor, 1 day	¼ bronze
Food & drink, average, 1 day	1 bronze
Food & drink, superior, 1 day	2 bronze
Trail rations, 1 day	1 bronze

Animals, Transportation & Slaves

Animal	Cost
Bison	200 bronze
Bull	250 bronze
Cart	75 bronze
Cat	2 bronze
Chariot	600 bronze
Cow	150 bronze
Dog, domestic	2 bronze
Dog, hunting	25 bronze
Fowl	1 bronze
Goat	50 bronze
Hawk	400 bronze
Horse, draft	400 bronze
Horse, riding	350 bronze
Horse, combat trained	500 bronze
Mule	125 bronze
Ox	200 bronze
Pig	50 bronze
Saddle & bridle	75 bronze
Sheep	30 bronze
Slave, adult	1,000 bronze
Slave, child	200 bronze
Slave, educated	5,000 bronze
Slave, skilled	2,500 bronze
Slave, youth	400 bronze
Travel (by coach)	15 bronze per kilometre
Travel (by post-horse)	20 bronze per kilometre
Travel (by ship)	10 bronze per kilometre
Travel (by wagon)	5 bronze per kilometre
Wagon	300 bronze

Equipment

COMBAT

*P*oignards glittered in the darkness and their owners wore the black hoods of professional assassins. There were at least a dozen of them. The young dandy must therefore be extremely rich, for assassins were expensive in Old Hrolmar. Moonglum had already drawn both his swords and was engaging the leader. Elric pushed the frightened girl behind him and put his hand to Stormbringer's pommel. Almost at its own volition the huge runesword sprang from its scabbard and black light poured from its blade as it began to hum its own strange battle-cry.
– The Vanishing Tower

Combat is a frequent occurrence in the Young Kingdoms. From battling creatures of Chaos to settling a dawn-called duel with a rival, it is a necessary evil for most adventurers although many, such as Moonglum and Smiorgan Baldhead, enjoy the heat, noise and sheer exhilaration offered by battle. And Elric, gripped by the demonic battle-fever so characteristic of his people, Stormbringer in hand, drenched in the gore of his foes, is the absolute epitome of how central combat is to the world in these final days.

Combat Time

Combat is divided into rounds. With 12 rounds in every minute, a single round roughly translates to five seconds of time, during which a character can perform one or more actions.

Each round is broken into Strike Ranks, which determine when a character can act. Quick and lithe characters will act first, while those wielding heavy weapons will act later. As characters are attacked, they will also have an opportunity to react to their enemies. Every Combat Round goes through the following steps:

1. **Determine Strike Ranks:** At the start of every Combat Round, roll D10 for each character and add the character's Strike Rank modifier. This will determine the character's Strike Rank – the order in which every character involved acts for the round.

2. **Characters Take 1st Action:** Each character involved in the combat performs one Combat Action in Strike Rank order. The character with the highest Strike Rank will act first, followed by the character with the second-highest Strike Rank, and so on until the character with the lowest Strike Ranks acts. Reactions, such as parries or dodges, are made during this process as appropriate.

3. **Characters Take 2nd Action:** After each character has completed his 1st action, characters with Combat Actions remaining (if any) may perform a second Combat Action, in Strike Rank order.

4. **Characters Take 3rd Action:** After each character has completed his 2nd action, characters with Combat Actions remaining (if any) may perform a third Combat Action, in Strike Rank order.

5. **Characters Take 4th Action:** After each character has completed his 3rd action, characters with Combat Actions remaining (if any) may perform a fourth Combat Action, in Strike Rank order.

6. **End of Combat Round:** Once all eligible characters have used up all their Combat Actions in the Combat Round, it is over. Fatigue is determined now, if applicable. If there are characters still engaged in combat with enemies, another Combat Round begins.

Strike Ranks

During every Combat Round, characters will act in order of Strike Rank, starting with the highest, resolving the actions of each character in turn. If two or more characters can act in the same Strike Rank, the characters will act in order of their DEX, with the highest going first. If two or more characters acting in the same Strike Rank have the same DEX score, they will act simultaneously.

A character's Strike Rank modifier is determined during character creation, as detailed on page 37.

Gaining Surprise

There will be times when one side in combat effectively gets 'the drop' on their enemies, launching an attack with surprise on their side. This may be because of a carefully planned ambush, the victims are just not paying attention or there may be a major distraction going on. Whatever the cause, surprise is gained whenever one side in a combat is completely unaware of the other when the first Combat Round begins. Whether a character is surprised or not is entirely down to the Games Master. He may require that the character makes Stealth tests to gain the edge on a victim or that the target of an attack may attempt a Perception test to avoid an ambush. Under other circumstances, there may be no tests to make – the Games Master can rule that surprise is automatic.

In combat as lethal as that of *Elric of Melniboné*, surprise can be a powerful ally or a terrible enemy. A surprised character suffers a –10 penalty to his Strike Rank during the first Combat Round. In addition, he may only use Reactions against actions that occur after his own Strike Rank. Reactions are discussed on page 69.

The effects of surprise generally only last for the first Combat Round of a combat.

Combat Actions

The actions a character may take when it is his turn to act are detailed here. Note that some actions may take more than one Combat Action to perform and these may be stretched across several Combat Rounds if need be – this is useful if a character is casting a particularly long spell or wants to spend more time aiming at a target before attacking.

Aim: If using a ranged weapon, a character may spend time aiming at a target in order to deliver a more accurate attack. Every Combat Action spent aiming adds a +10% bonus to the character's ranged Weapon skill. This bonus only applies to the first attack the character makes with the weapon, which must be at the target being aimed at. A maximum of three Combat Actions may be spent aiming, for a +30% bonus. A character can take no other Combat Action or Reaction while aiming without losing the aim bonus.

Change Stance: The character may shift from one of the following stances to another: standing, prone, kneeling or sitting. Any adjacent enemy may make a Reaction free attack in response to this action.

Charge: If a character can move a minimum of five metres, he can make a charge. He may move a distance up to twice his Movement. This must be in a straight line and he must end up adjacent to an enemy. When the move is complete, a close combat attack may be made against the enemy. If the attack is successful, the character gains a bonus of +1D4 damage.

Close Combat Attack: The character can make a single close combat attack. The full rules for close combat attacks are detailed on page 67.

Defend: A character may defend himself, effectively adding +20% to any Dodge skill tests or parrying Weapon skill tests he is called upon to make until the beginning of his next Combat Action.

Delay: A character may pause to assess the tactical situation around him, then choosing the precise moment to act.

* If a delaying character merely wishes to act after a specific character has acted, they wait until that character has finished their Combat Action. The delaying character's Strike Rank is then altered to reflect their new place in the Strike Rank order and they act as normal.

* If a delaying character wishes to interrupt a specific character's action as it occurs, or act immediately upon a specific trigger, the character must make a test appropriate to his interrupting action (a Weapon skill test if the character wishes to attack, for instance). If the trigger is capable of opposing the test with a test of its own relevant to its action, it may do so. Whoever wins the test acts first.

For Example: If Farric wishes to fire his bow at anyone who draws a knife in the group in front of him, he needs to make a Bow Skill test opposed by the opponent's Dagger Skill test. Failure means he is slightly late and acts after, rather than before, the dagger-wielder's Combat Action.

Combat

Regardless, once the character has acted, they are no longer delaying and their Strike Rank is modified appropriate to their new position in the Strike Rank order.

If a delaying character waits for an entire Combat Round and does not act at all, they may choose to either keep their current Strike Rank or re-roll at the beginning of the following Combat Round.

Fighting Retreat: The character backs away slowly from an opponent but does not lower his guard. He may move up to half his Movement directly away from an enemy he is fighting.

Flurry: A character may use all of his remaining Combat Actions at once, rather than waiting for other characters to act. Each blow struck in a flurry is at −20% to Weapon skill, since the character is sacrificing technique for speed.

Move: The character moves quickly but not at a flat-out run (that is fleeing or charging). Any adjacent enemy may make a Reaction free attack in response to this action.

The character may move a distance up his Movement score.

Ranged Attack: The character can make a single ranged attack. The full rules for ranged attacks are detailed on page 71.

Ready Weapon: Drawing a sword from its sheath, unhooking an axe from one's belt, nocking an arrow to one's bow – all these actions require the Ready Weapon Combat Action. A single Ready Weapon action can also include dropping a weapon currently held to the floor and then drawing a new one. Sheathing one weapon and drawing another takes two Combat Actions, as does readying two weapons. Ranged weapons can be reloaded with this action – this takes as many Combat Actions as noted in the weapon's description.

Skill Use: The use of skills during combat is covered in more detail in the *Skills* chapter.

Sprint: A character can run as fast as he can, regardless of threatening enemies. Any adjacent enemy may make a

Reaction free attack in response to this action and gains a +20% bonus for the attack. The character may move a distance up to twice his Movement score.

Other: The actions detailed above are the most common players will want to attempt in a Combat Round. However, the open-ended nature of roleplaying games, not to mention the ingenuity of players, means that characters may end up doing many different things not covered in these rules. When this happens, it is up to the Games Master to determine the effects of the attempted action and how many Combat Actions it will take to complete.

Close Combat Attacks

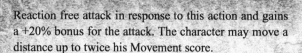

When a character is adjacent to an enemy, he may use a Combat Action to make a close combat attack. Alternately, the character may have charged an enemy or attacked with a flurry of rapid blows. Regardless of the specific Combat Action that initiates the attack, all close combat attacks are handled in the following manner:

1 - Making the Attack

An attack is made by simply rolling D100 and comparing it to the character's skill in the weapon he is using. If a character rolls equal to or lower than his Weapon skill, he has hit his target. Move on to Target Reaction. If he rolls greater than his Weapon skill, he has missed his target. The target may choose to react but otherwise the attack simply fails at this point.

2 - Target Reaction

If the target has any Reactions left, then they may declare they are reacting to the attempted attack at this point. The target may attempt to dodge or parry the attack. However, only one Reaction may be made to each attempted attack. See page 69 for more details on Reactions.

If the enemy has no Reactions left and the attack was a success, then the attack is unopposed. Move straight on to Damage Resolution.

3 - Damage Resolution

If the attack is successful, damage is rolled. Each weapon has its own Damage score, to which is added the attacker's Damage Modifier in order to determine the total damage being dealt. A D20 is rolled alongside the damage roll, in order to determine the location of the target being struck, as shown on page 73.

If the damage is greater than the target's SIZ at this point (before armour points are deducted), Knockback occurs (see page 75).

If the defender is armoured in the location that is hit, the armour may absorb some of this damage. Reduce the attack's damage by the armour points (AP) of the location's armour, to a minimum of zero damage.

4 - Damage Application

Apply any remaining damage to the location's hit points. Loss of hit points to a particular area may well have additional effects, especially if the total hit points in that location have been reduced to 0 or less. See page 73 for more details on damage and injuries.

Close Combat Situational Modifiers

There are various modifiers which may be applied when using a weapon, as shown on the Situational Modifiers table. These modifiers are applied to attacks, parries and dodges equally. The skill modifier applies directly to the skill in question.

Close Combat Situational Modifiers

Situation[1]	Modifier
Target is helpless	Automatic Critical Hit
Target surprised[2]	+20%
Target prone or attacked from behind	+20%
Attacking or defending while on higher ground or on mount	+20%
Attacking or defending while prone	–30%
Attacking or defending while on unstable ground	–20%
Free motion of weapon arm obstructed (for example, a wall on the right side of a right-handed swordsman)	–10%
Attacking or defending while underwater	–40%
Defending while on lower ground or against mounted foe	–20%
Fighting in partial darkness	–20%
Fighting in darkness	–40%
Fighting while blind or in pitch black	–60%

[1] These modifiers are cumulative – attacking a surprised target who is on lower ground increases the attacker's Weapon skill by +40%.

[2] A surprised character may only use Reactions against attackers with a Strike Rank lower than their own.

Combat

Critical Hits

Critical hits are strikes that cause exceptional carnage, causing the maximum possible damage for the weapon used. Such strikes often permanently debilitate the location struck and represent particularly crushing blows, powerful swings and lethally accurate strikes. Skilled warriors are more likely to deal critical hits to their enemies but even the lowest untrained peasant can sometimes surprise an opponent. A critical hit automatically causes maximum damage for the weapon in question. Damage Modifiers, such as that derived from statistics, are not maximised.

For Example: In combat with a clakar, Farric strikes a critical hit to the winged ape's chest. Farric's longsword inflicts 1D10 points of damage and he has no Damage Modifier due to his STR and SIZ. Thus, with his critical hit he wounds the clakar for 10 points of the damage, the weapon's maximum, without needing to roll a D10 to determine random damage. Had Farric been larger or stronger, thus gaining a Damage Modifier of +1D2, his damage would have been 10 plus the result of rolling the Damage Modifier (so either 11 or 12 points of damage in total).

Impaling Close Combat Attacks

Some thrusting and piercing weapons, such as spears and shortswords, do even more damage on a critical hit than other weapons, as the shaft or blade penetrates deep into the enemy's body and will quite likely stay there. A character that scores a critical hit with an impaling weapon causes maximum damage as normal. However, the character also has an additional choice – whether to yank the weapon free (causing more damage) or to leave the enemy impaled.

Yanking: Yanking the weapon free requires a *brute force* Athletics test. If successful, the character automatically causes normal (not maximised) damage for the weapon once more, to the same location as the original strike, and has also regained their weapon for use. If the *brute force* Athletics test fails, 1D4 damage is inflicted upon the impaled enemy's stricken location and the weapon remains stuck.

Impaled Enemies: Impaled enemies suffer from a –20% penalty to all skill tests, including Weapon skills, due to pain and physical difficulty. This penalty is cumulative – a character impaled by two arrows suffers a –40% penalty.

A successful unarmed close combat attack that targets an enemy's impaled location (using the precise attack rules detailed below) results in the attacking character laying hold of the impaling weapon. They may immediately attempt to yank it free (see above). The impaled creature may also spend a Combat Action to yank the impaling weapon free themselves (this does not require an unarmed attack), or, another character may remove the impaling weapon in a cleaner and less agonising manner through the use of the First Aid skill (see page 49).

Precise Attack

A character may make one precisely aimed attack in order to strike a specific hit location, bypass a target's armour, strike a target's weapon or disarm an enemy. Precise attacks are just like normal attacks, in that they can cause critical hits and be parried or dodged as normal.

Precise attacks may not be made as part of a charge or flurry. All precise attacks are very difficult; the character's Weapon Skill suffers a –40% penalty. Precise attacks cannot be combined in a single strike.

Bypass Armour: A precise attack can be used to find chinks in an opponent's armour, bypassing its protection. Instead of choosing a hit location, the character determines it normally but if successful in his attack, will ignore all AP (armour points, see page 73) of the location he hits.

Disarm: The attacker declares that he is attempting to disarm the target of a single held weapon. If the attack successfully strikes the opponent, no damage is caused and instead an opposed Weapon skill test is made (see page 48 in the Skills chapter). If either combatant is using a weapon in two hands, they gain a +20% bonus to this test. Should the attacker succeed, his opponent's weapon flies 1D6–1 metres in a random direction (a result of 0 metres places it at the defender's feet).

Location Strike: The attacker declares that he is aiming for a specific hit location of the target's body. If successful, this strike automatically hits the desired location, instead of using the normal Humanoid Hit Location table (see page 73).

Strike Weapon / Shield: The attacker declares that he is attempting to attack the target's held weapon or shield. If the attack is successful, any damage is dealt directly to the opponent's weapon, using the rules for attacking inanimate objects in the Adventuring chapter on page 82. Natural weaponry may not be attacked in this way.

Reactions

When a character is attacked, he will usually get the chance to make a Reaction. A character can make as many Reactions in a Combat Round as he has Combat Actions. Unlike Combat Actions, Reactions are not made during a character's Strike Rank but are made in response to the Combat Actions of enemies.

There are four types of Reaction – dodge, parry, dive for cover and free attacks.

Using a Reaction does not take away from a character's Combat Actions for the round. Thus, if Farric has three Combat Actions in a round, he may also make up to three Reactions. His Reactions in any given round could be three dives, three dodges, three parries, three free attacks or any combination of these, depending on the outcome of attacks made against him. Reactions are declared after the trigger event has occurred but before its effects are applied. For instance, the trigger event for a dodge or parry is an attack upon the character; the dodge or parry resolution occurs after the attack has been determined as a hit but before any damage is allocated.

Only one Reaction may be made in response to a single trigger event, no matter how many Reactions a character has available.

Dodge

Trigger Event: A ranged or close combat attack being made against the character.
Restrictions: Helpless characters may not dodge.
Penalties: A mounted character suffers a –30% penalty

to his Dodge skill. If a character has his back to a wall, cliff, more enemies or is otherwise impeded from freely dodging in any direction, he will suffer a –20% penalty to his Dodge skill.

A character may choose to try to move out of the way of an incoming attack, avoiding it altogether. This uses the Dodge skill. Note that dodging an attack usually does not mean a wild leap to one side, but rather the character shifts his body just enough (he hopes) to allow the blow to bypass him harmlessly.

A dodge opposes the attacker's attack roll to the target's Dodge skill in a roll similar to an opposed skill test, except that the attacking and defending players compare their results on the Dodge table.

Attack Succeeds as Normal: The dodge attempt failed and the attack resolves damage as normal.

Attack Succeeds and becomes Critical Hit: The dodge attempt was a disaster and the defender opens himself up for worse damage than he was otherwise exposed to – the attack is upgraded to a critical hit.

Attack Fails: The dodge is a success and the attack is evaded. The attack is considered to have missed and therefore causes no damage.

Attack Succeeds but Inflicts Minimum Damage; Defender Forced to Give Ground: The dodge is partially successful. The attack still causes damage, however the damage is the minimum possible for the weapon in question. Damage modifiers, such as that derived from statistics, are not minimised. If the attack being dodged was a critical hit, it instead inflicts normal damage. The defender must also Give Ground.

Dodge

Attacker's Roll (Weapon Skill)	Defender's Roll (Dodge Skill)		
	Failure	*Success*	*Critical Result*
Failure	Attack succeeds as normal	Attack fails	Attack fails; attacker Overextended
Success	Attack succeeds as normal	Attack succeeds but inflicts minimum damage; defender forced to Give Ground	Attack fails
Critical Result	Attack succeeds and becomes critical hit	Attack succeeds as normal	Attack succeeds but inflicts minimum damage; defender forced to Give Ground

Combat

Attack Fails; Attacker Overextended: The dodge is a success and the attack is evaded. The attack is considered to have missed and therefore causes no damage. If this was a close combat attack, the attacker has also dangerously Overextended his reach.

Giving Ground

A character forced to Give Ground immediately retreats his Movement directly away from the attacker. The attacker has the option of either immediately following up and remaining adjacent to the defender, by making the same Movement, or remaining where he is. Neither the movement of the defender or the attacker cost any Combat Actions or Reactions in this case.

If the defender cannot Give Ground their full Movement, they will move as far as possible and then stop.

Overextended

A character who attempted a close combat attack but Overextended themselves is thrown off balance, as he overreached in an attempt to hit the dodging character. This imposes a –20% penalty on the next Reaction the attacking character takes, as he tries to recover his balance. As soon as the Overextended character performs another Combat Action, he recovers from his Overextension.

Parry

Trigger Event: A close combat attack being made against the character.
Restrictions: Helpless characters may not parry. Ranged attacks may not be parried.
Improvisation: Parrying with improvised items, such as crossbows or fallen logs, is usually done using the Shield Skill, though the Games Master may decide a particular

Weapon skill is more appropriate in other cases (such as the Club Skill for tree branches).

To make a parry, a character must place his weapon or shield in the path of his attacker's and try to block or deflect the blow. As characters will soon discover when fighting, some weapons are better at parrying than others, just as some weapons are harder to block. As the player grows in experience with *Elric of Melniboné*, characters will begin to learn when it is best to parry an attack and when it is best to dodge.

A parry attempt is similar to a dodge attempt. A parry opposes the attacker's attack score to the target's Weapon skill (if parrying with a weapon) or Shield Skill (if parrying with a shield), in a roll similar to an opposed skill test, except that the attacking and defending players compare their results on the Parry table.

Attack Succeeds as Normal: The parry attempt failed and the attack resolves damage as normal.

Attack Succeeds and becomes Critical Hit: The parry attempt was a disaster and the defender opens himself up for worse damage than he was otherwise exposed to – the attack is upgraded to a critical hit.

Attack Fails: The parry is a complete success and the attack's energy is diverted entirely away from the defender. The attack is considered to have missed and therefore causes no damage.

Attack Succeeds but AP of Parrying Weapon/Shield is Deducted from Damage: The parry is at least partially successful. The attack still causes damage, however the

Parry

Attacker's Roll (Weapon Skill)	Defender's Roll (Weapon or Shield Skill)		
	Failure	*Success*	*Critical Result*
Failure	Attack succeeds as normal	Attack succeeds but 2xAP of parrying weapon/shield is deducted from damage	Attack fails; defender may Riposte
Success	Attack succeeds as normal	Attack succeeds but AP of parrying weapon/shield is deducted from damage	Attack succeeds but 2xAP of parrying weapon/shield is deducted from damage; defender may Riposte
Critical Result	Attack succeeds and becomes critical hit	Attack succeeds but ½ AP of parrying weapon/shield is deducted from damage	Attack succeeds but AP of parrying weapon/shield is deducted from damage

damage is reduced by the AP of the parrying weapon or shield. The amount deducted from the attack's damage may also be the ½ or double the parrying weapon/shield's AP, depending on the specific result on the Parry table.

Riposte

Successfully parrying an opponent can sometimes leave him off balance and in a vulnerable stance, making it easier to strike him. A Riposte is a free attack against the attacker. In order to make the free Riposte attack, the defender must have an available Reaction to spend. Free attacks are discussed below.

Free Attacks

Trigger Event: Free attacks are made in response to certain adjacent enemy actions (see below).

Restrictions: Helpless characters may not make free attacks. Free attacks must always be close combat attacks.

There are situations in which a character may gain one or more free close combat attacks in a round because of the actions of enemies adjacent to him. Basically, certain physical acts leave the enemy open to opportunistic strikes. The following situations will grant a free attack, as long as the reacting character is adjacent to the acting enemy:

* If the enemy makes a ranged attack. If the free attack causes damage, the ranged attack fails.
* If the enemy casts a spell. If the free attack causes damage, the caster must make a Persistence test or the spell fails.
* If the enemy readies a weapon. If the free attack causes damage, the enemy must make a Dodge test or drop the weapon instead of readying it.
* If the enemy stands from prone. If the free attack causes damage, the enemy must make an Athletics test or remain prone.
* If the enemy moves away from the character without using the Fighting Retreat Combat Action. If the free attack causes damage, the enemy's Movement for that particular move is halved.
* If the enemy moves adjacent to the character without using the Charge Combat Action (which must be targeted at the character). This includes enemies who move through an adjacent area to the character en route to a further destination.
* If the enemy leaves himself open for a Riposte.

Free attacks are always single close combat attacks – they may not be charges, flurries or precise attacks. Enemies may parry or dodge free attacks with Reactions as normal.

Dive

Trigger Event: An area effect taking place that encompasses the character.

Restrictions: Helpless characters may not dive. Targeted attacks may not be evaded with a dive. A character that has nowhere to dive to (balancing on a rope above a lake of lava for example), may not dive. A prone character cannot dive.

Penalties: A mounted character may not dive and remain mounted. A mounted character may dive with a –30% penalty to Dodge skill, but automatically dismounts when he does so.

Some attacks, such as dragon's breath and many destructive spells, will affect an entire area rather than just target a single character. These attacks can be very difficult to avoid and all a character can do is hurl himself to the ground to escape the worst of the effects. Area effects apply their damage to every hit location and thus are incredibly dangerous to characters.

To dive for cover against an area attack, a character must succeed in a Dodge skill test. If successful, he will halve the damage dealt by the attack. A critical success avoids all damage dealt by the attack.

Any character that attempts a dive, whether successful or not, becomes prone.

Ranged Attacks

Ranged weapons such as slings, bows and even the occasional pebble make attacks a little differently from close combat weapons. Ranged weapon attacks are usually initiated through the Ranged Attack Combat Action. Ranged attacks may not be used as part of a charge or flurry. Regardless of the specific Combat Action that initiates the attack, all ranged attacks are handled in same manner as close combat attacks, with the following exceptions:

Loading Ranged Weapons: When a ranged weapon is readied, it is either in hand (for throwing weapons) or loaded (for bows and other projectile weapons). While

Combat

readying most ranged weapons take only a single Combat Action, others take more than one Combat Action to reload. The number of Combat Actions it takes to load a ranged weapon is listed in its statistical entry in the Ranged Weapons table, page 60.

Ranged Attack Situational Modifiers

Situation	Skill Modifier
Wind[1]	
Strong wind	−10%
High wind	−20%
Fierce wind	−40%
Hurricane	Attack automatically fails
Target Movement[1]	
Target has moved 10m or more since attacker's last Combat Action	−10%
Target has moved 30m or more since attacker's last Combat Action	−20%
Target Visibility[1]	
Target obscured by smoke, mist or is in partial darkness	−20%
Target obscured by thick smoke, fog or is in darkness	−40%
Target Size[1]	
Per 1 SIZ target is under SIZ 5	−10%
Per 10 SIZ target is above SIZ 20	−10%
Target Condition[1]	
Target is helpless	+10%
Target surprised[2]	+10%
Target prone	−20%
Attacker Condition[3]	
Attacker is prone	−20%
Attacker is underwater[4]	−20%
Attacker is on unstable ground	−20%
Attacker is blinded	−40%

[1] Modifiers within these sections are not cumulative. However, modifiers from different sections are cumulative. Therefore, shooting at a target within a mist that has moved more than 10m since the attacker's last Combat Action imparts a −30% penalty.

[2] A surprised character may only use Reactions against attackers with a Strike Rank lower than their own.

[3] Attacker condition modifiers are cumulative.

[4] Only thrown weapons may be used underwater. Bows and other projectile weapons will automatically miss if fired underwater.

Range: A target within the weapon's Range may be attacked without penalty. A target within double the weapon's Range may be attacked, but the attacker's effective Weapon skill is halved (before other modifiers are applied). Attacks against targets beyond the weapon's Range automatically fail.

Dodging and Parrying: The target may attempt to dodge the attack, but may not normally parry it unless using a shield.

Damage Modifier: A character's Damage Modifier applies to the damage a ranged weapon inflicts, providing the weapon is thrown or the projectile is drawn (such as with a bow). Blowpipes do not use a character's Damage Modifier. If the Games Master desires, other small projectiles of negligible mass (darts or throwing stars for example) might only be granted half the Damage Modifier.

Impaling Ranged Attacks: A character that impales an enemy with a ranged attack (a thrown spear or fired arrow) obviously does not have the option of immediately attempting to yank out the projectile.

Precise Attacks: A character may not attempt to disarm targets with ranged attacks, nor may he attempt to strike to damage a target's weapon or shield. Precise ranged attacks made to bypass armour or hit a specific location operate normally.

Cover

If a target is in cover or partially covered by an object (such as a wall, door or fence), any attack that hits a covered location will instead hit the object. See Inanimate Objects on page 82. Cover affects both ranged and close combat attacks.

For Example: Three Dharijorian archers launch arrows at a Jharkorian guardsman standing at a window. This particular window is small and narrow, obscuring the guardsman except for his Head and Chest, which are visible. All three archers roll successful attacks, then roll to see which hit locations the arrows strike.

The first hit location rolled is the Left Leg, the second is the Abdomen and the third is the Head. The arrows destined for the Left Leg and Abdomen bounce harmlessly off the stone sill of the window, as both those locations have cover. The third arrow, however, strikes the Head as normal, as it is not behind cover.

The normal method of overcoming the impediment of cover is to use precise attacks to aim for specific uncovered locations.

Firing into a Crowd

When firing a ranged weapon into a crowd, close combat or any group where the target is adjacent to one or more other potential targets, there is always a chance the character will hit someone other than the target he was aiming at. When firing into a crowd, the Games Master will determine which locations of the target have cover from the ranged attack. The ranged attack is then resolved as normal for a target behind cover.

If a covered location is hit by the attack, the firer has hit one of the individuals adjacent to the target (the Games Master will decide who). The accidental target may use Reactions against this attack as normal. If the attack damages the accidental target, roll the hit location randomly. If the accidental target successfully dodges a ranged attack, the projectile continues on its original path and may strike the intended target. The intended target may use Reactions against this attack as normal.

A character may not make a precise attack when firing into a crowd.

Armour

Any good adventurer knows that even a thin layer of leather can make the difference between life and death in combat, and thick plate armour can make a good fighter almost invulnerable. Whenever a character is hit, the damage is reduced by the armour point score of the location struck. This can reduce the damage to zero (but not to less than zero).

Wearing Armour

While the protective qualities of armour are obvious, the sheer bulk of heavy leather or metal can slow a character down drastically. Characters will often have to balance the protection granted by armour with the ability to move speedily when needed. The penalties armour can inflict upon a wearer depend on its weight (ENC) and its restrictiveness (Skill Penalty). The different types of armour can be found on page 61.

Damage

When a character successfully scores damage against a target, the damage must be deducted from a specific hit location. Every weapon has a damage rating, which is listed in its statistical entry in the relevant Weapons table in the Equipment chapter. This is the amount of dice rolled when the weapon successfully hits a target, to which is added the attacker's Damage Modifier.

Hit Locations

A successful attack will damage a specific hit location. To determine which location has been hit, roll 1D20 and compare the number rolled with the Humanoid Hit Location table.

Humanoid Hit Location

D20	Hit Location
1–3	Right Leg
4–6	Left Leg
7–9	Abdomen
10–12	Chest
13–15	Right Arm
16–18	Left Arm
19–20	Head

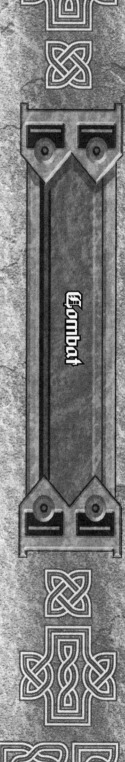

Some unusual creatures have slightly different hit location tables to reflect their own unique physiology. Such creatures will have their modified Hit Location tables listed with their description.

The amount of damage is deducted from the hit points of this location. So long as the location has hit points remaining, the character will suffer no further effects. If the location is reduced to zero hit points or less, then the character is injured:

Location's Hit Points reduced to 0

The location has suffered a Minor Wound. The location will be permanently scarred and the character loses his next Combat Action.

Location's Hit Points reduced to -1 or more

The location has suffered a Serious Wound. The location is permanently scarred and the character loses his next 1D4 Combat Actions.

Limbs

A limb will be rendered useless by a Serious Wound, until the location is restored to 1 hit point or more, or if the character receives First Aid (see page 49). If a leg is rendered useless, the character drops prone.

Abdomen, Chest or Head

A character suffering a Serious Wound to the Abdomen, Chest or Head must immediately make a Resilience test or fall unconscious. If the character remains conscious, this test will have to be repeated at the end of every Combat Round, until the location is restored to 1 hit point or more, or the character receives First Aid (see page 49).

Location's Hit Points reduced to a negative score greater than its starting Hit Points

The location has suffered a Major Wound. The location is permanently scarred and the devastating extent of the injury may well maim or kill the character.

Limbs

A limb will be either severed or mangled by a Major Wound. The limb is considered to be either missing (severed) or maimed. The character drops prone and must immediately make a Resilience test or fall unconscious.

If the character remains conscious, this test will have to be repeated at the end of every Combat Round, until the location is restored to 1 hit point or more, or the character receives First Aid (see page 49). If the location does not recover within a number of Combat Rounds equal to the character's CON+POW, the character dies from blood loss and shock.

Abdomen, Chest or Head

A character with either the Abdomen, Chest or Head suffering a Major Wound must immediately make a Resilience test or die. If the character lives, another Resilience test must be made to stay conscious. Both tests will have to be repeated at the end of every Combat Round, until the location is restored to 1 hit point or more, or the character receives First Aid (see page 49). If the location does not recover within a number of Combat Rounds equal to *half* the character's CON+POW, the character dies from blood loss, shock and internal injuries.

One Useless or Missing Arm

A character that has one arm rendered useless drops anything held in that arm's hand. The character may not use any weapon that requires two hands, such as great axes or bows. They also suffer a –20% penalty to any Skill that normally relies upon using two arms or hands, such as Athletics tests to swim or Boating tests to paddle.

Two Useless or Missing Arms

A character that has both arms rendered useless drops anything held in either arm's hand. The character may not use any weapon. Most Skills based on STR or DEX are impossible, though some (such as Athletics and Dodge) only suffer a –30% penalty.

One Useless or Missing Leg

A character that has one leg rendered useless may only stumble along. This halves their Movement score. They also suffer a –10% penalty to any Skill that relies upon physical mobility, such as Athletics, Dodge, Stealth and most Weapon skills.

Two Useless or Missing Legs

A character that has both legs rendered useless may only crawl – their Movement is reduced to 1 metre and they

called Knockback and a clever adventurer can often use it to his advantage. Knockback can occur when a character is hit by ranged or close combat attacks. Knockback occurs after Reactions (if any) have been completed, but before armour points are deducted from the attack's damage. If the damage at this point exceeds the target's SIZ, the target is knocked backwards 1 metre by the force of the attack.

For every five full points the damage exceeds the target's SIZ, they are knocked back an additional metre. For Example: Farric is struck by a ballista bolt launched by a band of Pikaraydian raiders besieging Raschil that causes 18 damage. Farric only has a SIZ of 9 and is therefore knocked back 2 metres.

A character that suffers from Knockback must also succeed at an Acrobatics test or fall prone.

If a character is knocked back into a wall or other solid object, he must make a Dodge skill test or suffer 1D4 damage to a random hit location as they slam into the obstruction.

If the character who caused the damage did so as part of a Charge Combat Action, the distance the target is knocked back is doubled.

Mounted characters suffering from Knockback can add the SIZ of their mount to their own if they make a successful Riding Skill test. If this roll is failed, only the character's own SIZ is used and any Knockback will cause him to be knocked off his mount.

will be prone until at least one leg is restored. Most Skills that rely upon physical mobility are impossible, though some (such as Dodge and Stealth) only suffer a –30% penalty.

One-Armed Warriors

Characters seriously injured in past combats may enter battle missing the odd limb – this is by no means unusual in *Elric of Melniboné*! If such a character is hit in a location that he no longer possesses, the attack misses. Note that if the character has replaced his lost limb with an artificial version – such as a wooden leg – then the attack does not miss – it strikes the replacement limb and causes damage as normal.

Knockback

As well as causing great amounts of damage, exceptionally powerful attacks can send a character sprawling backwards under the force of the blow. This is

Two Weapon Use & Shields

If a character is not harnessing the raw power of a two-handed weapon, then he will usually take either a second weapon or a shield into combat.

Two Weapon Use

A character wielding two weapons or a weapon and a shield may use the off-hand item to either: Parry one additional attack per Combat Round (over and above the normal Reaction allowance) OR gain a single bonus Close Combat Attack action. This bonus attack may not be a precise attack and suffers a –20% penalty to the relevant Weapon or Shield Skill.

Mounted Combat

The best way to fight is from horseback, or the local equivalent. The mounted warrior's view of the battlefield is better and he has the 'high ground' over his infantry opponents. However, that advantage depends on the mount as much as it does the man, and a wise knight remembers this. The following rules assume that the mount is trained for combat.

A mounted adventurer can use no weapon at a Skill level greater than his Riding skill score.

For Example: If Sir Gharhir of Malador has a 1H Sword skill of 58%, but a Riding skill of 45%, while he is on horseback his 1H Sword skill is only 45%.

A mounted warrior has a +20% bonus to his attacks and parries (though not his dodges) against adjacent opponents on foot; a character on foot defending against a mounted attacker suffers a –20% penalty to his Reaction skill. These modifiers are summarised in the Close Combat Situations table (see page 67). These modifiers do not apply if the target on foot is as tall as the mounted character is while mounted. For instance, for a normal human cavalryman, an opponent three meters tall or taller will cancel these modifiers.

A mounted warrior is prohibited from using weapons dependent on a 2H Weapon skill, Polearm or Staff while mounted.

A mounted character uses his mount's Movement score when moving rather than his own.

Hit Locations in Mounted Combat

A mounted warrior striking downward will usually hit only the top half of the target. Unless the mounted combatant is using a weapon dependent on the Spear skill, re-roll the location for all Leg hits by mounted attackers against opponents on foot.

A footsoldier striking upward will usually be unable to hit the target's head. Unless the footsoldier is using a weapon dependent on the Spear, Polearm or a 2H Weapon skill, re-roll the location for all Head hits by footsoldiers against mounted combatants.

Untrained Mounts

The rider of a mount unused to combat must make a Riding Skill test at the start of each Combat Round. Failing this test will cause the horse to automatically use the Move Combat Action at every opportunity for the remainder of the Combat Round. Succeeding this test allows the horse to be treated as a trained mount for the remainder of the Combat Round.

Unarmed Combat

A character forced to fight with just his fists and feet can be at a real disadvantage. Unarmed attacks deal 1D3 points of damage on a successful strike. In addition, an unarmed attack may only parry another unarmed attack. They may never parry weapons.

Parried Unarmed Attacks

If an unarmed attack is parried (the opponent's parry test is a success or critical success) by a crafted or natural weapon, the attacker will immediately suffer the rolled damage of the parrying weapon, with no damage modifier, to the limb he is using. This is in addition to the normal effect of the parry.

Natural Weapons

Natural weapons such as the teeth and claws of monsters are counted as weapons and not unarmed attacks. The damage they deal is listed in the monster's description. They may parry other natural weapons or unarmed attacks, but not crafted weapon attacks. Strikes using Martial Arts (page 52) count as natural weapons rather than standard unarmed attacks.

Grappling

Sometimes an adventurer will be interested in restraining an enemy rather than slaying them outright – this is where grappling comes in. A grapple attack is made in the same way as a normal unarmed or natural weapon attack but must be declared as such before any dice are rolled.

Should the attacker hit with his grapple attack, no damage is initially caused. Instead, the attacker then opposes their attack score to the target's Unarmed skill, Weapon skill or Dodge skill (target's choice), in a roll similar to an opposed skill test, except that the attacking and defending players each roll D100 and compare their results on the

Grapple

	Defender's Roll (Dodge, Unarmed or Weapon Skill)			
Attacker's Roll (Unarmed Skill)	*Failure*		*Success*	*Critical Result*
Failure	Grapple fails		Grapple fails	Grapple fails; defender may Riposte
Success	Grapple succeeds		Grapple fails	Grapple fails; defender may Riposte
Critical Result	Grapple succeeds; attacker may immediately make Immobilise or Throw attempt (attacker's choice)		Grapple succeeds	Grapple fails; defender may Riposte

Grapple table. Resisting a grapple attempt is a Reaction (failing to use a Reaction to the resist the attempt counts as if the defender had failed their skill test).

Grapple Fails: The grapple attempt fails and the attack is considered to have missed.

Grapple Succeeds: The grapple attempt is successful and the two combatants are now grappling.

Grapple Succeeds; Attacker may Immediately make an Immobilise or Throw attempt (attacker's choice): The grapple is a phenomenal success. The two combatants are now grappling and the attacker may immediately follow up on this success by attempting either a Throw or Immobilise manoeuvre.

Grapple Fails; Defender may Riposte: The grapple fails badly. The attack is considered to have missed and therefore causes no damage. The attacker has also left himself wide open for a Riposte, which the defender may immediately take advantage of. See page 71 for details on Ripostes.

Martial Arts

Note that a character with Martial Arts may use his Martial Arts skill rather than any other skill in the grapple rules.

Grappling Combatants

Grappling combatants will remain locked together until one combatant breaks free or is thrown out of the grapple. Grappling combatants suffer a –20% penalty to any tests that do not target or directly respond to their grapple partner. Grappling combatants may not use Reactions.

A grappling combatant is restricted to the following special Combat Actions.

Break Free: To break out of a grapple, the character makes a grapple attempt, designating himself as the defender. The character may only use the Unarmed skill or a Natural Weapon skill in this case. Compare the opposed results on the Grapple table – a result of 'grapple fails' means the character has succeeded in breaking free and the combatants are no longer grappling, though they will be adjacent.

Immobilise: This is simply holding the enemy in place so they can attempt no actions other than to break free of the grapple. While immobilised, enemies are considered helpless. It takes a successful Unarmed skill test to immobilise an opponent – this test suffers a penalty equal to the opponent's DEX+STR.

Inflict Pain: By exerting pressure at key points or cutting off air supply, a character can cause serious damage to his opponent while grappling. It takes a successful Unarmed skill test to inflict pain – this test suffers a penalty equal to the opponent's DEX+CON. If this skill test succeeds, the damage is 1D6 + damage modifier, applied to a random location.

Throw: By using leverage and a modicum of brute force, a character can throw his opponent away from him. It takes a successful Unarmed skill test to throw an opponent – this test suffers a penalty equal to the opponent's DEX+SIZ. If this skill test succeeds, the opponent is thrown 2 metres and suffers 1D6 damage, applied to a random location. The grapple ends in this case.

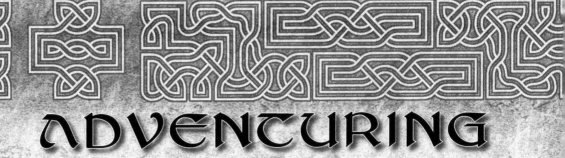

ADVENTURING

This chapter discusses a series of rules covering general situations adventurers are likely to encounter in the course of a campaign, and how the Games Master should resolve such situations.

Movement

The Movement table shows how far adventurers with a variety of Movement scores can travel over various periods of time. Groups of adventurers travelling together will move at the speed of the slowest member. Unless otherwise stated, all human Player Characters have a Movement of 4m

Movement in combat assumes a character is moving as fast as possible given his particular Combat Action. Movement over any period other than combat (minute or longer) assumes a character is walking at a sustainable rate, though it is possible to run instead. This sustainable walking is considered light activity, though a full day (12 hours) of walking will count as medium activity.

Running

Running is easy enough for short periods; a character can run for a number of minutes equal to his CON before suffering from any tiredness. Once this time period has elapsed, the running counts as medium activity.

Terrain & Weather

Movement rates can be hindered by terrain and other adverse conditions such as wind, rain and hail. These conditions are divided into three categories, Slight, Moderate and Great Adversity.

Slight Adversity: Reduce the adventurer's distance moved by 25%.

Moderate Adversity: Reduce the adventurer's distance moved by 50%.

Great Adversity: Reduce the adventurer's distance moved by 75%.

Chases & Pursuits

If an adventurer succeeds at a Difficult (−20%) Athletics test, they may treat their Movement as one higher than normal for a single Combat Action or minute.

Sprinting is very tiring when chasing and counts as heavy activity.

If mounts are being used by adventurers in a pursuit, then the Athletics skill of the mount should be used rather than that of the character.

Illumination & Darkness

Night Sight allows the adventurer to treat partial darkness as illuminated and darkness as partial darkness. Nocturnal creatures usually possess this ability.

Illuminating Items

Example	Radius
Candle or embers	1m
Flaming brand or lantern	3m
Campfire	5m
Bonfire	10m

Movement

Time Period	Movement 1m	Movement 2m	Movement 3m	Movement 4m	Movement 5m	Movement 6m
Combat Action	1m (2m if running)	2m (4m if running)	3m (6m if running)	4m (8m if running)	5m (10m if running)	6m (12m if running)
Minute	12 (24m if running)	24m (48m if running)	36m (72m if running)	48m (96m if running)	60m (120m if running)	72m (144m if running)
Hour	0.7km	1.4km	2.2km	2.9km	3.6km	4.3km
Day (12 hours)	8.4km	16.8km	26.4km	34.8km	43.2km	51.6km

Illumination & Darkness

Environment is...	Example	Effects
Brightly Illuminated	Blazing summer day.	+10% to Perception tests to spot hidden characters or items.
Illuminated	Heavily candlelit room, overcast day, within radius of illuminating item.	None.
Partial Darkness	Cavern mouth, misty day, within 3 x radius of illuminating item.	–20% to vision-based Perception tests.
Dark	Large cavern illuminated only by embers, foggy day, within 5 x radius of illuminating item.	–40% to vision-based Perception tests. Movement penalised by –1m.
Pitch Black	Sealed room with stone walls, cavern many kilometres underground, mountaintop whiteout.	Perception tests reliant on vision impossible, as are ranged attacks. –60% to close combat attacks. Movement halved.

Fatigue

At noon of the next day the mercenary army rode swaggering into the city. Elric met them close to the city gate. The Imrryrian warriors were obviously weary from a long ride and were loaded with booty since, before Yishana sent for them, they had been raiding in Shazar close to the Marshes of the Mist.
– Stormbringer

Physical activity is divided into three categories; light, medium and heavy. The length of time a character can engage in physical activity without running the risk of becoming Exhausted is determined by his CON. Once this time has elapsed, a character must begin to make skill tests in order to resist the effects of exhaustion.

Light Activity: Adventurers never risk Fatigue while engaging in light activity.

Medium Activity: Includes running, fighting in combat, climbing or swimming at a rapid rate. A character can engage in medium activity for a number of minutes equal to his CON before risking Fatigue. Once this time has elapsed, the adventurer must immediately make a Simple (+20%) Athletics test or begin suffering the effects of Fatigue. So long as the activity continues, he must make another Simple (+20%) Athletics test every time a number of minutes equal to the adventurer's CON elapse.

Heavy Activity: Includes back-breaking manual labour, sprinting and climbing at a rapid rate. A character can

Fatigue Levels

Level of Fatigue	Effects
Fresh	None.
Winded	All skill tests (including further tests to resist Fatigue) suffer a –10% penalty.
Tired	All skill tests (including further tests to resist Fatigue) suffer a –20% penalty. Movement suffers a –1m penalty.
Wearied	All skill tests (including further tests to resist Fatigue) suffer a –30% penalty. Movement suffers a –1m penalty. Strike Rank suffers a –2 penalty.
Exhausted	All skill tests (including further tests to resist Fatigue) suffer a –40% penalty. Movement is halved. Strike Rank suffers a –4 penalty. DEX is considered 5 points lower for the purposes of determining Combat Actions. Adventurer must make a Persistence test every minute or fall unconscious for 1D3x2 hours
Debilitated	All skill tests (including further tests to resist Fatigue) suffer a –50% penalty. Movement is halved. Strike Rank suffers a –6 penalty. DEX is considered 10 points lower for the purposes of determining Combat Actions. Adventurer must make a Difficult Persistence test every Combat Round or fall unconscious for 1D6x2 hours.

engage in heavy activity for a number of Combat Actions equal to his CON score before risking Fatigue. Once this time has elapsed, the adventurer must immediately make a Normal (+0%) Athletics test or begin suffering the effects of Fatigue. So long as the activity continues, he must make another Normal (+0%) Athletics test every time a number of Combat Actions equal to the adventurer's CON elapse.

Effects of Fatigue

If a character fails a test while engaged in medium or heavy activity, he will begin to show Fatigue. Every time a Fatigue test is failed, the adventurer will drop down one level of Fatigue, as shown on the Fatigue Levels table.

Time & Fatigue

Once a character has been awake for 10+CON hours, they must make a Persistence test or drop one Fatigue level. This test must be repeated for every hour the character remains awake.

Recovering from Fatigue

A character will move up one level of Fatigue for every two hours of complete rest or four hours of light activity. A successful First Aid or Healing test can raise a character by one level of Fatigue once per day, but cannot raise a character above Winded.

Exposure, Starvation & Thirst

A character can normally survive for a number of hours equal to his CON before suffering from exposure.

A character can survive for a number of days equal to his CON before becoming starved, though after three days they will begin to suffer a –10% penalty to Fatigue tests.

A character can survive for a number of hours equal to his CON x 4 before becoming chronically thirsty, though particularly arid environments may reduce this to CON x 3 or even CON x 2.

Whenever a character is suffering from exposure, starvation or thirst, the Fatigue test penalty immediately doubles to –20%. In addition, the character will automatically suffer one point of damage to all locations every day, for every condition he is experiencing. Natural or magical healing will not heal this damage – only sufficient shelter, food or water can remedy the problem and allow natural or magical healing to take place.

Healing

Healing can be performed in one of three ways – using the First Aid skill, through sorcery, or through natural healing, resting while the injuries heal themselves.

Natural Healing

A character's injured locations (any location that has 0 hit points or more) regain one hit point per 24 hours, as long as the character does not engage in anything more than light activity.

A character's badly injured locations (any location that has –1 or fewer hit points or more) regain one hit point per location per day, as long as the character does not engage in anything more than light activity, and the character succeeds at a Resilience test.

Natural healing will not heal a Major Injury until that location has either been treated with a successful Healing test or some exotic form of magical healing has been applied.

Magical Healing

The Elric saga is curiously devoid of healing magic. Elric, the greatest sorcerer of his age, never uses healing magic upon himself or upon others, having to rely on restorative herbs and potions to regain his own, feeble strength. Certain rare artefacts, such as the Nanorion Elric plucks from the corpse of Ashaneloon's guardian, may have healing qualities, but there are no healing runes or spells.

Encumbrance

Every piece of equipment in the Equipment chapter has an Encumbrance (ENC) score, though some items are too small or light to have an ENC score. Characters can usually ignore the effects on Encumbrance that these have unless they start carrying a lot of them – assume that an average of 20 such items will equal 1 ENC, so long as the character has a suitable means of carrying them, such as a sack or backpack.

A character can carry equipment whose total ENC is less than or equal to his STR+SIZ without penalty.

Overloading

A character carrying total ENC greater than his STR+SIZ is Overloaded.

Overloaded characters suffer a –20% penalty to all tests that require physical actions, including Weapon skill tests and most tests that have DEX or STR as a Characteristic.

Overloaded characters have their Movement halved. They also suffer a –20% penalty to all Fatigue tests.

A character cannot carry more than twice his STR+SIZ in ENC.

Falling

A character that takes damage from a fall ends up prone. Armour points do not reduce falling damage. Falls of a metre or less do not incur any damage. Falls of greater than a metre incur 1D6 points of damage for every *5 metres* fallen.

An Acrobatics test can be attempted to mitigate falling damage – a successful test allows the character to treat the fall as if it were two metres shorter than it actually is. In addition, as long as this test is a success and the character is not reduced to 0 hit points in a location due to the fall, the character lands safely and is not prone.

Characters falling onto soft surfaces may have the distance they fall effectively halved for the purposes of damage.

Suffocation

While performing medium activity, a character can hold his breath for a number of Combat Rounds equal to his CON. Characters engaging in light activity can double this time, while characters performing heavy activity will halve it.

Once a character has surpassed the time for which he can hold his breath, he must make a Resilience test every round with a cumulative –10% penalty. If he fails, he automatically starts inhaling the suffocating substance, which automatically damages his Chest location once every round.

Anaerobic environments causes 1D6 damage to the Chest location. Suffocation due to smoke or smog causes 1D3 points of damage; and, if the smog is poisonous, then the effects of the poison take effect in addition to the general suffocation damage.

Armour points do not reduce suffocation damage. The damage will only cease once the character can draw breathable air once more. Even then, the character will require a Resilience test to be able to do anything other than wretch or gasp for breath for 1D4 Combat Rounds.

Fire, Heat & Freezing

A character will normally take damage from fire or heat to a specific hit location. However, if a character is immersed in the source of the damage, then all locations will suffer from the damage the fire causes. The amount of damage suffered from fire or heat will depend on its intensity, as shown on the Fire and Heat table.

Fire & Heat

Damage Source	Example	Damage
Flame	Candle	1 point
Large Flame	Flaming brand	D4 points
Small Fire	Camp fire, cooking fire	D6 points
Large Fire	Scolding steam, large bonfires, burning rooms	2D6 points
Inferno	Lava, inside a blast furnace	3D6 points

A character who takes more than 10 points of damage from a fire in successive rounds is set alight, and takes 1D4 points of damage per round until the flames are put out.

Poison

Every type of poison has the following information detailed:

Name: The poison's name. Also, if the poison is magical in nature, it will be mentioned here.
Type: Lists whether the poison is ingested, used on a weapon or inhaled.
Delay: The time between the poison's introduction to a character, to the time its effect takes hold.
Potency: This is a number between 10 and 100 that measures the strength of a poison. Some magical poisons have even higher Potencies. A character must make an opposed Resilience test versus the poison's Potency test in order to avoid or mitigate the damage of the poison.
Effect: Usually hit point damage that affects all locations of the victim, though this is not universal. Some poisons cause a character to sleep for a period of time. More exotic poisons may cause hallucinogenic effects, paralysis or a combination of effects. These take place after the delay noted above.

Adventuring

81

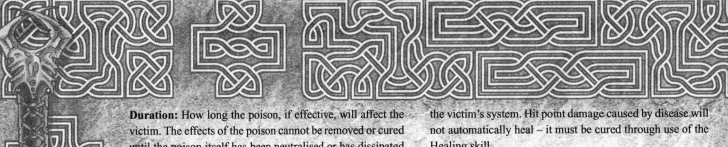

Duration: How long the poison, if effective, will affect the victim. The effects of the poison cannot be removed or cured until the poison itself has been neutralised or has dissipated in the victim's system. Hit point damage caused by poison will not automatically heal – it must be treated with the Healing skill.

Poison Succeeds, Character Fails

If the poison succeeds its Potency test and the character fails his Resilience test, the poison has its full effect.

Character Succeeds, Poison Fails

If the character succeeds his Resilience test and the poison fails its Potency test, the poison has no effect.

Both Poison and Character Succeed

Whoever rolled the highest in their test wins.

Both Poison and Character Fail

Whoever rolled the lowest in their test wins.

Disease

Every type of disease has the following information detailed:

Name: The disease's name. Also, if the disease is magical in nature, it will be mentioned here.

Type: Lists whether the disease is spread through contamination, touch or is airborne.

Delay: The time between the disease's introduction to a character, to the time its effect takes hold. It is also the time following disease contraction that a victim will be forced to make follow-up opposed disease tests.

Potency: This is a number between 10 and 100 that measures the strength of a disease. Some magical diseases, like the shining plague, have even higher Potencies. A character must make an opposed Resilience test versus the disease's Potency test in order to avoid or mitigate the damage of the disease.

Effect: Usually hit point damage that affects all locations of the victim, though this is not universal. Many diseases will apply a penalty to Characteristics or skills. More exotic diseases may cause hallucinogenic effects, paralysis or a combination of effects. These take place after the delay noted above.

The effects of the disease cannot be removed or healed until the disease itself has been neutralised or has dissipated in the victim's system. Hit point damage caused by disease will not automatically heal – it must be cured through use of the Healing skill.

Disease Succeeds, Character Fails

If the disease succeeds its Potency test and the character fails his Resilience test, the disease has its full effect.

Character Succeeds, Disease Fails

If the character succeeds his Resilience test and the disease fails its Potency test, the disease has no effect.

Both Disease and Character Succeed

Whoever rolled the highest in their test wins.

Both Disease and Character Fail

Whoever rolled the lowest in their test wins.

Unlike a poison, diseases will progress if a character does not resist its effects. Once the first opposed test is failed by the victim, they will have to make an additional opposed test (after an amount of time determined by the disease's delay statistic). If the victim succeeds this second opposed test, he has overcome the worst of the disease and will no longer suffer its effects (other than remaining hit point damage) after while (use the disease's delay statistic to determine how long this takes). If the victim fails this second opposed test, he falls deeper into the disease. Apply all of the disease's effects again to the character. Once the delay period has elapsed once more, the victim will have to make a third opposed disease test, and so on.

Inanimate Objects

All inanimate objects have armour points and hit points. Except for the most unusual of circumstances, attacks on inanimate objects will automatically hit – characters simply need to work out how much damage they deal.

The object's armour points are deducted from any damage dealt as normal, with the remainder being applied to its hit points. Once an object's hit points have been reduced to zero, it is smashed and useless.

Inanimate objects likely to block or restrain characters, such as doors or ropes, have Strength scores. To break down a door, or burst one's bonds, a character must succeed at a brute force Athletics test. This automatically reduces the object's hit points to 0.

LORDS OF THE MILLION SPHERES

The gods described in this chapter are the Lords of the Higher Planes; living, intelligent entities with murky agendas and schemes ignoring the requirements of mortals, but having implications for every single one of them. These gods make frequent appearances; Arioch is the most famous example, but Grome and Straasha also manifest in response to Elric's calls, compelled by ancient pacts forged in the Bright Empire's earliest days. Why do mortals need such mercurial gods? They need to believe that there is purpose to life and a reward (or punishment) after it. They wish to believe in, and witness, miracles. They want to call upon something by name as they engage in deeds of good or ill, in the hope of gaining some kind of approval, whole-hearted or slender, for what they are about to do or have done already. And gods, being as vain and arrogant as humans, welcome such attention and flattery. In return they offer certain gifts, facsimiles of their own powers, but typically attached with conditions and side-effects that result in binding mortals to courses of action they might not otherwise have chosen. This chapter discusses the various divine powers at work in Elric's world, and some of the cults worshipping them.

The Elements

The elements rule over the four domains of the physical world: Air, Earth, Fire and Water. They control the beings that manifest as the winds, the soil and rocks, the seas and rivers, and the fires of the tribal hearth. The materials of air, earth, fire and water are elementals that lack spirit and intellect, and so can be easily manipulated by mortals.

Lady Lassa, Ruler of the Air, Bringer of Storms, Mother of Breath

Without her the Earth would be devoid of life for it is her realm that brings air to the world. She controls the sylphs, spirits of the breeze; the sharnah, builders of gales; the h'haar shan, makers of whirlwinds. The birds and other flying creatures are her children and she abhors anything that would cause them harm. Lady Lassa has two unruly and destructive brothers; Misha of the West Winds, who creates the sharnah gales, and Graoll of the East Wind who raises the whirlwinds and tornadoes. From time to time they grow bored and release their creations upon the earth, until Lassa berates them and sends her calming breath to restore order. There is also her sister, Shaarnasaa, the life-giving and blessing queen of the South Winds. Certain tribes of Dorel, Pikarayd and the Weeping Waste venerate Misha and Graoll as gods in their own right, and flattered, the brothers send sharnahs and h'haar shans as displays of their gratitude, with no inkling of the damage caused.

Lady Lassa's enemy is Lord Kakatal. Kakatal is greedy and would starve the world of air so his flame-children, the salamanders, might burn hotter and brighter. But though they are enemies, they have maintained a respectful distance and have only rarely battled directly.

Lord Grome, Earth-Father, Mover and Shaker, the Binder

Without Grome the world would fly apart in a storm of dust and rubble. Grome binds and makes solid. He gives form and meaning, expressing himself in the mountains and hills, great plains and calm valleys. His children are the gnomes, made from the stuff of the world, beings of immense strength that build and arrange, reshape and restructure as Grome desires. When the earth was young Grome was naked, so he called upon Lady Lassa and they made a daughter who lives with Grome as his consort; she is Ish'ish'a'maal, Lady of the Trees, and she clothes Lord Grome in the finery of the forests, giving homes to the animals and birds, which honours her mother.

Twenty thousand years ago Lord Grome went to war with Straasha, seeking dominance over which element should cover the surface of the earth. Their war reshaped the world, moving continents, raising and submerging islands, creating huge ranges of mountains and flattening hills. Whilst they know peace during Elric's time, their enmity is as strong as ever; Grome builds and Straasha erodes the edges of what is built, either through the slow drip of the rains or the battering of the waves against coastlines.

Lord Kakatal, the Fire Heart, Giver of Warmth and the Hearth of the World

Kakatal surrounds the Earth and gazes upon it with his single brilliant eye, which is called the sun. He gave the world the gift of fire, so that mortals might worship him in their homes and make edible the things they caught or grew to eat. In his carelessness he neglected to restrict fire's power and so it is a force for destruction unless strictly controlled. His servants, the salamanders, lurk at the molten heart of the Earth, and can be called forth to channel Kakatal's powers. But they are unruly children, revelling in their power to consume and destroy, and Kakatal, neglectful still, refuses to admonish them.

Lord Kakatal seeks to dominate Lassa for she provides the stuff his fires and salamanders need to consume to live. She has an abundance of air, and recognises fire's importance, but refuses to feed his salamanders more than the merest scraps. Resentful, Kakatal challenges her now and then by inflicting forest fires upon her daughter, Ish'ish'a'maal, forcing her to call upon Lord Straasha to quench them with his tears, which angers jealous Lord Grome.

Lord Straasha, the Water Father, King of the Waves and Currents

Straasha's domains are the upper waters of the world, the oceans, seas and rivers. His children, the undines, move the waters of the Earth in tides and currents, causing seas to swell and retreat and rivers to flow. He cannot understand why the entire world cannot be flooded because his waters are filled with life, and he constantly challenges Lord Grome's creations by gradually eroding them, reclaiming the world inch by inch. His war with Grome, twenty millennia ago, created the oceans of the Young Kingdoms. But parts of his kingdom, the deepest reaches of the ocean, were stolen from him by Pyaray, a duke of Chaos who now rules a dread realm of undead sailors and sea monsters. Alone Straasha cannot challenge Pyaray and must cede this domain to the tentacled whisperer. Straasha is too proud to seek aid from any of the other elemental rulers, and must therefore accept the presence of Chaos within his beloved oceans.

Straasha believes in life and respects all its mortal forms. He is sympathetic to the humans of the earth and would preserve them from the horrors of Pyaray's hellish depths. His love for life is recognised by the sailors of the Young Kingdoms, many of whom have been saved from a watery death (claimed by Pyaray for his undead fleet) by either Straasha's undines or the hand of the water father himself.

The Beast Lords

The Beast Lords represent the natural creatures of the Earth. They are the archetypes of the beasts of the world, the primal definition from which the natures of all animals emanate. Earthly cats behave in the way they do because Meerclar behaves that way. If his behaviour changed, the cats of the Young Kingdoms would naturally follow. This is true for all Beast Lords; they are creatures and the very essence of creatures, abstractions and natural forms at the same time. In this sense they are elements; indeed, Elric refers to them as such on several occasions. There may even be some relation between the beast and Elemental Lords; if there is, it is cryptic and known only to them.

For the most part the Beast Lords slumber in their individual realms allowing their subjects to go about their business. The earthly creatures represent their Beast Lords simply by being themselves; they have no other agendas or motives, save doing what their natures dictate. If those natures are threatened in some extreme way, and on a species-wide level, only then would a Beast Lord be roused into action.

Melniboné holds ancient pacts with all the Beast Lords, just as they do with the elementals. Each has aided the other over the millennia (although how and why is not understood), and as a result, Melniboné's emperors have the power to rouse a Beast Lord from its rest and seek its direct intervention in the mundane world. Elric summons Fileet, Lady of the Birds, to rescue him from the Oonai; he calls upon Haaashaastaak Lord of Lizards, to devour the chaotic winged creature sent against him, Yishana and Moonglum by Theleb K'aarna; and Nnuuurrrr'c'c, King of Insects, is called to subdue the olab on his expedition to R'lin K'ren A'a. Other Beast Lords mentioned by name in the saga are Meerclar, Lord of Cats, Roofdrak, Lord of Dogs, Muru'ah, Lord of Cattle and Ap-yss Alara, Queen of Swine.

Beast Lords of the Elric Saga
Haaashaastaak, Lord of Lizards

The entity was called Haaashaastaak; and it was scaly and cold, with no true intellect, such as men and gods possessed, but an awareness, which served it as well if not better… It did not really hear words in the exact sense, but it heard rhythms which meant much to it, even though it did not know why…'

'Haaashaastaak, Lord of Lizards,
Your children were fathers of men,
Haaashaastaak, Prince of Reptiles.
Come aid a grandchild now.
'Haaashaastaak, Father of Scales,
Cold-blooded bringer of life...'
– The Weird of the White Wolf

Meerclar, Lord of Cats

Far beyond the Earth, dwelling within a world set apart from the physical laws of space and time which governed the planet, glowing in a deep warmth of blue and amber, a manlike creature stretched itself and yawned, displaying tiny, pointed teeth. It pressed its head languidly against its furry shoulder – and listened. The voice it heard was not that of one of its people, the kind he loved and protected. But he recognised the language.

He smiled to himself as remembrance came and he felt the pleasant sensation of fellowship. He remembered a race which, unlike other humans (whom he disdained) had shared his qualities – a race which, like him, loved pleasure, cruelty and sophistication for its own sake.
– The Bane of the Black Sword

Nnuuurrrr'c'c, Lord of Insects

'King with Wings! Lord of all that work and are not seen, upon whose labours all else depends! Nnuuurrrr'c'c of the Insect Folk, I summon thee!'

In his ears now Elric heard a buzzing and gradually the buzzing formed itself in words. 'Who are thou, mortal? What right has thou to summon me?'
– The Sailor on the Seas of Fate

Roofdrak, Lord of Dogs (and by extension wolves and foxes)

Elric does not summon Roofdrak during the saga, but the ancient pacts which bind Melniboné and Roofdrak together will be known to him. From the incantations the albino uses for other Beast Lords, one can surmise that Roofdrak's will be similar, and his ethereal home will be a place of rosy warmth, akin to the hearth-side, where languid Roofdrak dozes and dreams of chasing Meerclar through the Multiverse, or chewing on the marrowbones of the enemies of canine-kind.

Nuru'ah, Lord of Cattle (and all ungulates)

No summoning of Nuru'ah is mentioned in the saga, although Melniboné has long enjoyed a pact with the Cattle King, having used immense oxen in times past to draw the war chariots of the Bright Empire in their subjugation of the old human kingdoms.

One can imagine Nuru'ah's realm as a place of soft, verdant pastures, peaceful and vast, where the Cattle Lord grazes steadily, immense tail swishing away the motes and spirits of Nnuuurrrr'c'c's insect-kind.

Ap-yss-Alara Lady of Swine (pigs and boars)

'...and even Ap-yss-Alara, Queen of the Swine, who was said to refuse all mortal advances and would continue to do so while one of them still ate pork. Since pork was not eaten by any Melnibonéan of the higher castes, my folk had first made their accommodation with the queen.'
– The Skrayling Tree

Ap-yss-Alara is never summoned in the saga, but it is obvious that such creatures were once useful to Melniboné – perhaps in the form of savage battle boars, used to shatter the formations of armies who dared to defy them. The home of the Lady of Swine is a dark, shady forest. Its dappled roof a tangle of ancient gnarled trees that drop acorns and nuts, and its moist floor covered with flavoursome fungi. There she is attended by litters of her devoted children.

Creating Other Beast Lords

As there is a Beast Lord for every natural beast upon the Earth, creating new additions is a matter only of imagination. Names for these beast-kings reflect the sound of the animal and their home realms reflect the conditions favoured by the creature. Their enemies and prey are the natural enemies and prey of their kind, and no Beast Lord will stir himself to deal with anything less.

Summoning Beast Lords

Though the Dharzi once possessed the knowledge to summon the Beast Lords, only Melnibonéans still retain the ability. No Beast Lord stirs without a Pact, and only then when the identity of the summoner can be established. Elric's command of the

Lords of the Million Spheres

Beast Lords stems from his peoples' age-old relationship and his wearing of the Actorios, the ring of kings, identifying him as one with a right to call for aid. At the Games Master's discretion human sorcerers may be permitted to attempt to form a Pact with a Beast Lord. A sorcerer needs to know High Speech, the Beast Lord's name, and the Summoning Ritual skill (which, when summoning a Beast Lord is always at *half* the usual base percentage). A bonus can be gained from sacrificing enemies, or prey, relevant to the lord being summoned. Nominally, each animal slaughtered adds 1% to the chance of success, up to a maximum of the sorcerer's original Summoning Ritual skill.

The sorcerer must also dedicate characteristic POW in return for the Beast Lord's aid, thereby forming a Pact with it. The compulsion imposed by such a bond is always that the sorcerer protects and nurtures the offspring of the Beast Lord.

For example Malagan of Pan Tang requires the help of Roofdrak to assist with a plague of cats sent by a rival sorcerer. He is fluent in High Speech and his base Summoning Ritual skill is 35%. To attempt the summoning, this will be halved to 18% (rounding up). Malagan barks out the incantation whilst wringing the neck of a cat which is trying to claw out his eyes, gaining a bonus of 1%. The dice roll is 19 – a success, but only just. Roofdrak's voice, a panting, breathy sound, echoes in Malagan's mind wanting a reward for his help. Malagan pledges it and dedicates 1 point of POW. Roofdrak calls forth a pack of street-hounds to savage the cats that are clambering over Malagan's body and the sorcerer is left battered and scratched, but with his eyes still in their sockets. He now has Pact (Roofdrak) 12% (his CHA plus the amount of POW dedicated to Roofdrak).

The Plant Lords

'They sang together, sending their song through all the dimensions of the Multiverse, to where a dreaming creature stirred and lifted up arms made of a million woven brambles and turned faces which too, were of knotted rosewood, in the direction of the song it had not heard for a hundred thousand years… the Tangled Woman shifted her brambly body, arm by arm and leg by leg, then head by head, and, with a rustling movement which made all her foliage shudder, she formed herself into a shape very like a human shape, though somewhat larger'.
– The Revenge of the Rose

The Plant Lords represent the myriad plants of the world in the same way the Beast Lords represent the beasts. Each species of plant has its own guardian who defines what that plant is and how it behaves. The Tangled Woman, for example, represents brambles and thorns. Even Melniboné has forgotten much of what it ever knew about the Plant Lords, but they are clearly a powerful, if dormant force. Treat their summonings and pacts in precisely the same way as Beast Lords.

Chaos

There are many Lords of Chaos, some of which are minor dukes of Hell acting on certain agendas, such as Narjhan and Balo. The most powerful, like Arioch and Xiombarg, are akin to gods with complex agendas and motives concerning the overthrow of Law and the domination of earth. They seek to establish realms of Chaos throughout the Multiverse, creating an entropic empire where all life, save their own, is an unstable, constantly changing melange of the beautiful and the horrific.

Chaos has been prevented from manifesting directly on the earth for the past five hundred years, due to the actions of the Lords of Law who created a barrier around the Earth's plane to limit the Chaos Lord's interference. Before that, battles between the Lords of Chaos and Law were played-out across the Young Kingdoms. The bay of Dhakos, for instance, is said to have been created when Lord Tovik of Law defeated Mabelode, King of the Swords, some 5,000 years ago. With Melniboné as their enthusiastic mortal servants the Lords of Chaos helped create the majesty and terror of the Bright Empire, but with the Barrier of Law preventing further direct intervention, their influence declined and so did their direct worship by the Dragon Lords. Consequentially the empire fell.

The Lords of Chaos can still manifest upon the Earth, but their direct powers are limited. They can, and do, aid their mortal servants but as is the nature of Chaos, the type and level of aid is inconsistent. A mortal worshipper may be called beloved by a Chaos Lord one day, only to fall from favour the next. The Lords of Chaos do not truly care; all that matters is their own agenda and mortals are only useful if they can advance it in some way. If they cannot, they are an irrelevance.

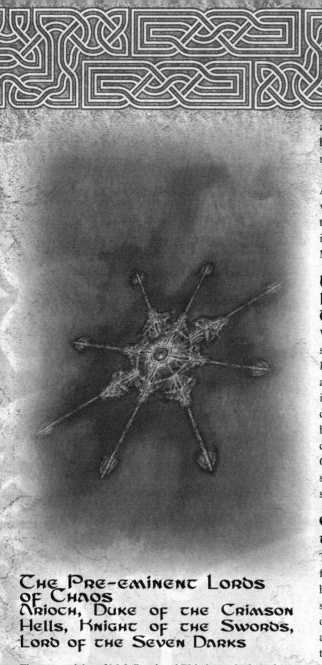

and takes delight in rendering entire worlds parched and barren. When it is through, it spits what it has drunk at the sun, perhaps to spite it, or perhaps to extinguish it.

Artigkern's last manifestation on the Earth was during the very first decades of Melniboné's rule, before it truly became the Bright Empire. It stole Lord Straasha's sister, becoming infatuated with her, but was defeated by the silver-skinned Mernii hero, White Crow.

Balaan, The Grim-Faced, Lord of Ecstatic Agony and Unbearable Pleasures

With his face hidden behind a mask of black iron, bolted to his skull, Balaan is the god of torturers, sadists and masochists. He is worshipped widely on Melniboné as both the torturer and the giver of pleasure through pain where his adherents include Doctor Jest, amongst others. Balaan's worshippers consider the inflicting of pain, and its receipt, as one of the highest art forms, as demonstrated in the altered eunuch choirs of Imrryr who sing Balaan's hymns of suffering. On Pan Tang, Balaan is god of torturers and the bringer of suffering, an implacable deity who seeks only to hear the screams of the unholy.

Chardros, The Reaper, Lord of the Graves

Taking many forms (a shrouded, skeletal figure; a gaunt-faced, emaciated Melnibonéan; a vast, vulture-headed human, to name but a few), but always with his immense iron scythe, Chardros is the lord of death, undeath and the reaping of souls. Shunned in Melniboné but welcomed in Pan Tang and Dharijor, Chardros remains aloof from mortal affairs for the most part, awaiting his hour in the final battle where he will engage with Donblas the Justice Maker.

Demons of combat and war are Chardros's foot soldiers and those pledging their souls to his worship are taken to the Gates of Hell where he patrols, to be made into the demonic spawn he unleashes at the end of the world.

The Pre-eminent Lords of Chaos
Arioch, Duke of the Crimson Hells, Knight of the Swords, Lord of the Seven Darks

The patron deity of Melniboné and Elric in particular, whom he 'loves above all other mortals'. Arioch takes many forms, from swarms of insects or a jade statue, to beautiful, fair-skinned children, but his favoured manifestation is as a Melnibonéan male of brilliant, blinding beauty. Lord Arioch is cruel, fickle and, on this plane, the most powerful of the Chaos Lords. Arioch guards the runeswords Stormbringer and Mournblade, which may only be wielded by the royal line of Imrryr.

Artigkern, Drinker of Oceans, Drainer of Worlds

The vast maw of Artigkern, brother to Arioch, can drain entire seas in a few days, as it sups voraciously. Artigkern exists solely to consume every last drop of water in the Multiverse

Eequor, Blue Lady of Dismay, Goddess of Sorrowing Solitude

Eequor dwells in a realm decorated solely in shades of blue. She is a self-pitying and jealous Lady of Entropy, forever scheming and seeking ways of improving her rule over the Earth. Images of her are always carved from blue stone or sapphires and in each she is always of a beautiful, melancholie countenance. Many female sorcerers are drawn to her

worship, for she promises many gifts and secret knowledge that may be put to bitter ends. One of her worshippers is Sorana, the duplicitous lover of Rackhir the Red Archer; she has many other such acolytes.

Hionhurn, The Executioner, Lord of the Gallows

Another god of death, Hionhurn is the brutish executioner of Chaos, his huge axe sharpened and ready to sever heads and souls alike. He manifests as a giant, shaggy-haired axeman, his lime-green skin as gnarled and twisted as an ancient tree, his expression jovial. Hionhurn promises a pleasant death but eternal suffering and torment.

Mabelode, The Faceless, King of the Swords, Ruler of Shadows

Mabelode is worshipped across many planes of the Multiverse, and on some, his power exceeds that of Arioch and Xiombarg, his fellow Sword Rulers. Mabelode's face is always wreathed in shadow, however it is viewed, and this has led to the soubriquet of 'faceless'. A cunning and manipulative deity, he numbers Prince Yyrkoon amongst his devotees, and his schemes are concerned with deception, stealth and the advancement of shadow. He bears an immense sword of dazzling gold that sings through the air, and delights in securing the worship of powerful individuals who can be easily twisted into acting as his followers.

Maluk, The Silent Watcher of the Single Eye, Lord of Treachery

A favoured god of Pan Tang, Maluk has but a single, staring eye gazing from his slender, androgynous face, and his mouth stitched-shut so that none of his secrets may escape his thin, bloodless lips. Adherents of Maluk are known to put out an eye and stitch-shut their mouths in homage to his ghastly visage.

Maluk adores treachery and betrayal for selfish gains. He grooms those who show such qualities and shows them tantalising glimpses of how much better their lives will become if they carry out their schemes to the full. As a guardian of secrets his province is knowledge and subversive power, seeking not to command directly but to control through others.

Pyaray, Tentacled Whisperer of Impossible Secrets, Lord of the Fleets of Chaos

Lord Pyaray lurks in the planes of Hell that intersect with the deepest reaches of the ocean. He receives the souls of

drowned sailors and adds their wrecked ships to his ever-growing fleet that, at the end of the world, arises from the depths and commands the seas of the Young Kingdoms. He is worshipped by pirates and other sea-borne reavers, but he fears, and avoids, Lord Straasha, who does all in his power to prevent Pyaray's undead crews from growing.

When he manifests it is as a huge, blood-red octopus with many tentacles and several eyes of blue crystal. One, usually at the top of the head, is said to contain Pyaray's soul, and a special weapon, such as Stormbringer or Mournblade, can destroy him. Indeed, this is the tactic used by Elric when he battles Pyaray aboard his flagship in his quest to rescue Zarozinia.

Slortar the Old

Eldest and most sweet-tongued of the Hell Dukes, Lord Slortar is favoured in Melniboné and enjoyed its primary worship before Arioch replaced him in the nation's affections. He is a connoisseur of the debauched, depraved and decadent; a self-satisfied lord of indulgence who condones gluttony, greed and sloth in its myriad forms. Those who worship him tend towards the corpulent – a sharp contrast with Slortar's trim and beautiful frame.

Xiombarg, Queen of the Swords, Promiser of Eternal Life

On this Earth, Queen Xiombarg is no more powerful than Arioch, her brother, or Mabelode, but on other planes she is more powerful than Arioch and matched only by Mabelode the Faceless. Described as *she*, she can take the form of either sex, but when choosing to manifest prefers the female form: that of the most beautiful woman possible to imagine, her hair dark gold and streaked with red and black. Her form can switch abruptly – as can all the Lords of Chaos – into that of a man or a creature with a leering skull-face.

As a Sword Ruler she is beloved of warriors and soldiers. It is said she can control time to an extent, though has never done so upon the plane of the Young Kingdoms, but she can – and does – promise eternal life to those who serve her. One such recipient is Prince Gaynor the Damned, doomed to wander the Multiverse as the Eternal Enemy, undying yet not invincible, forced to experience every minute of every hour of every year without hope of rest.

Minor Nobles

These are the lesser lords, vassals of the major dukes of Chaos. Some are worshipped in their own right whilst others are worshipped through a more pre-eminent deity.

Balo, Insane Jester and Minstrel, of neither Chaos nor Law

Balo belongs to neither Chaos nor Law and is the only supernatural entity permitted to cross the divide between them (although neither is he of the Balance). An insane prankster, he is most commonly attributed to Chaos, but the guise of a simple fool with a love of vicious pranks, often at the expense of the Lords of Chaos, masks a complex and confused mind that has, perhaps, been driven mad by both the chaotic and lawful secrets he has been privy to.

As a result, Balo has few formal worshippers in the Young Kingdoms. Those that do offer him allegiance have been approached directly by him to aid in one of his 'jokes' or schemes. Becoming involved with him is to risk his infectious insanity.

Checkalakh the Burning God

A minor Chaos Lord made entirely of fire, he was once summoned to Nadsokor to burn disease from the city, but ran amok. He was imprisoned within a labyrinth in the city by Lord Donblas, sealed within it by a one-way membrane. His essence is fire, and, like his essence, he is constantly hungry. The beggars King Urish of Nadsokor offers to him

are poor food and he constantly craves more. He has almost no influence in the Young Kingdoms, save to strike fear into the beggars who gaze upon the treasure hoard of Urish, and is little stronger than a powerful salamander.

Count Mashabak

A pretender, on some planes, to Lord Arioch, Mashabak was a patron, of sorts, to Sadric 86th, Elric's father, and laid claim to Sadric's soul upon his death. Mashabak, commanding Prince Gaynor, has the temerity to challenge Lord Arioch for power in the Multiverse and, in some realms, can neutralise Arioch's potency. However, whilst he has all Arioch's cruelty, Mashabak lacks his subtlety, and is sublimely unaware of how the forces of Chaos are marshalling for the Great Struggle. For this reason, he will ever be a minor noble of Chaos, and not the great and powerful lord he yearns to be.

Narjhan, Lord of Beggars

Narjhan of Chaos is worshipped by the beggar-hordes of Nadsokor and he leads them against Tanelorn, manifesting as a suit of armour from which emanates a booming voice. He fosters and encourages the deceptions of beggars and blesses them with disease and suffering.

Law

Law has dominance in the Young Kingdoms. Melniboné's decline and the imposition of the lawful barrier around the plane of the Earth has allowed the worshippers of Law to move into the partial vacuum. The promise is of a freedom from the hellish practices of Chaos, from the tyranny of the all-changing, and for a better world founded on the fundamental principles of nature, as described through the Lawful sciences of physics, mathematics, chemistry and biology. Deviation from these underlying principles is deemed a heresy, and this has been logically extended to include those unfortunates born with deformities and disabilities, or afflicted by diseases that cause the same. The exodus from the city of Nadsokor, fleeing the ravages of plague, was initiated by Lawful priests. Its subsequent colonisation by the beggars and wretches of the world is the result of those same priests expelling those from the Vilmirian cities who were, in some way, disfigured or considered abnormal – in other words, Chaos-tainted.

Law need not be this way. In some places, such as Ilmiora, Jharkor and Lormyr, lawful worship is of a liberal, accepting kind, but that does not mean that lawful zealots and logic-obsessed proselytisers do not exist; they are simply outnumbered by those who have not yet immersed themselves in Law's true meaning, and can maintain a healthy balance

The Lords of Law

When appearing before mortals, the White Lords of Law are perfection personified: more than simply beautiful, they are the absolute pinnacle of appearance and integrity. But, as Elric ruefully notes, such perfection must be at the price of progress. Their home realm is a featureless expanse, perfectly flat, representing the ultimately barren nature of complete uniformity.

Arkyn The Meticulous

Lord Arkyn governs the realm of scientific thought and endeavour, embodying the underlying symmetries of all things in the natural world, the application of logic, the development of theory and proof over superstition and supposition. Arkyn manifests himself through his writings and theories. The priests of Law scour them intimately, attempting to find the one, true rule within the equations, logical arguments and complex geometries that illustrate these huge tomes of densely written script. His worship is strong amongst philosophers, mathematicians, inventors and logical theorists. His teachings propose the four-fold approach: *Method, Observations, Results and Conclusions*.

Donblas The White Lord, Justice Maker

Donblas represents the Rule of Law; doctrine, legislation, enforcement. His realm is that of codes and constitutions, the impartiality of rational systems against the inherently biased anarchy of Chaos. Great tracts of legal script and complex rules are his gift to his followers. The absolute certainty of the Law and its innate justice is theirs to administer.

Donblas manifests as a beautiful, glorious, human shimmering with a disturbing symmetry and perfection. Manifestations are rare, but his voice sings out to his followers in dreams and meditations.

Miggea The Mad, Duchess of Dolwic

Considered senile, but nevertheless, powerful, Miggea reaches out from her realm of Dolwic to destroy those worlds she considers in any sense chaotically influenced – which is to say, most of them. Her myth has gone through several cycles in the Earth's history and as a White Lord she can claim only a small influence at the time of the Young Kingdoms, but she still attracts active worshippers, themselves unreasoning zealots who cannot contemplate deviation from the laws and philosophies of Donblas and Arkyn.

of belief in the human condition, accepting a certain degree of deviation as a perfectly natural state of being. Most priests of Law begin thus, but those who study further and deeper begin to find patterns and recurring themes. They see, and embrace, the perfection absolute Law has to offer and its inherent power.

So begins the corruption of Law. Priests enthralled in this way can accept nothing less than perfection and compliance. Disagreement and dissent cannot be tolerated, even within their own kind. Enclaves of the like-minded form, consolidating power which they wield as far and wide as they can. The virtues of Law are lost; in its place is drab, miserable, conformity, a route march towards an unknowable destination along a featureless road that winds across a featureless plain, blistered feet stamping in unison for eternity.

Miggea, alone amongst the White Lords, despises Tanelorn and gathers her best soldiers and champions from across the Multiverse to challenge the Eternal City. One such champion is Prince Gaynor the damned, once of Xiombarg and Mashabak, who now enjoys her patronage. She inspires utter loyalty in her servants and commands a vast troop of knights prepared to fight to the death in her name. In times such as these she manifests as a knight of Law, riding a pure white she-wolf endowed with the power of speech. In human guise she has a radiant complexion and black, glaring eyes, with pale lips and pointed teeth.

Tovik The Relentless

A lord of righteous revenge, he is foremost of those who challenge Chaos, fighting with a berserk and terrible rage. He challenged Mabelode for the dominance of the western continent, besting him in a battle that created the bay of Dhakos. Sometimes a general for Duchess Miggea, and sometimes her opponent, depending on circumstances, he is a god of knights and warriors, worshipped in Lormyr, Jharkor and Vilmir with fervency.

His priests are warrior-priests, battle-hardened doomsayers who pray and fight with equal vitriol.

Cults of the Young Kingdoms

This section details the cults and religions of the Young Kingdoms. Each cult is prepared to a standard template explaining more about the cult, the training and gifts it offers, and the various stages of cult membership.

Souls

'A moment later Drinij Bara laughed wildly. 'My soul is mine again. Thank you, great Cat Lord. Let me repay you!'
'There is no need,' smiled Meerclar mockingly, 'and, anyway, I perceive that your soul is already bartered.'
– The Bane of the Black Sword

Souls are the currency of the higher powers. The value of a soul is both constant and priceless. For souls are the only worthwhile source of power and the Lords of Chaos and Law horde them jealously, to fuel their agendas and struggles across the Multiverse. Magic of great potency involves using the souls of others to summon forces beyond the ability of an individual sorcerer, as in the example of Yyrkoon who paid the demons which raised the pillars to support his ensorcelled mirror. Such uses are described further in *The Silver Grimoire* chapter.

Yet, the most disturbing aspect of souls is the ability to barter one's own in exchange for power. This is the path taken by sorcerers and priests, who promise parts of their own soul to form *Pacts* with the Lords of the Higher Planes. To barter away a soul does not necessarily imply an afterlife of hell and torment, rather it *enslaves* the soul to the servitude of the patron to which it was bartered. Souls taken usually end up as servants, endlessly labouring in the engines or mines of their lords' private worlds. In a few cases they are treated with some compassion, but generally souls are viewed at best as cheap drudges and at worst food. Favoured champions may be kept as lackeys to further their master's machinations, as they once did in life. The most fortunate who managed to accumulate the greatest power in life are sometimes raised to the position of a minor divinity. The bartering of a soul is represented by *dedicating* one or more points of POW to a particular entity. The character still possesses the POW for calculating skills, but upon their death, the entity to which they promised their soul will come to collect. Souls which are dedicated to more than one patron will be claimed by the entity with the greatest share. Only souls clean of such bargains are free to pass on to the realm of the Grey Lords, to experience true peace in the afterlife.

Available Magic Points are limited to the amount of *undedicated* POW. Thus, a sorcerer with a POW of 12 dedicating 7 points to Chardros would have only 5 Magic Points available for use elsewhere. Once a point of POW has been dedicated to an entity, it cannot be used for any other Pacts or Gifts. Thus, a follower of Chaos with a POW of 10 might dedicate 6 points to Chardros, but this would leave only a further 4 points to be dedicated to another Chaos Lord. The number of points of POW dedicated in this way defines the *gifts* one can obtain from the deity being worshipped. Gifts are described later in this chapter.

Joining a Cult

Any adventurer may join a cult simply by stating their intention to do so. Adventurers may be a member of any number of cults, as long as these do not conflict: no lawful cultist would ever join a chaotic cult, for instance; and no shaman of Grome would never affiliate themselves with Straasha. There is no requirement to find a temple or church, but such members are considered only as lay-members and do not derive any particular advantages or gifts from their membership.

Initiation and Pacts

To gain these benefits cult members must play a more active role in cult affairs; such agents are typically known

as initiates. There are no particular requirements, in terms of monetary donations or levels of skill, to become an initiate, but all initiates must undergo an initiation ritual resulting in the forming of a Pact with their chosen god or gods. They must also dedicate a certain amount of POW as part of the process of forming the Pact. Such a dedication is only required once, at the point the Pact is made.

The initiation rite accrues the Pact skill which measures their relationship both to the cult and the god(s) they worship. The initial level for the Pact is the adventurer's CHA plus whatever POW is *dedicated* to that entity. This is a momentous occasion for any cultist, identifying them to their deity and allowing them to start receiving that deity's gifts and compulsions. Gifts might be knowledge, such as sorcery; equipment, so they can carry through the cult's work; or training in a skill or skills. Some compulsions are extreme, for the Lords of the Higher Worlds are demanding creatures. Others are relatively benign.

The Pact skill can be advanced through the standard character improvement methods discussed on page 126. However, Pact always increases, automatically, by 1% each time a success is rolled when using the Summoning Ritual skill. For the cults of Law, which have few summonings, the Pact increases by 1% for every 10% increase in one of the cult skills, as listed for each cult. Lawful cult members *must always use at least one improvement roll to increase a cult skill*.

The Pact skill also increases if the souls of others are dedicated to a deity, or used during a summoning ritual to gain more Magic Points. For sapient creatures, such as humans, the Pact value increases by 1% per victim sacrificed.

Divine Intervention

The Pact skill allows the cultist to call upon their god for help. The rating in this skill reflects the intensity of the pact but does not guarantee that a Lord of the Elements, Beasts, Law or Chaos will ever keep their side of the bargain. The Lords of Chaos, in particular, are capricious beings that may ignore even their most faithful servants either due to preoccupation or simply for amusement. On many occasions Elric cries out for the aid of Arioch only to be politely declined or cruelly ignored. To gain the help of a specific deity, a successful Pact test is required. A failure results in stony silence whilst a fumble might indicate that the deity actively offers aid to whatever opposes the character. This is dependent on circumstances, of course, but the Lords of Chaos in particular, can be perverse when dealing with their

faithful using such an opportunity to test a worshipper's faith. However, calling for a god's intervention strains the Pact. Every time it is used to call for aid, successful or not, the rating decreases by 1D4 for elemental cults, 1D6 for Lawful cults and Beast Lords, and 1D8 for Chaotic cults. Even Elric found Arioch growing tired of his demands.

A Pact may only be called upon *once* for any situation. The god's actions when intervening are those satisfying *the deity's* desires, not necessarily the worshipper's. The summoner merely requests their patron's aid and cannot demand its form. Hence many interventions have serious consequences if the deity takes the opportunity to set in play their own machinations. When called upon to counter the supernatural powers of a conflicting entity, most Lords simply provide an equal force to oppose it.

Apotheosis

Although there is no upper level for a Pact skill, reaching 100% indicates the complete dedication of the worshipper to the god. At this stage, there is the likelihood that the worshipper will be called to the deity's service permanently – in which case they become a Non-Player Character under the control of the Games Master. This is called apotheosis, and the chance of it occurring is equal to the *current* POW dedicated to that god multiplied by 5%. Rolling this value or less on D100 means the adventurer's soul is claimed by the deity and whisked to the god's plane (or elsewhere in the Multiverse), either to reside with the god or do its bidding. The mortal body of the adventurer may be left behind, with the soul being granted a new body to the patron's liking, or it may be taken completely: the choice is at the Games Master's discretion.

If the apotheosis test fails, it will be tested again precisely one game year since the first test, and so on until the soul is finally claimed.

For example, Kerris of the Purple Towns, after many years of faithful service to Lord Tovik, is a Champion of the Knights of Tovik with a Pact rating of 100%. Kerris dedicated 8 POW to Tovik, which means there is a 40% chance of apotheosis. Kerris's player rolls a 16 on this fateful day. As Kerris settles into sleep, he hears his name called by a thousand separate voices echoing across the Multiverse. Lord Tovik rides into his dreams accompanied by a brilliant white stallion, equipped with a saddle of gold and a lance of bronze. Kerris's spirit mounts, and rides across the Moonbeam Roads beside Lord Tovik. In the morning, Kerris's companions find that the

Farric's Saga

Knowing he must seek revenge on Malagan, Farric decides to become an initiate of Tovik the Relentless. At one of the shrines to Tovik in Dhakos, he swears the oath of allegiance and undergoes a vigil of three days and three nights, and dedicates 7 points of POW. He experiences several visions of Tovik's struggle against Mabelode and emerges as a blooded initiate.

Farric has therefore developed a Pact with both cult and god. His Pact skill begins at 20, the sum of his dedicated POW and CHA of 13. This automatically entitles Farric to a gift *and* a compulsion. His gift is *Perfection*, allowing him to use part, or all of the 7 points of the dedicated POW to improve his Characteristics. His compulsion is to emulate Tovik's tenacity by never surrendering in any combat.

knight has died in his sleep, but the body wears a serene and peaceful smile...

It might appear that apotheosis can be averted simply by calling upon the patron frequently, thereby eroding the strength of the Pact. This is not the case. Gods become irritated with frequent interruptions and this certainly weakens their sympathy for the worshipper. If a character makes constant and frequent requests for divine intervention then it is quite possible, and even likely, that the patron will refuse *any* calls for aid, no matter how successful or persuasive, and even, perhaps aid the worshipper's foes directly instead. The only way to regain divine help in such cases would be for the worshipper to sacrifice more POW to strengthen the Pact and to refrain from constant impositions on the patron's time until it is *absolutely* necessary. This is the gods' way of ensuring that no promised soul escapes them. Clearly if the worshipper needs so much help he might be better employed in *permanent* service somewhere.

Gifts & Compulsions

Lords of the Higher Planes reward their followers with gifts, but the strength of the relationship always comes at a price, in the form of compulsions. Gifts vary in their power, as do compulsions, and what is offered depends on the god worshipped. A worshipper of a god is entitled to select one gift each time a compulsion is *imposed*: a worshipper *always* gains a compulsion every time he advances one rank within the cult. The maximum value of the combined gifts cannot

exceed the POW dedicated to the deity. A worshipper can always dedicate more POW, depending on how much they have remaining to dedicate, and always mindful that, as the Pact value rises, so does the chance of the god calling-in the debt.

In certain circumstances, such as successfully completing a mighty quest for the god or its cult, the Games Master might offer the faithful worshipper a chance to accept a new gift. If accepted, the gift always comes with a further compulsion.

Stages of Cult Membership
Lay Members

The vast majority of members of a cult are lay members, casual worshippers who follow the basic doctrine of the cult and attend regular ceremonies, where required.

Duties: There are very few duties required by lay members – they will be expected to attend celebrations on special Holy Days but unless they are aiming to rise in the ranks of the cult, they will not even be expected to attend regular ceremonies.

Benefits: The character will automatically be able to find tutors for any skills the cult teaches. They must still pay the normal rates for these services.

Initiates

Also known as agents, initiates are active in serving the cults aims and observing its rites and practices.

Requirements: All initiates receive the Pact skill for their deity. The initiate must also accept one compulsion and may choose to receive one gift.

Duties: Initiates are expected to follow any orders or commands given them by the cult or by the deity (although direct instructions from a god are extremely rare). Failure or refusal results in the Pact skill decreasing by 1D4 for elemental cults, 1D6 for Lawful cults and Beast Lords, and 1D8 for Chaotic cults. If the initiate continually refuses a cult's commands, he can be expelled from the cult completely.

Benefits: Initiates are able to find tutors for any skills the cult teaches. They must still pay the normal rates for these services.

Acolytes

Also known as devotees, acolyte is a rank requiring dedication and service but where the inner secrets of the cult begin to be revealed. Acolytes can be lay members and even initiates of other cults but cannot be acolytes of more than one cult.

Requirements: Pact skill of 50% or greater. All acolytes must also have completed at least two tasks or missions for the cult. On promotion to acolyte they automatically gain one compulsion and may, if they wish, receive a gift from their patron.

Duties: Acolytes are expected to donate half of all income to the cult and attend services at their place of worship at least one day every week. They must also attend all ceremonies during Holy Days.

Benefits: As well as all the benefits enjoyed by initiates, acolytes may begin to learn magic, as taught by their cult.

Warrior-Priest/Sorcerer-Priest

The most senior acolyte of each congregation of the cult, the title depends on the specific cult.

Requirements: Candidates must have been an acolyte of the cult for many years and know at least half of the cult's skills (need only learn a single Weapon skill) at 50% or greater. At least one Sorcery skill (see page 54) must be 50% or greater. On promotion to priesthood they automatically gain one compulsion and may, if they wish, receive a gift from their patron.

Duties: Priests are expected to donate all income to the cult, in return for being maintained by it; and are expected to make new converts to the faith. They are accorded more difficult tasks and missions and expected to support Champions of the cult in their own quests. Failure to do so always incurs cult retribution.

Benefits: One Priest-level benefit is granted.

Champion

The highest level of cult attainment, Champions are the heroes of the cult and are considered masters of everything the cult stands for. Champions are responsible for furthering the specific agendas of the gods themselves and have singled themselves out for special attention by the Lords of the Higher Worlds – and others who serve them

Requirements: Candidates must have been a Warrior-Priest or Sorcerer-Priest of the cult for at some years and know all of the cult's skills (need only learn a single Weapon skill) at 50% or greater. On promotion to Champion they automatically gain one compulsion and may, if they wish, receive a further gift from their patron.

Duties: Champions are expected to donate all wealth and conquests to the cult, and in return may call upon the cult's resources for their quests. Champions must accept every command or mission given to them, whether this is by a higher ranking Champion or the deity they serve. Failure to do so always incurs cult retribution.

Benefits: Champions can command priests, acolytes and initiates, calling upon their support for any missions they must personally fulfil. Champions receive one Legendary Ability appropriate to their cult, and may attain others through the normal Legendary Ability process described in *The Seventh Dark* chapter beginning on page 126.

Training Costs

Most cults offer training in certain skills. Whilst this differs from country to country and sect to sect, it typically costs the following to buy training from a cult:

* 10 Bronze per 1% of increase in Basic skills (double if the skill is not a cult speciality).
* 15 Bronze per 1% of increase in Advanced skills (double if the skill is not a cult speciality). Learning a new Advanced skill costs 500 Bronze to attain the skill's starting percentage.
* 500 Bronze per 1% of increase in Sorcery skills. Learning a new sorcery skill, such as a new summoning, costs 2,000 Bronze to attain the magic's starting percentage.

Cult Gifts

As briefly discussed, a gift is a power or ability, usually of a permanent nature, granted to faithful cult members. The opportunity to receive a gift is only granted to those who have shown dedication, or performed a major service for their deity, and only one gift is permitted each time. Characters are not required to *accept* the gifts of their patron lords, and indeed it is wise to avoid such bargains since each gift costs a further part of their soul, which is promised to the deity at their demise. But the powers offered are seductive, and few can resist their lure. Once all available POW has been bartered for gifts, not only may they not receive any further gifts, but their patron lord might be tempted to end their live

Example Gifts

Gift	Effect	Cost
Abstinence	Exist without one requirement, for example air, food, water, sleep	1 POW
Animal Familiar	The recipient receives the companionship of a *natural* animal with a SIZ in D6 no greater than the POW spent on this gift. The familiar obeys simple commands but will not go against its nature. If a further point of POW is invested, the creature can speak with its master.	1 POW per D6 of SIZ; additional 1 POW for a talking creature.
Automaton	Gain a self powered automaton as a servant. See page 121 for how to create automata.	1 POW per 20 Characteristic/ Armour Points invested in the automaton's assembly
Change Gender	The character changes from male to female or vice-versa. All characteristics and skills remain the same but the voice and physical functions of the new sex are gained.	1 POW to change gender once 2 POW to change a second time, 3 POW to change a third, and so forth.
Chaotic Blessing	Roll once on the Chaotic Features table (pages 117-118)	1 POW
Divine Training	Raise a cult skill to 100%.	1 POW the first skill, 2 the second, and so forth.
Elemental	Gain an elemental helper which may be called once per adventure	1 POW per metre of the elemental's size
Endurance	Endure any pain. Never needs to test *Resilience* to prevent unconsciousness when wounded, and immune to torture.	1 POW
Eternal Life	The recipient will not die of natural causes during the lifetime of the gift, although they are still vulnerable to death through violence.	Costs 1 POW
Horde	May at a future point, when summoning *a* demonic or elemental being, call forth an army of the same entities, equal in number to the sorcerer's remaining Magic Points, per POW invested in the gift	One use
Perfection	Raise a characteristic by 1D6 (any POW gained is automatically forfeit to that deity).	Costs 1 POW the first time, 2 the second, etc.
Return Loved One	A loved one is brought back from death. Their POW automatically belongs to the god, and the resurrected person serves the patron's agenda completely.	1 POW the first time, 2 the second, and so forth. The cost increases even if used on *different* loved ones.
Sanctuary	The deity provides the recipient with a magical structure or plane as a residence. 1 POW buys a villa or manse; 2 POW buys a castle; 3 POW a city, and so forth. The property always belongs to the deity and can be removed at any time if the deity so chooses. The residence may have further powers as desired.	Initial cost is variable. 1 POW for Hidden (residence itself cannot be perceived); 1 POW for Movement (flying, rolling, crawling, etc); 1 POW for Shifting (interdimensionally); 1 POW for Isolation (residents cannot be located magically); 1 POW for Impregnability (access cannot be forced, save at the deity level), 1 POW for Peacefulness (residents suffer no violence or insanity)
Second Life	Return from the dead once (all POW sacrificed to *other* entities, and their Gifts are lost)	1 POW the first time, 2 the second, forth.
Slave	Gain a demonic servant (available to the cult) which may be summoned for one task per adventure	1 POW per Magic Point required to summon such a demon
Summon	Some cults have a specific creature from the Creatures chapter that can be summoned. This gift allows one creature of the particular type mentioned to be summoned. No summoning roll is necessary, but the Command skill is still used to direct the creature's actions.	1 POW for the first summoning 2 POW for the second, and so forth.
Ward	Gain total invulnerability to one form of harm. Each time this gift is taken a new form of harm is selected (for example: swords, spears, arrows, fire, poison, and so forth)	1 POW the first time, 2 the second, 3 the third, and so forth.
Youth	Return to a young body, reversing all aging effects	1 POW

prematurely in order to reap the promised reward. The list of gifts on page 95 is far from exhaustive. Games Masters should feel free to create their own gifts to supplement the ones presented here.

The Elemental Cults

Cult of Grome

The elemental cult of Grome has been worshipped constantly across the world. Shrines to Grome belonging to the extinct Pukwadji tribe of the Silent Lands have been found, and cave writings show they were a beloved race of the Earth King. The worship of Grome is still found mainly in the barbarian regions of the Young Kingdoms and rarely in the cities and towns. Cult practices are standard across different cults: respect for the land, protection of Grome's interests, and the disruption of Straasha's. Dedicated cultists – initiate and above – mark themselves with ritual scars and tattoos, wear their hair long and matted, often with twigs, pebbles or iron rings woven in, or daubed with mud to form imposing coxcombs and spikes.

Temples are little more than caves adapted to the purpose or simple shrines of heaped stones. In civilised areas temples are always in basements or constructed underground. In barbarian regions each member of the tribe is a Dust Son or Daughter, with perhaps Earth Sons and Daughters numbering 25% of the total, three or four Earth Brothers or Sisters, a single Earth Father and, sometimes, an Earth Shaker. Tribes affiliated to Straasha are hated; raids are frequent and bloody affairs. Prisoners are sacrificed to Grome by being buried alive.

Cult Skills

1H Spear, 2H Spear, Engineering (civilised regions only), Language (High Speech*), Lore (Animal), Lore (Plant), Lore (Grome), Stealth, Survival, Tracking

Principal Duties

Maintaining the land taking only what is needed for survival, herd Grome's creatures (cattle, goats, sheep and so forth), and restrict the activities of Lord Straasha.

Cult Ranks

Lay Member	Dust-Son/Dust-Daughter
Initiate	Earth-Son/Earth-Daughter
Acolyte	Earth-Brother/Earth-Sister
Priest	Earth Father/Earth-Mother
Champion	Earth Shaker

Cult Summonings

Command, Summoning Ritual (Gnome)

Gifts

Animal Familiar, Elemental (Gnome), Divine Training (Cult skills), Perfection, Sanctuary

Compulsions

* Must never come into contact with water, save for drinking.
* Never eat fish or other creature of the water.
* Develop fear of water (cannot approach large bodies of water; must make a Persistence test to avoid fleeing in fear or being rooted to the spot in terror).
* Eat only vegetables.
* Sacrifice 1 point of CHA (through ritual scarring).
* Never wear footwear or armour on the limbs.
* Bury all foes alive, in sacrifice to Grome.

Cult Secrets

King Grome was the custodian of the Black Blade which he bartered with the Mernii people before the reign of the Bright Empire. When the Mernii refused to return the Black Blade Grome threatened to destroy their ships. The Mernii hero, White Crow, kept his oath to Grome Earth King and returned the Black Blade so that Grome could re-entomb it, keeping its evil isolated. For keeping the Mernii oath, Grome entered into the compact that remains with Melniboné to this day.

Cult of Kakatal

Kakatal is not widely worshipped in the Young Kingdoms. Some tribes of the Sighing Desert and the Weeping Waste offer worship and tribute, but they are small in number. There is an isolated cult in Yu that believes the Boiling Sea is the result of Kakatal fighting a battle for control of the Earth with Straasha, but worship has not spread far. He has been worshipped primarily in Melniboné but even now, that worship has been mostly forgotten. Where he is worshipped his symbol is often considered to be sun, the great eye of Kakatal that watches over the Earth and gives it life. Most temples or shrines are filled with braziers burning night and day, creating a barely endurable heat. Worshippers are often burned or scorched across their bodies and must undergo some form of trial by fire to advance within the cult.

Cult Skills

1H Spear, Bow, Craft (Blacksmith), Influence, Language (High Speech), Lore (Kakatal), Lore (Haborym), Mechanisms, Resilience

Principal Duties

Sustain the eternal fires of Kakatal, extinguish the dominance of Lassa, and maintain the sun's journey through the sky.

Cult Ranks

Lay Member	Brand
Initiate	Fire Starter
Acolyte	Flame Breather
Priest	Sun Mover
Champion	Fire-Son

Cult Summonings

Command, Summoning Ritual (Salamander)

Gifts

Divine Training (Cult Skills), Elemental (Salamander), Eternal Life

Compulsions

* Skin becomes cracked and broken, as though scorched, –1 CHA.
* Develop Agoraphobia. Cannot abide wide-open spaces where Lassa's spies can watch.
* Become obsessed with starting fires, opposed to all those who try to extinguish them.
* Singe the skin from the body, leaving the flesh raw, –1HP to all locations.
* Donation of 1D4 points of permanent POW to sustain Kakatal's eternal flame.
* Never enter into hand-to-hand combat.

Cult of Lassa

Lassa is a dominant elemental in the Young Kingdoms. She is worshipped widely across the Weeping Waste, Dorel, Pikarayd and in Myyrrhn, where she is the sole deity. There are several sects within her cult, worshipping Misha, the West Wind, maker of gales; Graoll, the East Wind, bringer of hurricanes; and Shaarnasaa, the blessing and life-bringing Southern Wind whose soul was once held captive by the Karasim Horde. The cult of Lassa is a largely benign cult, concerned with life and freedom. As such, she and her worshippers are considered peaceful, and indeed they are, unless provoked into wrath. On these occasions Lassa's worshippers can be every bit as terrifying as Kakatal's destruction, which they oppose.

Temples of Lassa and her various sects are always open air and frequently at the top of hills or mountains.

Cult Skills

1H Spear, 1H Sword, Bow, Acrobatics, Athletics, Boating, Dance, First Aid, Healing, Language (High Speech), Lore (Lassa), Lore (Weather), Play Instrument, Shiphandling, Throwing

Principal Duties

Preserve freedom, heal the sick.

Cult Ranks

Lay Member	Breath of Lassa (or sub-cult name)
Initiate	Wind Bearer
Acolyte	Wind Holder
Priest	Wind Singer
Champion	Wind Dancer

Cult Summonings

Command, Summoning Ritual (Sylph), Summoning Ritual (Sharnah), Summoning Ritual (h'Haar'shann)

Gifts

Abstinence (Air), Divine Training (Cult Skills), Elemental (Sylph), Perfection, Sanctuary, Ward (Fire), Youth

Compulsions

* Develop claustrophobia. Cannot enter any space of less than 3 times SIZ willingly; stricken with panic if forced into such a space.
* Unable to concentrate for long periods. Tasks requiring periods of concentration take twice as long to complete.
* Cannot wear armour of any kind; must always wear loose-fitting clothes or robes.
* Never eat the flesh of any bird.
* May not kill any enemy, no matter how hated.
* Must always offer healing to those who need it.

Cult of Straasha

Like Lassa, the cult of Straasha seeks to preserve life but places the dominion of water above that of the land or air. Straasha is worshipped throughout the Young Kingdoms, including civilised ports and trading centres, as well as the river traders of Lormyr. The cult has no particular sects or subdivisions; King Straasha is present wherever there is water.

Cult Skills

1H Spear, 1H Sword, Bow, Boating, Dodge, Language (High Speech), Lore (Straasha), Lore (Sea and Tides), Lore (Fish), Shiphandling

Lords of the Million Spheres

Principal Duties

Preserve the seas, lakes and rivers

Cult Ranks

Lay Member	Stream Son/Daughter
Initiate	River Son/Daughter
Acolyte	Lake Son/Daughter
Priest	Ocean Son/Daughter
Champion	Straasha Son/Daughter

Cult Summonings

Command, Summoning Ritual (Undine)

Gifts

Abstinence (Water), Second Life, Return Loved One, Ward (Poison)

Compulsions

* Craves the seas or rivers. If confined to land for more than a few days, becomes panicked and sullen.
* Develop a fear of dirt and the soil. Must bathe or wash regularly (every few hours).
* Unable to cross any stream or river via a bridge, must always wade or swim.
* Weeps almost constantly at the injustices Grome has heaped on Straasha by cutting-off lakes from the sea.
* Drink only water.
* Eat only fish.
* Fear of Chaos and Pyaray's undead fleet.

The Chaos Cults
Arioch

Arioch is only worshipped as a singular deity on Melniboné and even there his cult has receded in power and importance as the Bright Empire has waned and his worshippers have lapsed into solipsism. When Elric takes the Ruby Throne worship of Arioch is almost forgotten, and those who do worship the Lord of the Seven Darks do so in isolation and futility: as they have forgotten Arioch, *he* has forgotten *them*. A few isolated Arioch cultists and would-be sorcerers can be found around the Young Kingdoms, but these are mere parodies of the true cult and studiously ignored by him. Once Elric has rekindled their ancient pact, Arioch has time for only one man; cults are irrelevant to the Chaos Lord's schemes. Where these cultists are active they teach that Lord Arioch is the general of the Chaos armies, preparing to overthrow the Lords of Law.

Cult Skills

1H Sword, 2H Sword, Athletics, Dodge, Language (High Speech), Lore (Arioch), Lore (Chaos)

Principal Duties

Prepare for the war with Law.

Cult Ranks

The cult of Arioch has no special titles for its ranks. Cults are so small, ranks are meaningless.

Cult Summonings

Command, Summoning Ritual (Demon of Combat)

Gifts

Change Gender, Eternal Life, Perfection, Second Life, Youth

Compulsions

* Blood sacrifice to Arioch every week.
* Human sacrifice to Arioch every week.
* Develop an irrational fear of three separate things: the dark, the cold, spiders, rats, and so forth.
* Become increasingly morose. As the Pact skill increases, behaviour becomes more depressive until it reaches the suicidal at the 95% level or greater.
* Develop a nervous tic, mannerism or speech impediment.
* Develop the overwhelming desire to slay loved ones.

Cult Secrets

The end of the world is coming. The prophecy of the White Crow's treachery will be re-enacted. The Seven Darks shall be manifest on Earth.

Sword Rulers

This is a popular cult in Dharijor and amongst the martial ranks of Pan Tang. Its members are forbidden to use any weapon other than the sword, and to dedicate all kills to their chosen deity. The cult of the Sword Rulers recognises three gods: Mabelode and Xiombarg, as King and Queen of the Swords respectively, and Arioch as the Knight of the Swords. Sects for all three exist; they all follow similar practices. Mabelode is a male-only sect; Xiombarg and Arioch accept males and females.

The Sword Rulers are preparing for war against Law. The war is perpetual and being fought constantly across the

Multiverse. Adherents of the cult believe themselves to be the reincarnations of the Sword Rulers' champions from across the Million Spheres, fighting the eternal war against Order.

The infamous *Straw Dogs* mercenaries of Dharijor are all Champions of the Sword Rulers Cult.

Cult Skills

1H Sword, 2H Sword, Dagger, Athletics, Dodge, Language (High Speech), Language (Low Speech), Language (Mabden), Lore (Sword Rulers), Resilience, Throwing

Principal Duties

Victory in battle. Vanquish Law. Die Bravely.

Cult Ranks

Lay Member	Sword Son/Daughter
Initiate	Sword Brother/Sister
Acolyte	Sword Singer
Priest	Sword Blesser
Champion	Sword Master

Cult Summonings

Command, Summoning Ritual (Demon of Combat), Summoning Ritual (Demon of Protection), Summoning Ritual (Demon of Transport), Summon Hunting Dog of the Dharzi, Summon Elenoin

Gifts

Abstinence (Sleep), Change Gender (Xiombarg aspect only), Chaotic Blessing, Divine Training (Cult Skills), Sanctuary, Slave, Ward (Swords)

Compulsions

✳ Uncontrollable, irrational obsession over some trivial matter: a jealousy over a lover, or the tendency to find a slight where none occurred.

✳ Develop a vile, argumentative and violent temper threatening to destabilise all attempts to remain calm.

✳ A constant and gnawing fear of death – something no Sword cultist could ever admit, but one that drives the individual to distraction and growing anxiety.

✳ Visions of terrible carnage that disturb the sleep and leave the dreamer feeling worthless and drained.

✳ Develop the overwhelming belief that one is invulnerable to mortal weapons.

✳ Never wear armour.

✳ Never use a shield.

✳ Never dodge a blow.

✳ Develop a nervous tic, twitch, mannerism or other physical condition (constant blinking; a stammer, an inability to leave any door unlocked, for instance).

Cult Secrets

The Sword Rulers hold dominion over three planes close to this world, where Mabelode is undisputed king and Xiombarg his queen. A hero is emerging to challenge their power, guided by the Lords of Law and equipped with the dreadful weapons of The Hand and The Eye.

Death Bringers

The Death Bringers cult venerates Chardros and Hionhurn, the two principal chaotic lords of death, dying, murder and undeath. Its members are not necessarily those with a death-wish, but those who revel not just in the heat of battle, but casual violence for its own sake, retribution, revenge, cold-blooded murder, execution, and, in a twisted way, the ultimate justice death offers. The cult predominates in Dharijor, Pan Tang and Pikarayd, and small enclaves are found in many Lawful cities, including Ilmar, Bakshaan and Cadsandria.

The sect of Chardros venerates the reaping of souls. All souls taken in whatever way are dedicated to Chardros with the blood-curdling battle cry, or soul-chilling whisper 'The Scythe! The Scythe' the moment before the killing starts. The undisputed aim of the sect is to damn as many souls as possible to Chardros' grim realms where they will be tortured and twisted into demonic servants, to serve in the Army of Chaos.

The sect of Hionhurn is every bit as chilling. It adherents are assassins, hangmen, executioners, and those who simply enjoy murder. The sect, echoing its master's methods, promises 'a pleasant death', but an unbearable time thereafter. 'Time to Die' is the single signal that one is dealing with a Hionhurn Death Bringer, before a swift, sometimes painless, death occurs. Those words, as spoken by Hionhurn cultists, speed the soul to the Executioner's hells where all manner of tortures await.

Cult Skills

1H Axe, 2H Axe, Dagger, 2H Flail, Garrotte/Strangle Cord, Dodge, Language (High Speech), Lore (Chaos), Law (Death Bringers), Perception, Resilience

Principal Duties

Send souls to Hell. Kill all who oppose Chaos.

Cult Ranks

Lay Member	Stalker
Initiate	Stealer of Life
Acolyte	Maker of Knots
Priest	Maker of Chains
Champion	Lord of Death

Cult Summonings

Command, Summoning Ritual (Demon of Combat), Summoning Ritual (Demon of Knowledge), Summoning Ritual (Demon of Protection), Summon Elenoin

Gifts

Animal Familiar, Chaotic Blessing, Divine Training (Cult Skills), Endurance, Horde, Slave, Ward (Poison)

Compulsions

* Kill once per week. Failure to do so results in loss of 1 point of POW.
* Desire to murder a loved one.
* Collect and constantly count, the bones of dead things. Wear prized bones around the body.
* Expose a section of own skull (–1HP to Head Hit Location).
* Increasing fear of death. As the Pact skill increases the fear of death grows stronger until the individual is unable to act for fear of accident, murder or assassination.
* Morbid fascination with bringing the dead back to life to question them on Chardros or Hionhurn's plans. Spends hours with corpses trying to revive them. As Pact skill increases, develop physical affection for one particular corpse.
* Unable to sleep for fear of never waking. Become gaunt-eyed, cadaverously thin and intensely paranoid of even one's closest associates.
* Obsession with self-harm. Arms and legs constantly cut and sliced, hair pulled out at the roots, teeth self-extracted, and so forth.

Cult Secrets

The horrors visited upon dead souls in the torture chambers of Chardros and Hionhurn are beyond compare. All demons are the twisted souls of those slaughtered in the name of Chaos. There is no escape from eternal agony. Hell spills-over and soon the demons will seek a way to Earth.

Ecstatic Indulgence

The cult of Balaan and Slortar the Old. Worshipped enthusiastically on Melniboné and Pan Tang, this cult views Slortar as the master of unearthly, ecstatically painful delights, and Balaan his apprentice, although in some sects the two are equals and aspects of the same being where Balaan is the lord of pain and torture and Slortar the bringer of all indulgences. No perversion, predation or sado-masochistic act is too extreme, and in Pan Tang cult members seek to outdo each other in what they can endure or inflict on others (usually slaves) without the subject dying. Prayers are always offered to either Balaan or Slortar before acts of indulgence are committed. Blood sacrifices are frequent, and ceremonies venerating either god frequently descend into orgies of dreadful sexual depravity.

Cult Skills

Dagger, Craft (Torture), Evaluate, Influence, Language (High Speech), Language (Low Speech), Lore (Chaos), Lore (Balaan and Slortar)

Principal Duties

Pursue every pleasure and every pain to its fullest

Cult Ranks

The cult has no special names for its ranks.

Cult Summonings

Command, Summoning Ritual (Demon of Desire)

Gifts

Change Gender, Chaotic Blessing, Endurance, Perfection, Sanctuary, Second Life, Slave, Youth

Compulsions

* Overwhelming desire to commit rape on either sex. Requires Persistence test to control the desire. Subtract the Pact percentage from the Persistence skill before the test is made.
* Overwhelming desire to kill the person one has just enjoyed carnal relations with. Requires Persistence test to control the desire. Subtract the Pact percentage from the Persistence skill before the test is made.
* Driven to self-mutilation on a daily basis. Lose 1 CHA for every 10% of the Pact skill. Mutilations become more bizarre and extreme.
* Unable to derive self-sexual gratification under any circumstances. Become enraged and over-more obsessed with sex and self-gratification as a result.
* Can only be happy when inflicting physical pain on innocents. Revel and delight in their screams. But these screams haunt the dreams leading to

development of fear of those tortured awaiting in Hell to inflict the same fate

* Cannot stop eating or drinking, becoming corpulently fat. +1 SIZ and –1 CON for every 20 points in Pact skill.

Azure Sisterhood

Eequor's cult consists entirely of women. The Blue Maidens revel in the duplicity and deceit their goddess embodies and traditionally dress in nothing but the colours of Eequor. The core belief is that men are weak and malleable, there to be used and exploited whenever the opportunity arises. Worship is popular in all chaotically-aligned nations of the Young Kingdoms.

Blue Maidens are dedicated to Eequor's dominance over the male Lords of Chaos and, of course, the male Lords of Law. The Earth is destined to be inherited by women, for they are the bearers of life.

Eequor is the one Chaos ruler who allows her faithful to step into her azure realm from time to time. Acolytes and above can, through a deep sleep achieved through inhaling the burned petals of the blue lotus, enter Eequor's house where they may seek her advice and be directed by her agenda.

Cult Skills

1H Sword, Dagger, Artistic Expression, Evaluate, Influence, Language (High Speech), Lore (Plant), Lore (World), Lore (Chaos), Lore (Eequor), Seduction, Stealth

Principal Duties

Be the lackey of no man, ever.

Cult Ranks

Lay Member	Azure Sister
Initiate	Sister of the Azure Veil
Acolyte	Sister of the Azure Robe
Priest	Sister of the Azure Sceptre
Champion	Sister of the Azure Crown

Cult Summonings

Command, Summoning Ritual (Demon of Desire), Summoning Ritual (Sylph), Summoning Ritual (Gnomes), Summon Elenoin

Gifts

Animal Familiar, Perfection, Return Loved One, Sanctuary, Second Life, Youth

Compulsions

* Aversion to the colour red, in all its forms. Cannot wear red or stand to be in the company of any who does so.
* Uncontrollable, irrational obsession over some trivial matter: a jealousy over a lover, or the tendency to find a slight where none occurred.
* Develop a vile, argumentative and violent temper threatening to destabilise all attempts to remain calm.
* Develop the need to kill any male lover. Requires Persistence test to control the desire. Subtract the Pact percentage from the Persistence skill before the test is made.
* Compelled to betray the plans and schemes of every man one encounters. Requires Persistence test to control the desire. Subtract the Pact percentage from the Persistence skill before the test is made.
* Irrational fear of rodents, spiders and insects, believing them to be the spies of the male Lords of Chaos (which, of course, they may be).
* Destined to sorrow. Nothing brings comfort or pleasure. All dreams are nightmares, all experiences fleeting and unfulfilling. Life is futile. Retirement to the Azure realm of Eequor is the only solace.

Cult Secrets

The secret dreams of the Blue Realm, allowing women to prepare blue lotus and then pass into Eequor's house.

The Whisperers

The Whisperers primarily worship Pyaray, Lord of the Chaos fleet, the commander of all souls lost to the sea and its depths. The cult is found amongst the Dharijorian and Pan Tangian navies, although there is a growing sect in Pikarayd and amongst the many renegade pirates roaming the Young Kingdoms' seas and oceans. The sign of the Whisperer is the many tentacled octopus associated with Pyaray, and worshippers' ships carry the symbol as their figurehead. Human sacrifice is common – captured sailors or slaves – with drowning and keel-hauling the favoured forms of execution. Worshippers nevertheless fear their god, knowing that their souls are damned to crew the war galleys of Chaos on these seas or others where Pyaray holds dominance.

Several land-based sects venerate Artigkern, Drinker of Oceans, in his capacity to drain life from worlds and the god's enmity with Straasha. Artigkern covets Straasha's unnamed sister, mistress of the upper currents and favourable tides,

and seeks to capture her soul once more and reunite it with Artigkern. They also believe the sun should be extinguished and abhor Kakatal's power over it.

Cult Skills

1H Axe, 2H Axe, Spear, Athletics, Boating, Language (High Speech), Lore (Chaos), Lore (Pyaray/Artigkern), Lore (Deep Water), Shiphandling, Survival

Principal Duties

Maintain dominance of the seas. Deliver souls to Pyaray. Thwart the schemes of Straasha.

Cult Ranks

The cult of the Whisperer has no special names for its ranks.

Cult Summonings

Command, Summoning Ritual (Demon of Combat), Summoning Ritual (Demon of Protection), Summoning Ritual (Demon of Transport)

Gifts

Abstinence (Water), Chaotic Blessing, Divine Training, Horde, Ward

Compulsions

✳ Hatred of land. One cannot abide the solidity of the ground for any length of time and must return to the list and sway of the deck to gain comfort.

✳ Skin becomes bloated, blotched and translucent, as though submerged in brine for months. –2 CHA.

✳ Sleep is disturbed by the moaning of the souls drifting down to Pyaray, calling for mercy and screaming as they are chained to the oars of the undead galleys. The sounds stay within the mind long after sleep has passed.

✳ Develop a nervous tic, twitch, mannerism or other physical condition (constant blinking; a stammer, an inability to leave any door unlocked, for instance).

✳ Growing compulsion to join with the undead fleet. As the Pact skill rises, so the calling of Pyaray becomes ever stronger until, at 100%, it becomes irresistible, and the individual throws himself into watery oblivion.

✳ Develop gills and vestigial fins, accompanied everywhere by the dreadful smell of rotting fish.

✳ Develop fish eyes, –3 CHA, perfect underwater vision

✳ Tentacles form in place of a beard, –3 CHA.

✳ Desire to consume gallons of water at a time to slake an unquenchable thirst. +1 SIZ, –1 CON for every 20 points of the Pact skill.

Cult Secrets

Pyaray's soul is held in one of the jewel-like eyes covering his squid-like body. Location of the major ship graveyards, although these may only be reached with Pyaray's blessing.

Silent Watchers

The Silent Watchers are dedicated to the worship of Maluk. This is a cult of arcane secrets, forbidden research, and attempting to understand the agenda of Chaos and its true nature. The cult predominates in Pan Tang, Pikarayd and is gaining ground in Argimiliar, especially in Cadsandria where the university offers fertile conditions for pursuing such knowledge and gaining new adherents.

Silent Watchers are often used as ambassadors and advisers to those Chaos wishes to corrupt. Cultists are adept in handling knowledge and misinformation in the pursuit and exercise of power. They tend to be shadowy, unseen manipulators, the quiet whisper in the ear of a noble at a crucial time, or the source of a decision that appears beneficial but serves to further only Chaos. Silent Watchers love to gather secrets and information from other cults, including Chaos, and to place their own people in influential positions to secretly manipulate the agendas of even their supposed allies.

Of particular interest is the knowledge being compiled by the cults of Arkyn and Donblas, and how these lawful secrets can be perverted to the services of Chaos. Agents of the Silent Watchers are abroad in Vilmir and Ilmiora, quietly observing and, where possible, corrupting those who handle such knowledge.

Cult Skills

Artistic Expression, Courtesy, Evaluate, Influence, Language (High Speech), Language (Low Speech), Lore (Chaos), Lore (Cryptography), Lore (Maluk), Lore (Million Spheres), Lore (World), Perception, Stealth

Principal Duties

Gather information. Exert the influence of Chaos.

Cult Ranks

Lay Member	Reader
Initiate	Borrower
Acolyte	Understander
Priest	Interpreter
Champion	Grand Master of Whispered Knowledge

Cult Summonings

Command, Summoning Ritual (Demon of Desire), Summoning Ritual ((Demon of Knowledge), Summoning Ritual (Demon of Transport)

Gifts

Divine Training (Cult Skills), Eternal Life, Sanctuary, Slave

Compulsions

- ✳ Must put-out one eye (–1 DEX, –1 CHA).
- ✳ Must stitch-shut the mouth (–1 CHA). Must communicate through half-audible mumbles, the written word, and sign language.
- ✳ Develops overwhelming desire for self-harm and mutilation, carving knowledge and secrets into the skin in High or Low Speech.

- ✳ Refuse to speak in any language other than High or Low Speech.
- ✳ As above, but High Speech.
- ✳ As above but in Mong, which has no written form.
- ✳ Become intensely secretive and jealous of information gained. Takes unusual and risky measures to protect even the most trivial knowledge.
- ✳ Fixate on a single individual, becoming increasingly obsessed about what they do or don't know. Jealous to the point of murder.
- ✳ Overwhelming desire to consume brains, intent on the belief that the knowledge they contain can be absorbed.

Cult Secrets

The sum of the cult's knowledge is held in the vast underground libraries of Maluk beneath Hwamgaarl. These chambers contain a million books and scrolls, protected by demons sensitive to the scent of the soul and pursue any intruder relentlessly.

Narjhan (Beggars)

All Nadsokor's beggars worship Narjhan, who promises many things: freedom from drudgery, disease and servitude, the riches of Tanelorn and a dozen other cities; beggars to become princes in the new empire arising from Chaos. Beggars, seeking whatever scraps they can, fall for Narjhan's promises heavily, but rarely, if ever, will they be held true. Narjhan is viewed as the one god who can, and will, alleviate misery. He is considered a god of righteousness where many others have failed. He is a faint beacon of hope in a city and world where little exists. Beggars bless their bowls in his name and offer 'Narjhan's blessings' to all those who deposit a coin, but their worship is typically fair-weather, since all beggars seek proof above reassurances (of which they have had plenty).

All those who wish to reside in Nadsokor must pledge allegiance to Narjhan, in Urish's name, but that is the extent of their compact, usually. Urish hand-picks those he wants to progress in the cult, and, as a selfish king, the one person he wants to progress the most is himself.

Members of the cult of Narjhan are expected to give half their earnings to King Urish. In return they gain free training in the cult's skills.

Cult Skills

Club, Staff, Evaluate, Influence, Language (Opish), Lore (Chaos), Lore (Nadsokor), Lore (World), Streetwise

Principal Duties

Collect money for Urish. Spy, learn secrets

Cult Ranks

None

Cult Summonings

None taught

Gifts

Abstinence (beggar's choice), Animal Familiar, Endurance, Ward

Compulsions

* Show devotion to Urish by cutting off 1D3 fingers (–1 DEX).
* Develop foul body odour.
* Develop unsightly sores and buboes (–1 CHA).
* Lose short-term memory.
* Fear clean water.

The Cults of Law

Whilst the cults of Law predominate in the Young Kingdoms, there are fewer of them than for Chaos, and they are less secretive. The cults are represented by churches and temples of all shapes and sizes: the bland monolithic edifices of Vilmir, through the ornate cathedral halls of Ilmiora, to small, secluded chapels and way-side shrines of Lormyr; and, of course, the mighty castles of Ashaneloon and Kaneloon. The functionaries found in these places of worship vary in number and type. In Vilmir there are hundreds of priests and cult members. In some places, such as Filkhar and Argimiliar, the method of worship is based on a monastic tradition with members dedicating their lives to study and living communally. In Jharkor, where Tovik is revered, martial academies double as temples of Law, training those who would fight the righteous fight against Chaos.

Arkyn

The cult of Arkyn is found across the Young Kingdoms. Larger temples include laboratories where priests experiment with their latest discoveries whilst smaller ones are dedicated to more bibliographic study. As Lord Arkyn embodies symmetry, his temples are built to strict symmetrical and geometric templates, wonders of engineering and architecture.

Arkyn's worshippers are both scientists and philosophers. They seek to understand the underlying principles of the Multiverse and put them to practise in the every day. This cult embodies thinkers and doers, numbering scholars, philosophers, mathematicians and engineers amongst its ranks. It offers a rational, considered approach based on the Four Fold Way with conjecture being either proved or disproved.

Cult Skills

Craft, Engineering, Evaluate, Healing, First Aid, Language (High Speech), Language (Low Speech), Lore (all basic Lores), Lore (Arkyn), Lore (Logic), Lore (Mathematics), Lore (Million Spheres), Lore (Philosophy), Lore (Physics), Mechanisms

Principal Duties

Study the works of Arkyn, following the Four Fold Way.

Cult Ranks

No special names for cult ranks

Gifts

Automaton, Second Life, Perfection, Sanctuary, Youth

Compulsions

* Becomes obsessed with the shapes and geometries of things, seeking to study and understand every nuance and every angle.
* Collect and catalogue obscure objects constantly.
* Become an oppressive bore on one particular subject, imparting all knowledge about it in long, rambling, tedious eulogies.
* Develop nervous tics and mannerisms which grow steadily more pronounced with the increase of the Pact skill.
* Develop an uncontrollable anger and violent temper if things are not done perfectly – and they never are. No one can meet the cultist's impossibly high standards.

Donblas

Donblas's worshippers are concerned with law, doctrine and applying the letter of such things specifically and precisely. They are advisers, counsellors, magistrates and judges. Frequently they are the power behind the throne and, at their most extreme, proponents of expulsions, purges and, sometimes, executions in the course of achieving purity and perfection. The cult is widespread across the Young Kingdoms. Every lawful nation has at least one temple to Donblas that also serves as a courthouse. Guilds are regulated by the cult, with permits for trade and practise granted only to those who meet the stringent codes and guidelines decreed by the cult.

The cult is also concerned with rooting-out Chaos in all its forms. In Argimiliar's later years it is the cult of Donblas that leads the pogroms against anyone considered to be chaotically tainted. At such extremes the cult maintains networks of spies and informers to bring all pertinent information to the cult's leaders, so that confessions, trial and punishments may be carried through according to Donblas's doctrines.

Cult Skills

1H Sword, 2H Sword, Bow, Influence, Language (High Speech), Language (Low Speech), Lore (Donblas), Lore (Law), Perception

Principal Duties

Administer the laws and codes of Donblas. Ensure order. Seek out and destroy all aspects of Chaos and those who sympathise with it.

Cult Ranks

Lay Member	Fellows
Initiate	Brother
Acolyte	Magistrates
Priest	Judge
Champion	Grand Master of Justice

Cult Summonings

Command, Summon Oonai (Law Speakers and Champions only)

Gifts

Abstinence (Sleep), Animal Familiar, Automata, Divine Training (Cult Skills), Second Life

Compulsions

✳ Obsessed with detail. Study every word and every letter without fail. Tasks involving study and concentration take twice as long to accomplish.

✳ Become increasingly paranoid about the influence of Chaos, seeing it everywhere; in secret symbols, the way people talk; the things they do.

✳ Quote laws and doctrines at people *ad nauseum*. Constantly correct the use of grammar, pronunciation, and so forth.

✳ Notice every transgression of every law no matter how small or inconsequential. Seek the maximum punishment possible in every instance and develop an ongoing grudge against these law-breakers.

✳ Develop obsessive/compulsive disorder. Must check everything several times. Must complete simple, everyday tasks in a set order. Eat the same foods in the same places at the same times.

✳ Develop nervous tics and mannerisms which grow steadily more pronounced with the increase of the Pact skill.

✳ Develop an uncontrollable anger and violent temper if things are not done perfectly – and they never are. No one can meet the cultist's impossibly high standards.

Cult Secrets

Only Donblas has any true power in this realm of Earth. He stands alone against Chaos.

Miggea

Miggea's worship has dwindled in the Young Kingdoms, but her cult still exists in remote places. Her worshippers are fanatics and zealots, often finding Arkyn and Donblas's cults too lenient or unexacting. They seek the absolute imposition of Law, its complete dominance of the Multiverse, and the eradication of all opposition to Law's aims. There can be no exceptions; all beliefs are heretical in Miggea's eyes, and there can be no surrender in the fight against Chaos. Even the Cosmic Balance is irrelevant.

Miggea's cultists are responsible for initiating crusades against those who reject Law. Purges of barbarian lands have seen elemental-aligned tribes crushed or scattered for defying the White Lords. Suicidal attacks against Pan Tangian and Dharijorian pirates might have been attributed to Donblas, but Miggea's fanatics have been the motivators. Her agitators and insurgents are everywhere, watching, waiting and striking without mercy.

A sect of Miggea is growing steadily in Argimiliar under the direction of Duke (later to be King) Hozel.

Cult Skills

1H Sword, 2H Sword, Dagger, 1H Flail, 2H Flail, Polearm, 2H Hammer, Athletics, Influence, Language (High Speech), Lore (Law), Lore (Miggea), Resilience, Unarmed

Principal Duties

Eradicate Chaos

Cult Ranks

Lay Member	Son/Daughter of Dolwic
Initiate	Brother/Sister of Dolwic
Acolyte	Magistrate of Dolwic
Priest	Law Speaker of Dolwic
Champion	Knight of Dolwic

Cult Summonings

Command, Summon Oonai

Gifts

Abstinence, Animal Familiar, Perfection, Return Loved One, Sanctuary, Second Life, Ward

Compulsions

* Become increasingly paranoid about the influence of Chaos, seeing it everywhere; in secret symbols, the way people talk; the things they do.
* Develop obsessive/compulsive disorder. Must check everything several times. Must complete simple, everyday tasks in a set order. East the same foods in the same places at the same times.
* Develop nervous tics and mannerisms which grow steadily more pronounced with the increase of the Pact skill.
* Develop an uncontrollable anger and violent temper if things are not done perfectly – and they never are. No one can meet the cultist's impossibly high standards.
* Never surrender or accept the surrender of any foe.

Cult Secrets

Knights of Dolwic can be summoned to any plane of the Multiverse where Miggea has influence, to fight in her crusades.

The Unrelenting Knights of Tovik

Tovik is a purely martial cult of Law. Its members follow strict codes of honour and chivalry, but train and fight with fervour in the name of the White Lords. The cult serves as guards for the cults of Arkyn and Donblas, and carries out missions and quests on their behalf. In Lormyr this cult is known as the Knights of Malador.

Knights of Tovik believe in rigour and discipline. The anarchy of Chaos is abhorrent to them, and they see the forces of the chaotic cults as an undisciplined, but dangerous, rabble. The codes of warfare and valour instilled into the Knights of Tovik convince them that any Chaos foe cannot possibly be a match for their righteousness.

Members of the cult are expected to fight Chaos wherever it arises. Initiates are often hired out as bodyguards, mercenaries, explorers, trouble-shooters and men-at-arms. This is an adventurous cult that honours its members and trains them well.

Cult Skills

All weapons, Dodge, Language (High Speech), Lore (Law), Lore (Tovik), Martial Arts

Principal Duties

Protect the churches and temples of Law. Do the bidding of the cults of Arkyn and Donblas

Cult Ranks

Lay Member	Shield of Tovik
Initiate	Sword of Tovik
Acolyte	Hammer of Tovik
Priest	Battle Priest of Tovik
Champion	Knight of Tovik

Cult Summonings

None

Gifts

Automaton, Perfection, Divine Training (Cult Skills), Ward

Compulsions

* Undergo a regular vigil of 3 days and 3 nights.
* Undertake a vow of chastity.
* Wear only leather armour, as Tovik himself wore.
* Develop nervous tics and mannerisms which grow steadily more pronounced with the increase of the Pact skill.
* Develop an uncontrollable anger and violent temper if things are not done perfectly – and they never are. No one can meet the cultist's impossibly high standards.
* Never surrender to Chaos, but always accept the surrender of an unarmed opponent.

THE SILVER GRIMOIRE

When he had meditated for more than five hours Elric took a brush and a jar of ink and began to paint both walls and floor with complicated symbols, some of which were so intricate, that they seemed to disappear at an angle to the surface on which they had been laid. Elric sent his mind into twisting tunnels of logic, across endless plains of ideas, through mountains of symbolism and endless universes of alternate truths; he sent his mind out further and further and as it went he sent with it the words which issued from his writhing lips – words that few of his contemporaries would understand, though their very sound would chill the blood of any listener. And his body heaved as he forced it to remain in its original position and from time to time a groan would escape him. And through all this a few words came again and again. One of these words was a name. 'Arioch'.
– Elric of Melniboné

THE NATURE OF SORCERY

Sorcery is the ability to control the energies of the Multiverse and, through that control, create powerful effects. As such, it has no allegiance to either the powers of Law or Chaos, and indeed is used by both in their eternal struggles. However, magic is a perversion of the natural order of things in the Young Kingdoms, and sorcerous knowledge is dangerous to sanity, soul and life. In *Elric of Melniboné* sorcery is difficult to master and the costs of its use high. Learning it takes years of study and usually involves entering into a Pact with the Lords of the Higher Planes to secure the knowledge. Once understood, sorcery's rituals take time to prepare and execute and there is *always* a cost to the sorcerer that goes beyond the mere spending of Magic Points.

Human sorcerers are rare. Melniboné, the grand master of sorcery, guarded its knowledge jealously and never taught sorcery to humans. Yet in the twilight years of the Bright Empire humans have been intrepid enough to go in search of sorcerous knowledge, combing the abandoned buildings and settlements of Melnibonéan rule, finding

scraps of spells here and incantations there. With careful and deliberate study some have been able to replicate certain spells and rituals, but the human grasp of sorcery is shaky and clumsy. The human mind is simply unable to cope with the insights it offers into the nature of the Multiverse. To study sorcery is to gaze into an abyss and comprehend its unending nature. It is to peer into realms that men call Hells and witness the creatures dwelling there and the depravities they commit. A Melnibonéan mind can take these punishments – indeed, welcome them – but for humans, sorcery is a path to madness and ruin.

Many different forms of sorcery appear throughout the Elric saga: from simple charms that induce sleep through to spells that resurrect the dead for a short time; from summoning simple elementals to aid in a battle through to calling upon Arioch himself; and strangest of all, the twisting of reality by manipulation of dreams. The most fearsome and potent magics, such as the making of Stormbringer, forged to slay a race of gods and a drinker of souls, are mysteries now lost to the past and only alluded to in the stories. The themes here are *summoning* and *dreaming*. There are also two other issues that greatly influence the others: *Pacts* and *language*.

SUMMONING

Summoning is ritualistic and involves calling to a creature or higher power, opening a gateway in the fabric of reality, and inviting it through. Once summoned, the entity may or may not do the summoner's bidding; much depends on the task and the whim of the creature. Many beings, like the Beast Lords, simply will not heed a summons unless a Pact has already been established. Some, like demons and elementals, are driven by agendas and desires alien to the human psyche and may react violently to the summons.

DREAMING

Dreaming as a potent magical force is developed throughout Elric's saga and, indeed, that of the Eternal Champion. The Dreamthieves of the Sighing Desert come and go between the dream realms, bartering stolen

dreams at the market where they are bought and sold like apples. Melniboné's dream couches train its Emperors for the task of ruling the mighty Bright Empire, as well as offering an escape from reality for Melniboné's citizens. And, frequently, adventurers find themselves in dream-like landscapes, either slight shifts in reality, gates into nearby planes of existence, or the dream realms themselves.

The Making of a Sorcerer

All sorcerers, with the exception of Dreamthieves, must fulfil certain pre-requisites. They must have:

* Language (High Speech)
* Membership of a cult that teaches sorcery OR
* An active pact with a Lord of one of the Higher Powers OR
* A tome or grimoire containing sorcerous knowledge

The importance of High Speech is discussed below. Cult membership is of particular importance because it is usually the only way for a person to develop a Pact with a higher being and thus learn the sorcerous arts. Pacts can be developed without cult membership, but the circumstances are rare and need to be carefully adjudicated by the Games Master.

If one can read High Speech, certain spells can be learned from books, grimoires or scrolls. Such tomes are exceedingly rare and always unique. One will not find the same spell repeated in several grimoires although subtle (and not so subtle) variations might be found. Cults very often control access to grimoires and adventurers are frequently employed to go hunting in crumbling, monster-infested ruins of the Bright Empire in search of new secrets. Occasionally, grimoires are found in the hands of private collectors, many of whom have become gibbering madmen, having tried, and failed, to comprehend the awful knowledge they have paid so much to attain.

Cult membership is of particular importance because it is usually the only way for a person to develop a pact with a higher being and thus learn the sorcerous arts. Pacts can be developed without cult membership, but the circumstances are rare and need to be carefully adjudicated by the Games Master, since this normally requires the summoning of a Lord of the Higher Worlds

without aid; a task which was difficult even for Elric to achieve.

Importance of High Speech

Dyvim Slorm also called to Mournblade in the Ancient Tongue of Melniboné, the mystic, sorcerous tongue which had been used for rune-casting and demon-raising all through Melniboné's ten thousand years of history.
– Stormbringer

The ancient tongue, High Speech, is essential to sorcery. High Speech is more than just a language; with the right words, runes and inflections it is a way of breaking down and reshaping reality. All sorcerers need to be able to communicate in High Speech and sorcery is simply impossible without it. High Speech defines the competency of the magician. Neither the skills of Command nor Summoning Ritual, described below, can ever exceed the sorcerer's High Speech percentage.

Playing a Sorcerer

A freshly created *Elric of Melniboné* character may only begin the game as a sorcerer with the Games Master's approval. Otherwise sorcery must be learned and developed during the course of a campaign and, of course, the pursuit of sorcery can form the basis of many exciting adventures. Games Masters are cautioned against allowing unfettered access to sorcery. As depicted in the Elric saga sorcery is rare and the privilege (or curse) of only a very few. And, as will become evident later, sorcery demands a high toll on the sorcerer.

One benefit that sorcerers gain once they set foot on the path of damnation is that the strength of their mind continues to grow throughout their life. Sorcerers have no upper limit to training their POW characteristic.

Summoning

'As you know, sorcerer, the Lords of Law and Chaos are usually in perfect balance, neither tampering directly with our Earth. Evidently the balance has tipped a little way to one side, as it sometimes does, favouring the Lords of Disorder – allowing them access to our realm. Normally it is possible for an earthly sorcerer to summon aid from Chaos or Law for a short time, but it is rare for either side to establish itself so firmly as our friend in the citadel evidently has.'
– The Weird of the White Wolf

Summoning is complex and dangerous. It has many dependencies and requires several different skills working in combination. If it goes wrong, the sorcerer's very soul is at risk, let alone his life; demons, in particular, are reluctant servants and slaves. They take their vengeance swiftly and brutally if the chance presents itself.

SUMMONING PROCEDURE

'I know only a fragment of the spell for summoning the Water King,' Dyvim Slorm said.

'I know the whole rune. I had best make haste to meditate upon it, for our fleets will clash in two hours or less and then I'll have no time for the summoning of spirits but will have to keep tight hold on my own lest some Chaos creature releases it'

– Stormbringer

The procedure depends on the creature being summoned.

✳ **Elementals.** To summon an elemental of any kind the sorcerer must be surrounded by the element in question; in a wide open space or atop a mountain for a sylph; underground or in a cave for gnomes; submerged in water for an undine; surrounded by burning braziers for a salamander.

✳ **Demons.** The sorcerer needs seclusion and privacy. Having decided on the nature and power of the demon he wishes to summon, he spends 1D8 hours preparing the area, inscribing the enchantments, protections and other glyphs necessary to breakdown the fabric of reality, then casts his mind into the spheres and planes of the Multiverse, searching for an entity which meets his requirements. A sacrifice of some kind is usual.

✳ **Beast Lords.** The Beast Lords are usually summoned via the Pact skill. Except to initially create a Pact, they cannot be called upon in any other way (see Summoning Beast Lords in the *Lords of the Million Spheres* chapter, page 85).

✳ **Specific creatures.** Elric summons many distinct creatures in the saga, most of whom are clearly inhabitants of other planes that have established pacts with the Emperors of Melniboné: the Creatures of Matik and the Grahluk, from the 8th Plane, for instance. Such entities are summoned with a *specific* Summoning Ritual spell which has a fixed cost in Magic Points, and does not require the careful preparations necessary for demon summoning, as the spell is inherently bound to the nature and

location of that being. Such conjurations can, if the sorcerer is desperate enough, take only 1D8 minutes to invoke. However, failing such a summoning can have dreadful consequences for the sorcerer since they lack the mental protections normally gained from the wards and glyphs inscribed during a full ritual.

In game terms, the summoning procedure is as follows:

✳ The sorcerer's Summoning Ritual skill is limited by the value of the High Speech skill (to correctly prepare and either speak or draw the complex wording necessary for the summoning).

✳ The sorcerer should already have decided what type of creature to summon. These are described in the Sorcerous Creatures section starting on page 112. He decides how many Magic Points will be invested in the summoning, limited only by how many he has available. The number of Magic Points invested defines the characteristics and features of the demon or elemental being summoned. More Magic Points brings forth a stronger entity, but these are harder to bargain with. The Summoning Ritual skill test is made, with applicable modifiers. If it succeeds, the desired entity forms in front of the sorcerer and must then be commanded using the Command skill.

✳ If the sorcerer can invest enough Magic Points, say from the addition of extra points from sacrifices, then they may call forth multiple demons of the type required. Command of the demon horde is the same as control of a single individual of that type.

✳ If the summoning test fails, the sorcerer loses all the Magic Points invested in the ritual but may try again if he has sufficient Magic Points remaining. If the summoning test fails whilst using a *specific summoning spell* to call forth an entity without using a ritual, then the failure is treated as a fumble.

✳ If the Summoning Ritual test is a fumble, there may be catastrophic results through psychic backlash. Consult the Summoning Backlash table below.

Summoning Backlash

01-25	The summoning has failed normally with no further effects.
26-35	The sorcerer temporarily loses 1 POW.
36-45	The sorcerer is rendered unconscious for 1D8 hours.
46-55	The sorcerer loses *all* Magic Points for 1D8 days.
56-65	The sorcerer is reduced to a drooling, gibbering idiot for 1D8 weeks.
66-75	The sorcerer takes 1D6 damage to the Head Hit Location
76-80	The sorcerer loses 1D8 POW permanently.
81-85	The sorcerer loses 1D8 INT permanently.
86-90	The sorcerer loses 1D8 x 5% from their Persistence skill permanently.
91-95	The sorcerer's soul is ripped from their body and cast into the Multiverse.
96-00	The sorcerer's soul is consumed by the entity being summoned.

Sacrifices

The Magic Points available for a summoning can be boosted by making a sacrifice. As most creatures of the otherworld like souls as much as Lords of Law and Chaos, it is usual to sacrifice a living creature. Sacrificing an animal, or sentient creature, adds half the animal's POW in additional Magic Points. Sacrificing a sapient creature, or human, adds the full POW in additional Magic Points.

Every sacrifice of a human or similar, sapient creature, increases the sorcerer's Pact skill by 1%. Sacrificing animals does not influence Pact in this way.

It should also be stressed that human sacrifice is viewed very much with disdain and revulsion within the Young Kingdoms, even amongst some chaotic cults. Constant sacrificing to boost temporal power will lead to quicker day of reckoning with the patron deity.

Once Summoned

A successful summoning brings forth the creature, ready to be instructed using the Command skill (see Sorcery Skills page 54). The form the creature takes is defined either in its description (see Sorcerous Creatures starting on page 112) or, where demons are concerned, in a form the sorcerer specifies as part of the Summoning Ritual. Demons take countless forms: drooling monsters; beautiful, iridescent humans; horrific mixtures of different, sometimes alien, animals and creatures; pillars of smoke; formless, writhing, constantly shifting globes of flesh and sinew. Let the imagination run riot. Upon their death demon bodies dissipate slowly in various vile manners, occasionally leaving exotic remnants, Nanorian stones for example.

Irrespective of physical form, all creatures are defined by the standard characteristics. Elementals calculate their characteristics using a D6. Demons use a D8. Certain modifiers are applied to these characteristics according to type, and some characteristics may have fixed values. The number of dice rolled for each characteristic is equal to the number of Magic Points allotted for characteristics during the summoning; thus, more powerful spells bring forth more powerful creatures. In the case of elementals, the Magic Points invested determine SIZ only. Other characteristics are determined in the method detailed in the elemental's description. Attributes and skills are based on the creature's characteristics as defined in that creature's description.

A summoned creature awaits the sorcerer's command, and if none is forthcoming it returns to the sphere from which it was called. But, a summoning is not a permanent arrangement. After it has been commanded, the sorcerer retains the creature's service for but a single hour. The duration of the creature's stay can be extended by spending another Magic Point for each additional hour they desire to keep it in the Young Kingdoms. Once the sorcerer ceases to expend Magic Points the creature returns to whence it came.

Example of a Summoning: Malagan and Deadwing

Malagan of Hwamgaarl is a sorcerer of Pan Tang and worshipper of Chardros the Reaper. His POW is 15 and his sorcerous skills are: High Speech 60%, Summoning Ritual 58%, and Command 54%. He wants to summon a demon of combat to smite a merchant who cheated him out of a particular grimoire in an auction in Gromoorva recently. He has 10 available Magic Points, having dedicated 5 points of POW to the worship of Queen Xiombarg.

Malagan takes to his basement and begins his preparations by burning incense and coating the stone floor with the symbols and runes for the summoning. He sacrifices a cockerel for good measure, adding a further 2 Magic Points to his total. This takes 6 hours (rolled on 1D8). Ready, he begins his incantations, choosing to invest 4 Magic Points to bring forth a really efficient combat demon.

His Summoning Ritual test succeeds on a roll of 41 – lower than both skills needed for a summoning. An acrid stench fills the room and the demon materialises. The Games Master decides that the demon is a mixture of fox and a skeletally-winged eagle with razor-sharp teeth. Its characteristics are STR 26, CON 22, DEX 19, SIZ 13, INT 14, POW 23, and CHA 10, rolled using 4D8 with the appropriate modifiers for a Combat Demon.

Malagan is disappointed in its diminutive size, but encouraged by the teeth. He now has 8 Magic Points. Deciding that he likes the look of this beast, and certain it will terrify the merchant who dared cheat him, he names it Deadwing. Wasting no further time admiring Deadwing, he commands it to seek Arjhan the Pernicious (who resides in the golden tower of Gromoorva's harbour district) and tear his head off. An opposed test occurs, between Malagan's Command of 54% and Deadwing's Persistence of 69% (POW x3). Dice are rolled; Malagan rolls 31, but the Games Master, rolling for Deadwing, rolls 68. Deadwing has prevailed in the contest and ignores Malagan's shrieked orders, eating the remains of the sacrificed cockerel instead.

Malagan adopts a different tone, expends a further Magic Point (he now has 6 and is feeling weary from the exertions). The negotiation begins again and this time Malagan wins. With a snarl and a flurry of bushy tail and eagle feathers, Deadwing goes off to murder Arjhan the Pernicious. The Games Master decides this task will take 4 hours or so to complete. Malagan relaxes in his throne made of human bones and pours himself a goblet of yellow wine, awaiting Deadwing's return, hoping that the demon will bring back Arjhan's head clutched in its maw, before he runs out of Magic Points in six hours time.

Regaining Magic Points

Magic Points are expended quickly but regenerated slowly as the sorcerer is drawing upon the energy bound into the relationship with his god, and gods do not give up that energy lightly. Under normal conditions 1 Magic Point is regained for every 12 hours of complete, undisturbed rest. If the sorcerer engages in *any* form of mental or physical activity, the rate of regeneration falls to 1 Magic Point every 24 hours. Magic Points regenerate back to their original level; that is, equal to the sorcerer's POW less that POW dedicated as part of a Pact. *For example, Malagan, following his summoning of Deadwing, has 6 Magic Points left. It will take 48 hours to regenerate the Magic Points used in his summoning if he rests completely. As it turns out, there are things he must attend to, and so his Magic Point regeneration is slowed – it will take 96 hours for Malagan to regain what he has expended.*

The Silver Grimoire

Sorcerous Creatures

The creatures described below reside outside the sphere of the Young Kingdoms and must be summoned forth via magical means. They fall into three categories: Elementals, Demons and Unique Creatures.

Elementals

Elementals are creatures composed entirely of the element they represent. Some believe that elementals are a tiny part of the elemental ruler, a portion of the substance sent in lieu of their full presence, whilst others maintain elementals are discrete entities under the ruler's control.

In the case of salamanders, sylphs and undines, which do not have fixed bodies, SIZ is represented as a volume rather than a number. For example, an elemental may be described as having a SIZ of three cubic metres. When a numerical value is needed for an elemental's SIZ, the elemental's normal hit points may be used. For example, if an elemental with 10 hit points climbed into a box and was lifted by an adventurer, its SIZ could be treated as if it was 10. Normally, however, salamanders and sylphs have little or no mass, composed as they are of fire and air.

When an elemental is summoned, there must be enough of the appropriate raw material or force present to enable manifestation. For example, a 10 cubic metre salamander would require an inferno, and would be unable to manifest in a rainstorm with no source of nearby flame larger than a lantern. Likewise, a one cubic metre undine would require a tub or cauldron filled with water, and would be unable to manifest in the desert. No matter how much of the element is available, an elemental may not be larger than its SIZ. If insufficient material is available, the elemental will not form at less than full size – instead, it simply will not appear.

All elementals, regardless of their composition, may be struck and damaged with normal weapons. Elementals have only one hit location and no armour. When an elemental is reduced to zero hit points, its body immediately dissipates (or collapses, in the case of gnomes and undines) and its essence returns to its plane of origin.

Air Elementals

Lesser elementals are known as sylphs, elements of the breeze. They assume hazy, indistinct forms, but are also known to assume the form of delicate humans, adults or children according to size and whim. They are restless creatures, forever darting and whirling, creating eddies and sudden gusts as they writhe with the air. Sylphs are voluble, chattering in a hushed, whistling tongue that sounds almost like a distant echo.

Their cousins, the Sharnah and the h'Haar shanns (known as the Wind Brothers) are terrifying forces of nature, unruly, destructive and temperamental. It is the latter that Elric summons to cross the Oldest Ocean on his return trip to Melniboné before the Sea Lords sack Imrryr. These elementals are not controlled by Lassa, empress of the air, but by her more fickle and destructive brothers, Graoll (who begets the Sharnah) and Misha (who begets the h'Haar'shann, sometimes known as Shoashoon).

Air elementals have no fixed volume and SIZ is primarily used to determine how much damage the creature can inflict in combat.

Abilities

Sylphs can create a breeze, gale or whirlwind, moving objects equal in SIZ to the sylph's STR and for minutes equal to its hit points. An air elemental can also increase a ship's speed by filling its sails; though to do so, the sylph must have one cubic metre for every three metres of the vessel's length to increase the vessel's propulsion.

It can also create enough air to keep a person breathing in an anaerobic environment for minutes equal to its hit points, but at its own expense – deplete its hit points by 1 for every minute it provides breath to someone else.

Sylphs are the enemies of salamanders, as fire consumes oxygen. Sylphs and salamanders can never co-operate and always seek to destroy each other.

The Sharnah and the h'Haar shanns are notoriously capricious. If the sorcerer fumbles his Command test when trying to direct either, the elemental will turn upon the sorcerer and launch one attack before departing from service altogether. Even Elric, who was a master of such summonings, feared the unpredictability of the wind elementals and remained highly vigilant when commanding their aid.

Characteristics and Attributes

Air elementals' characteristics, except its DEX, are based on the size of the sylph. Each cubic metre the elemental possesses gives it 2D6 STR, 1D6 POW, one point of fixed INT, half a point of CHA and 1D6 hit points. All elementals have a DEX of 4D6. The Damage Modifier is the elemental's STR x 2, rather than STR + SIZ.

Sample 3 Point Sylph

STR	6D6	(21)
DEX	4D6	(14)
SIZ	3 cubic metres	
INT	3	(3)
POW	3D6	(11)
CHA	1	(1)
HP	3D6	(11)

Combat Actions: 3
Strike Rank: +8
Movement: 10m
Skills: Athletics DEX x4%, Dodge DEX x 3%, Persistence POW x3%, Stealth DEX x3, Throwing DEX x3%

Earth Elementals

Brutish, functional, taciturn and mud-caked, gnomes are as strong, tough and unyielding as the stuff they are born from. Human form is preferred, though it is rough-hewn, blocky and almost a parody of the human shape. Facial features are either absent or represented by cracks in the mud, soil or stone that makes them; moss, twigs, gravel and sludge might serve as a rudimentary head decoration. Earthworms and other insects skitter about their craggy bodies, burrowing into and out of the many pits, holes and fissures each gnome is covered in. When a gnome speaks it is a combination of the sound of rocks scraping together and gravel crunching underfoot. The words are slow, ponderous and indelicately formed.

Gnomes are ancient enemies of the element of water, a relic of the times when Grome and Straasha fought to reshape the world. A gnome will never co-operate with an undine and the two, if brought together, fight without hesitation.

Abilities

A gnome can open up pits in the soil, make tunnels and find buried objects. It can also be used for holding objects stuck into the dirt, keeping tunnel roofs from collapsing and forming mounds, ridges and ditches in the soil no larger than the elemental's volume. A gnome has many handy uses, from uprooting a stubborn tree stump in a field to ploughing fields and preparing foundations for buildings. In warfare, a gnome can undermine an enemy's fortifications, or even construct new ones, in moments for the sorcerer commanding it. A gnome can shift a cubic volume of earth or stone equal to its STR every minute.

Gnomes know the terrain of the Young Kingdoms intimately and innately. They can locate passages, mountain passes, sources of minerals and precious gems. They sink into and rise from the earth at will and they always seem to merge with it, rather than standing upon it.

A gnome can carry a person with it as it swims through the soil, provided it has the STR. The gnome cannot provide air for that person, and unless the person being carried has some magical means of breathing, he may suffocate during the trip. A gnome can only carry an unresisting passenger in this manner. A gnome can carry as many people in SIZ equal to its STR.

Characteristics & Attributes

Characteristics, except DEX, are based on the size of the gnome. Each cubic metre the gnome possesses gives it 1D6+6 STR, 1D6 CON, 1D6 POW, one point of fixed INT and half a point of CHA. All gnomes have a DEX of 1D6. A gnome's Damage Modifier is calculated with the gnome's STR x 2, rather than STR + SIZ. Hit points are calculated on CON x3.

Sample 3 Point Gnome

STR	3D6+18	(29)
CON	3D6	(11)
DEX	1D6	(4)
SIZ	3 cubic metres	
INT	3	(4)
POW	3D6	(11)
CHA	1	(1)
HP	CON x3	(33)

Combat Actions:	1
Strike Rank:	+4
Movement:	2m
Skills:	Athletics STR+DEX, Dodge DEX, Persistence POW x3, Resilience STR x3, Throwing STR x3

Weapons

Type	Weapon skill	Damage / AP
Fist	STR x3	1D6 / 3

Fire Elementals

Salamanders are composed of living, writhing flame, and can assume any shape they wish although they invariably opt for something warlike. They must be summoned from an existing flame large enough to accommodate the salamander's SIZ. Once formed, a salamander can only be extinguished by either an air elemental or a large amount of water or earth (typically an amount three times the salamander's SIZ in cubic metres). Salamanders make reluctant servants and easily take offence. They are also vindictive, taking great glee in destruction and mayhem.

They are ancient enemies of the air elementals and will not co-operate with them, always seeking their destruction.

Abilities

A salamander ignites any flammable object it touches. It heats, and eventually melts, metal; it can bake stone, set fires and, naturally, burn people. The amount of burning damage a salamander causes is based on its SIZ, cross referenced on the table below.

Salamander Burn Potency

Salamander SIZ (cubic metres)	Burn Damage	Heat Radius (metres)
1	+1D4	4
2	+1D6	6
3	+1D8	8
4	+1D10	10
5	+1D12	12
6	+2D6	14
7	+2D8	16
8	+2D10	18
9	+2D12	20
10	+3D10	22
For every further Magic Point invested	As per progression on the Damage Modifier table	+2

The Heat Radius represents the maximum range at which a salamander can deliver a ranged burn attack (a gout of flame, a spat fireball, a wave of heat, for example).

A salamander can be used to absorb natural fires, so long as it has a cubic metre of SIZ equal to or greater than that of the fire. A salamander cannot douse other salamanders, nor can it extinguish magical flame.

Salamanders can float through the air at the same rate as they move on the ground. A salamander must touch an object to ignite it.

Characteristics & Attributes

All salamander Characteristics except its DEX are predicated upon its SIZ. Each cubic metre gives it 1D6 STR, 1D6 POW, one point of fixed INT, half a point of CHA and 2D6 hit points. All salamanders have a DEX of 3D6. A salamander's burn damage is based on its SIZ, as already discussed.

Sample 3 Point Salamander

STR   3D6   (11)
DEX   3D6   (11)
SIZ   3 cubic metres
INT   3   (3)
POW   3D6   (11)
CHA   1   (1)

HP   6D6   (21)

Combat Actions: 2
Strike Rank: +7
Movement: 4m
Skills: Athletics DEX x3%, Dodge DEX x3%, Persistence POW x5%, Resilience STR x3%

Weapons

Type	Weapon skill	Damage
Flame attack	DEX x3%	1D8

Water Elementals

Servants of King Straasha, water elementals come in countless forms, from the undines, the lesser elementals, through to the mighty Soon'a'moon, the bringers of tidal waves. Lord Straasha seems to have a certain affection for mortals and his undines tend be thoughtful and far less capricious than the elements of Air and Fire. They enjoy verbal engagement with long, convoluted debates in their watery, sibilant tongue.

Undines are held in reverence by the sailors of the Young Kingdoms, for King Straasha rules over the upper waters of the oceans, keeping at bay the Chaos Lord Pyaray who rules the deeper reaches. Water elementals share a kinship with the air elementals, and it seems Straasha, Lassa and her brothers, Graoll and Misha, are in some way related.

All water elementals are composed of a formless mass of liquid. Undines often take on a human semblance when communicating with humans, typically forming a watery, female face. Greater elementals might through-out the image of some great, wave-trapped sea beast, but otherwise remain a fearsome, amorphous mass of brine. An undine may form in any liquid that is at least 95% water, such as beer, diluted milk or diluted wine. An undine moves overland like a huge, amorphous amoeba, and moves through water like a rippling current. There is no difference between undines formed of fresh water and salt water; save for the powerful smell of brine that always accompanies salt water undines.

Abilities

An undine can purify itself of sediment and insoluble substances by sitting and churning for a full Combat Round per cubic metre of the elemental. It cannot remove dissolved chemicals such as salt or miscible liquids such as alcohol in this way, though it could purge itself of dirt or oil.

An undine can be used to propel a ship through the water. To do so, the undine must have one cubic metre for every three metres of the vessel's length to increase the vessel's propulsion.

An undine can carry objects or beings if its STR supports their SIZ. It can carry things either underwater, to any depth, or along the surface if carrying a creature who needs air to breathe.

All undines are hostile to gnomes. They will not co-operate with them and always attack any earth elemental they encounter, such is their enmity.

Characteristics & Attributes

All undines' Characteristics, except for DEX, are based on its size. Each cubic metre of the undine it 2D6 STR, 1D6 POW, one point of fixed INT, half a point of CHA and 1D6+6 hit points. All undines have a DEX of 2D6. An undine's Damage Modifier is computed with the undine's STR x 2, rather than STR + SIZ.

Sample 3 Point Undine

STR   6D6   (21)
DEX   2D6   (7)
SIZ   3 cubic metres
INT   3   (3)
POW   3D6   (11)
CHA   1   (1)

HP   3D6+18 (29)

Combat Actions: 2
Strike Rank: +5
Movement: 6m (water), 3m (land)
Skills: Athletics DEX x3%, Perception POW x3%, Persistence POW x3%, Resilience STR x3%

Demons

The word demon usually describes the chaotic entities inhabiting planes of existence that are ruled solely by the Lords of Chaos. As creatures of other worlds, chaotic demons manifest in myriad forms, ranging from the eerily beautiful through to the nightmarish, grotesque and insane. Some revel in their ugliness whilst others maintain a certain, mortal-like dignity and strive to appear serene, beautiful and highly cultured. Irrespective of their appearance, these demons have allegiance only to their Lords of Chaos. They might lend their services to mortals for a time and might even offer gifts and fabulous promises, but they are ultimately untrustworthy. By their very natures they are restless, selfish and oblivious to the consequences of their actions. Demons always assume an animate form; they do not, and cannot, take the form of an inanimate object, for that is against the nature of Chaos.

For the purposes of *Elric of Melniboné* demons are gathered together into certain types. These are demons of combat, demons of desire, demons of knowledge, demons of protection and demons of transportation. Whilst these categories might seem restrictive, given a demon's chaotic nature, they indicate only a demon's primary area of expertise or interest. Demons of combat can still protect; demons of knowledge might be every bit as seductive as a demon of desire. The Lords of Chaos also control different categories of demon, as discussed in the *Lords of the Million Spheres* chapter, and can only teach the summoning of demon types within their control. The demons described are all lesser varieties, irrespective of their power. These are the foot-soldiers of Chaos, occupying the lowest ranks of the chaotic dukedoms. More powerful demons exist but unlike the Lords of the Higher Worlds who occasionally desire to be called, such creatures cannot be summoned by human sorcerers. Only the Melnibonéans mastered the rituals necessary to call the greater demons to Earth, and even the most powerful Melnibonéan sorcerers (most of whom are long-dead) were wary of engaging their services.

Defining a Demon

When a sorcerer decides to summon a demon, he must decide how many Magic Points he will invest into the ritual. These Magic Points are then divided amongst the various aspects of the demon; that is to say, its Characteristics, its Abilities and its Chaotic Features.

Demon Characteristics

Demons have their characteristics rolled on XD8, where X represents the number of Magic Points assigned to Characteristics by the summoner. Certain characteristics may also have a positive or negative modifier, depending on the demon's type. If the modifier would take the characteristic below zero, give that characteristic the minimum value of the dice roll. For example, a demon with a STR of 3D8–8 might have a roll of 7, meaning that the –8 modifier would reduce its STR to –1. Instead, its STR is simply rated as 3.

Demon Abilities

Each type of demon has certain abilities it excels at. For example, Demons of Combat are good at damaging foes, and Demons of Transport are gifted at moving quickly. However, any Magic Points placed into these abilities must be taken from the total invested in the Summoning Ritual to initially conjure the demon. The abilities are explained under each demon type.

Chaotic Features

Demons may possess one or more chaotic features, as determined on the Chaotic Features table or according to the Games Master's preference (but use the effects from the table as a guide). A chaotic feature costs 1 of the Magic Points invested in the Summoning Ritual that calls the demon into existence.

A Games Master may either choose the features a demon displays, adapting them to the demon's type, or roll randomly. Note that the Heart of Nanorion feature should only ever be a random feature; it is very rare even amongst demons.

Rolling the same chaotic feature several times indicates that either the feature's ability stacks or its incidence is multiplied, according to the Games Master's desire.

Demon Attributes & Skills

Attributes are figured as for any *Elric of Melniboné* character. All demons have hit points, Magic Points, Strike Rank and a standard movement rate of 6m. Hit points per location are calculated using the standard method on page 36. If killed, only the demon's corporeal form remains, albeit briefly; its essence returns to its plane of origin.

Skills are based on a multiple of a particular characteristic, and the skills most common to a demon type are listed in

Chaotic Features

01-02	Absorbing	All opponents it comes into contact with are drained of 1D8 MP each Combat Action and are added to the demon as temporary Characteristic or Attribute points; roll a D10, 1=STR, 2=CON, 3=DEX, 4=SIZ, 5=INT, 6=POW, 7=CHA, 8=MP, 9=HP or 10=roll twice.
03-04	Acidic	Possesses acidic ichor which sprays whenever the skin is penetrated, causing damage to the attacker; roll a D4, 1=1D2, 2=1D4, 3=1D6 and 4=1D8 damage per wound.
05-06	Agile	+1D8 DEX.
07-08	Arms	Gain an extra pair of manipulation limbs from a random species.
09-10	Asymmetric	One half of the creature is larger, longer or taller than the other, double the hit points of locations in the larger side and halve the hit points of locations in the smaller.
11-12	Beaked	Gain a bite attack. Each additional incidence adds another toothed beak on a different location; roll a D4, 1=1D6 damage, 2=1D8 damage, 3=1D10 damage or 4=1D12 damage.
13-14	Beautiful	+1D8 CHA.
15-16	Blind	No vision organs.
17-18	Boneless	Can squeeze through any gap.
19-20	Broadcaster	Any damage inflicted on the creature is felt by everybody within 5m, who suffer the psychological, but not physiological effects as if they had been wounded too.
21-22	Chameleon	+1D8x5% bonus to Stealth when hiding.
23-24	Clawed	Gain a claw attack. Each additional incidence adds another set of claws on a on a different location; roll a D4, 1=1D6 damage, 2=1D8 damage, 3=1D10 damage or 4=1D2 damage.
25-26	Climbing	Has a spider or lizard like ability to scale surfaces, +1D8x10% bonus to Athletics when climbing.
27-28	Corroding	Weapons take 1D8 damage each time they strike the creature.
29-30	Crystalline	Gain 1D10 Armour Points from a crystalline crust.
31-32	Deaf	No hearing organs. Suffer a –40% penalty to the Command skill when trying to control a demon with this feature.
33-34	Disturbing	Creature is covered with unsettling forms, such as baby arms, or multiple eyes or mouths.
35-36	Hatred	Creature possesses unreasoning hatred of a particular species and will attack on sight.
37-38	Head	Gain an extra head, each one gets an independent Persistence test against mental effects and can control the entire body if one head is incapacitated.
39	Heart of Nanorion	The demon's heart is a Nanorion gem, which can heal as many HP as the demon had POW before it shatters.
40-41	Horned	Gain a gore attack. Each additional incidence adds another set of horns on a different location; roll a D4, 1=1D6 damage, 2=1D8 damage, 3=1D10 damage or 4=1D12 damage.
42-43	Icy	Radiates freezing coldness, injuring anyone within melee range; roll a D4, 1=1D2, 2=1D4, 3=1D6 and 4=1D8 damage per round.
44-45	Leaper	Has powerfully sprung legs, +1D8 x10% bonus to Athletics when jumping.
46-47	Levitating	Has the capability to move over any solid or liquid surface without sinking or leaving tracks.
48-49	Mimic	Changes into the shape of a creature it successfully touches, maintaining its own Characteristics, but assuming the locations and a duplicate image of the being contacted.
50-51	Nerveless	Cannot feel pain, and does not suffer the ill-effects of serious wounds.
52-53	Obfuscating	Produces a cloud of mist that blinds observers, who must succeed in an opposed test of Perception against the Obfuscation's potency of 1D8x10% every Combat Action to observe the creature.
54-55	Paralysing	Weakens the DEX of an opponent by 1D8 each successful hit. This lasts for 3 Combat Rounds.
56-57	Poisonous	One unarmed attack inflicts a venomous poison with a delay of 1D8 Combat Actions and a potency of 1D8x10%, which causes an extra 1D8 damage to the location struck.
58-59	Regenerating	Recovers 1 hit point per round to every location, except for Major Wounds.
60-61	Resistant	Invulnerable to one type of damage or weapon type; fire, cold, poison, disease, swords, spears, cudgels and so forth (also known as a Wardpact). The demon must declare its resistance or Wardpact to anyone preparing to use that form of attack.

Chaotic Features (continued)

62-63	Roaring	Produces a thunderous sound which deafens listeners, who must succeed in an opposed test of Resilience against the Roaring's potency of 1D8x10% to avoid becoming temporally stunned for 1D8 Combat Actions.
64-65	Screaming	Horrible screams which terrify listeners, who must succeed in an opposed test of Persistence against the Screaming's potency of 1D8x10% to avoid a –20% Skill Penalty.
66-67	Spores	Produces clouds of spores. If inhaled the breather must win an opposed test of Resilience against the Spore's potency of 1D8x10% to avoid suffering 1D8 Hit Points to the chest every round until successful; as the spores gestate into worms, flowers, vines, etc, that are coughed up, or grow out of their lungs.
68-69	Stalker	+1D8x5% bonus to Stealth when sneaking.
70-71	Stench	Gives off nauseating odours that sicken inhalers, who must succeed in an opposed test of Resilience against the Stench's potency of 1D8x10% to avoid dropping prone and vomiting.
72-73	Sticky	Secretes a strong glue or mucus of potency 1D8x10% which causes items to adhere to its skin, requiring a *Brute Force* Athletics test at a penalty of the potency to remove.
74-75	Sting	Gain a sting attack. Each additional incidence adds another stinger on a different location; roll a D4, 1=1D6 damage, 2=1D8 damage, 3=1D10 damage or 4=1D12 damage.
76-77	Strong	+1D8 STR.
78-79	Swimmer	Has webbed digits and gills, +1D8x10% bonus to Athletics when swimming.
80-81	Tailed	Gains extra unarmed attack, the damage is triple the creature's Damage Modifier but only for the purposes of calculating Knockback.
82-83	Tentacle	Gains grapple attack. If successful then the tentacles Inflict Pain each Combat Action thereafter.
84-85	Tongue	Gains grapple attack. If successful then the sticky tongue Immobilises the opponent, and they can be automatically bitten or swallowed the following Combat Action.
86-87	Toothed	Gain a bite attack. Each additional incidence adds another toothed maw on a different location; roll a D4, 1=1D6 damage, 2=1D8 damage, 3=1D10 damage or 4=1D12 damage – roll.
88-89	Tough	+1D8 CON.
90-91	Warded	Invulnerable to one form of material; steel, wood, stone, flesh, etc.
92-93	Warped	One random location changes to that of a random animal (see *Creatures* chapter).
94-95	Weakening	Temporarily weakens the strength of an opponent by 1D8 STR each successful hit.
96-97	Wilful	+1D8 POW.
98-00	Wings	Gains bat, bird, butterfly or insect wings granting a Flying Movement equal to normal Movement.

the description of each category. However, a demon has any unlisted basic skill calculated in the same way as an *Elric of Melniboné* character. Additionally a demon also has one additional Advanced skill, for each Magic Point invested in its Characteristics.

Demons of Combat

The soldiers of Chaos, demons of combat relish battle and bloodshed, and are the only demons that can be commanded to attack without provocation. They always ignore any command that does not involve physical violence in some way and, if they make a Persistence test successfully, break free from the sorcerer's control and run amok for the remainder of their summoned time. Attacks are only made against the summoner if no one else is in the immediate vicinity.

All demons of combat come equipped with natural weapons, be these fists, feet, claws, jaws or something else. If they have hands capable of grasping, they can wield any weapon they are given, although this is something the sorcerer must provide, along with any armour, suitably crafted to its form.

Characteristic Modifiers
STR +8, DEX +8, INT –8

Special Ability
All demons of combat add any extra Magic Points beyond those invested in their Characteristics and Chaotic Features to their Damage Modifier.

Skills

Athletics DEX x3%, Dodge DEX x3%, Persistence POW x3%, Resilience CON x3%, Unarmed STR x3%

Weapons

Demons of combat wield any weapon given to them at DEX x3%. If the demon does not have a weapon to wield, it has one natural attack for every Magic Point invested in its Characteristics, at its Unarmed skill percentage.

Demons of Desire

These demons offer gratification and wish fulfilment. They tend to be obsequious and fawning, although they may equally be arrogant and aloof, depending on mood and personality. Demons of desire fetch, carry and indulge almost any decadent or perverted whim, but they do not fight or protect their summoner. They make excellent thieves, spies and eavesdroppers. Their skills are tailored to such tasks, every bit as much as the more obvious talents a demon of desire might be called upon to demonstrate.

Demons of desire usually manifest in a human form of a gender desirable to the summoner, but are not compelled to do so and can take whatever form (as long as it is an organic, animate thing) the sorcerer prefers.

Characteristic Modifiers

STR –8, POW +8, CHA +8

Special Ability

A demon of desire can confer one gift, as described in the Example Gifts table on page 95 of the *Lords of the Million Spheres* chapter, appropriate to its cult. The gift is temporary and lasts for a number of days equal to the demon's POW.

Skills

Dodge DEX x3%, Influence CHA x3%, Perception POW x3%, Persistence POW x3%, Resilience CON x3%, Seduction CHA x3%, Stealth DEX x3%. Bonus Advanced skills are normally spent on artistic or performance skills.

Weapons

Demons of desire never enter into combat. They will defend themselves by dodging, but take no other action.

Demons of Knowledge

These demons are the teachers of Chaos, spreaders of blasphemous knowledge, gatherers of information and disseminators of lies. Sorcerers call upon such demons when they need a certain fact, wish to broaden their knowledge in a particular area or to have knowledge stolen. Demons of knowledge are accomplished in all these areas; but that does not make them reliable.

Knowledge demons do not fight and cannot be commanded to do so. However, acting as strategists and tacticians they can command others to fight – demons or mortals – although success is never guaranteed.

The form taken by demons of knowledge is purely dependent on whim. The image of the shrewd scholar, hunched of back, wizened of feature, is a popular semblance, but knowledge demons delight in taking animal forms, in which case they act rather like familiars.

Demons of knowledge are chiefly masters of ancient, arcane lore, but they are skilled in looking into both the future and the past, with some accuracy. As teachers they can communicate their knowledge to their summoner although this always involves a Command roll from the sorcerer.

Characteristic Modifiers

STR –8, INT +8, POW +8

Special Ability

For every extra Magic Point beyond those invested in their Characteristics and Chaotic Features a demon of knowledge can look up to 1 day into the future or 1 year into the past, describing events relevant to a particular place or person. The accuracy of their knowledge (or what they communicate) is equal to INT x3. No roll is required; this is a measure of the demon's accuracy of observation. For example, a demon of knowledge with INT 17 with 3 points dedicated to its prophecy can look 3 days into the future and be 51% accurate in reporting what it sees. It might be able to report specific events but be hazy about participants, or might mix-up the chronology of events but get the participant's details precise. Games Masters should feel free to use this level of accuracy according to the scenario and requirements of their campaign.

When acting as teachers, demons of knowledge can school a student in one subject, either language or lore,

up to a number of points equal to its INT characteristic, but only if the demon's ability with the skill exceeds the student's by at least 20%. This takes 1 hour for every point of INT it teaches and can never exceed the amount of time the demon has remaining for its summoning. It cannot teach new skills; it can only build a student's existing knowledge.

Skills

Evaluate INT x3%, Influence CHA x3%, Language (High Speech) INT x3%, Lore (choose 1 separate field of Lore for every Magic Point invested in its base characteristics) INT x3%, Persistence POW x3%, Resilience CON x3%

Demons of Protection

Demons of protection guard whatever they have been commanded to protect and to the degree they have been instructed. Sorcerers need to be careful with how they phrase commands. 'Kill everyone trying to enter my laboratory' means the demon will do precisely that – including the summoner.

Protection demons can manifest in any animate form desired; huge, burly humans; vile monsters; softly spoken gatekeepers. They are taciturn and precise. They will fight for their summoner but only when this constitutes protection. No demon of protection can be ordered to fight unless there is a distinct and perceivable threat to what it is guarding.

All demons of protection come equipped with natural weapons, be these fists, feet, claws, jaws or something else. If they have hands capable of grasping, they can wield any weapon they are given, although this is something the sorcerer must provide, along with any armour, suitably crafted to its form. Demons of protection never wander more than two or three metres from what they protect. If acting as bodyguards for a sorcerer, they move when the sorcerer moves but never stray far away – certainly not beyond close combat distances.

If a ranged attack is perceived or launched, the demon intersperses itself between missile and object. They have no qualms in laying down their lives for a summoner; that is part of their contract.

Characteristics

CON +8, SIZ +8, INT –8

Special Ability

A demon of protection has natural Armour Points equal to every extra Magic Point beyond those invested in their Characteristics and Chaotic Features.

Skills

Dodge DEX x3%, Perception POW x3%, Persistence POW x3%, Resilience CON x3%, Unarmed STR x3%

Weapons

Demons of protection wield any weapon given to them at DEX x3%. If the demon cannot wield weapons, it has one natural attack, based on its form, for every Magic Point invested in their Characteristics, again at DEX x3%

Demons of Transport

Demons of transport usually take the form of beasts used either for riding or drawing some other mode of transportation. Demon horses, cattle, or even more esoteric configurations, such as giant wolves or insects are common forms. Demons that are equipped with wings can fly, but note that flying is a strenuous activity The demon can only fly while carrying a light load, limited to its STR or less in ENC. Additionally, for a flying demon to be used as a mount, it must have a SIZ double or more than that of its passenger or passengers.

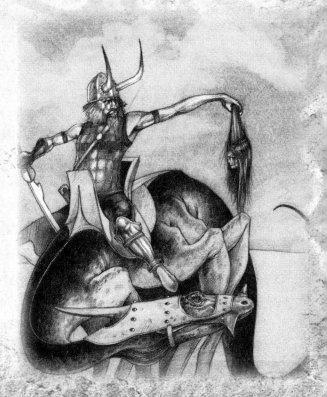

Transport demons will take the summoner anywhere they are commanded to, as long as the place can be reached within the time remaining for their summoning. If the destination exceeds the distance the demon can travel, it may not necessarily point this out and, instead, take the rider as far as it is able before leaving them stranded. Demons of transport stop at nothing to reach their destination leaping walls, gates and battlements. They ignore injuries if wounded and ignore threats of danger, but will not fight on behalf of the sorcerer. No demon of transport will ever try to bypass a demon of protection.

Characteristic Modifiers
STR +8, SIZ +8, INT –8

Special Ability
Demons of transport are preternaturally fast. Every extra Magic Point beyond those invested in their Characteristics and Chaotic Features adds +1m to their standard Movement rate. Demons of transport are tireless and suffer no fatigue effects while carrying out their duties. They can carry a maximum SIZ equal to their STR.

Skills
Acrobatics DEX x3%, Athletics DEX x3%, Dodge DEX x3%, Persistence POW x3%, Resilience CON x3%

Weapons
Although the demon may exhibit natural weapons due to its form, these are not used for combat purposes. However a demon can be commanded to charge at, or through, assailants. If the opponent(s) cannot dodge the charge they suffer damage equal to the demon's Damage Bonus and Knockback effects as described on page 75 of the Combat chapter.

Automata

The lawful cults, particularly Arkyn's, have their own versions of supernatural creatures: *automata*. Wrought from metal, wood, crystal or stone with internal gears, cranks, clockwork, springs and crude joints, these curious golems are given a rudimentary form of life through the inscription of runes upon the surface of the automaton. The most powerful versions, such as Myshella's bejewelled bird that carried Elric to Ashaneloon, may even have a certain level of sentience. The capabilities of these mechanical golems depend purely upon their shape and skills; automata cannot possess Chaotic Features. Their main benefit is that unlike summoned demons, automata can exist permanently within the Young Kingdoms.

Automata can be built and activated by human, lawful, sorcerers. Given the amount of time and Magic Points required to create and activate automata, it is common for teams of engineers and scholars to be working on such projects. This is the procedure:

It takes a number of weeks equal to the automata's total Characteristics and Armour Points to build and test the automata's armature. This requires both Engineering and Mechanisms tests each week during the construction. Thus, the builder needs to decide how strong, big, dexterous and so forth the automata will be in advance. A 70 point automaton would thus have 70 points to be distributed across the characteristics of STR, CON, SIZ, DEX, INT, CHA and its Armour Points, and would take 70 weeks to build. Each Characteristic must always have 1 point allocated, so that the automaton can function fully. The amount invested in CHA determines the finish and attractiveness of the final piece. Automaton's lack POW as they have no soul of their own. Divide the total build time by the number of people working on the automaton. However the minimum time to complete the automaton is always at least one tenth of the total build time (thus, 20 engineers working on the 70 point automaton above would still take 7 weeks to complete the machine).

All attributes are calculated from the characteristics in the usual manner.

Each point of INT allows the automaton to learn and perform one skill. Thus, an automaton with an INT of 1 could understand the command 'stack those crates into a pile' and execute the task using an Athletics test. The actual intelligence of the golem depends upon the value of its INT. An automaton with an INT of 8 (minimum human range) is capable of speech. Below this value the automaton has the mental ability of an equivalent animal and may only learn basic skills. The rating of each skill the automaton can perform is always a minimum of 25% plus the sum of the characteristics used to calculate the skill. Thus, an automaton with a STR of 10 and DEX of 10 would have an Athletics skill of 45%. Skills relying on POW are calculated using the INT characteristic instead.

The automaton is activated only when lawful sorcerers invest the creation with a number of Magic Points exceeding its *combined Characteristics and Armour Points*. After this moment, it functions for a further number of hours equal to the Magic Points invested *beyond* the activation total. At the end of this period the creature is completely discharged. Although automatons eventually run down, they can be reactivated once the sorcerer has recharged it, which usually requires multiple Magic Point investments. Immediately the reinvested Magic Points *exceed* the activation total, it begins to function again.

Automata are tireless and not subject to any form of fatigue. They are immune to mental effects, and therefore require no Persistence skill. Automatons only obey the commands of the person who inscribed their runes, unless that command is handed to someone else. Their hit points are calculated according to CON and SIZ, but Armour Points depend on how much effort is put into armouring the device and cannot exceed the automaton's SIZ. If an automaton ever runs down, it retains its skills and experience when it is next reanimated.

Stealing Dreams – Dreamthieves & Dream Realms

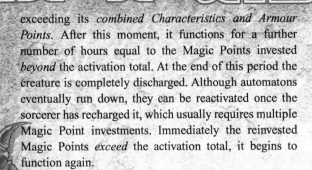

Dreams, their power, their significance and their explanation of the self, figure prominently in the Elric saga, particularly in the later Elric stories, which explore the dream worlds deeply and examine how Melniboné used them to equip its emperors with the skills and knowledge necessary to administer an empire as grand as the Bright Empire.

Like all magic, dream magic is rare in the Young Kingdoms. It is practised only on the Dragon Isle in the form of the dream couches and amongst the strange people called Dreamthieves, who wander the Million Spheres, occasionally pausing on this plane to acquire new dreams. Dreamtheft is recognised only in the Sighing Desert and Eshmir; it is barely known in the Young Kingdoms at large, although that might be due more to the absolute discretion of the practitioners – for they are thieves, after all.

Mastering dream magic is to become a wanderer of the Moonbeam Roads, the bright threads of the Multiverse that spin through the million spheres web-like, permitting their travellers to visit other realms and planes via their unconscious mind, experiencing these lands as though part of them and gaining from their experiences. Few have the faculties to do it, and dream magic is not taught by any of the cults of Law or Chaos. Indeed, Dreamthieves fear Chaos, and the dreams of those who bargain with it. Dreamtheft means imposing a kind of order on the chaotic nature of dreams, and this is dangerous for a Dreamthief.

Dreamtheft occurs when the Dreamthief uses his skills to physically and psychically bind with the dreamer. He enters the dream-consciousness, identifies the *source* of the dream, and thus its strength and nature, and then binds it into a form that can be carried away from the dreamer, ridding them of that dream or nightmare forever. Dreams are highly valued in some realms; by those who either cannot dream, or desire dreams of a certain type. Dreamthieves sell the dreams they have captured, unbinding them so that the new dreamer, the purchaser, may experience them fully.

Playing a Dreamthief

Dreamthieves as Player Characters are always at the Games Master's discretion. The vast majority do not hail from the Young Kingdoms, and all are able to wander the Multiverse, moving from plane to plane along the Moonbeam Roads, pausing for long enough in new realms to steal dreams for trade at the twice-yearly markets where such things are bartered to those who desire, and can afford them. Thus, Dreamthieves are transient characters who do not like to be confined to one place or realm for too long. Occasionally a Dreamthief might be searching for a specific type of dream, and that might confine him to a particular plane, realm or city for a lengthy period; or he might have chosen to remain. The reasons for the Dreamthief's presence in the campaign must be agreed in advance of the Dreamthief character being created, and it must satisfy both the Games Master's requirements and the general tenets as laid out here:

* The player must decide upon the Dreamthief's history – how he came to be a Dreamthief.
* He must determine what plane the Dreamthief comes from: if not the plane of the Young Kingdoms, he must describe something of that realm; its name, the name of, at least, the country where the Dreamthief was born, and the city, town or village of birth.
* He must decide what prompted the character to become a Dreamthief. Was it to save a loved one plagued by torment? Was it a natural talent spotted and nurtured by another Dreamthief?

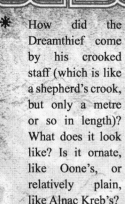

- How did the Dreamthief come by his crooked staff (which is like a shepherd's crook, but only a metre or so in length)? What does it look like? Is it ornate, like Oone's, or relatively plain, like Alnac Kreb's?

- What other planes has the Dreamthief visited? Precise details are not necessary, and it is completely acceptable, if not compulsory, to use any of the myriad worlds described in Michael Moorcock's books in whole or in part. Dreamthieves may have wandered Lwym-an-Esh, Granbretan or Garathorm. Anywhere is possible.

- He must detail at least two dreams, naming their realms and describing their content that he has stolen before adventuring. Here is an opportunity for the player to use his own dreams as the basis for the Dreamthief's.

- He must finally explain how the Dreamthief came to the Young Kingdoms and why. He must sketch a vague outline of how long he intends to remain, and what kinds of dreams he is looking to steal and then sell. These plans may change, of course. Fate plays many tricks.

Dreamthieves can come from any country, cultural background, or previous profession. However, as Dreamtheft is recognised only in the Sighing Desert and Eshmir, these are the principle countries where Young Kingdoms Dreamthieves are found. Experienced Dreamthieves are always searching for new thieves and anyone displaying the talent for dreamtheft might be approached secretly by a Dreamthief (and perhaps even via dreams) offering the opportunity to train. Dreamthieves appear to be more common beyond the plane of the Young Kingdoms and so it is quite plausible for a thief working in the Young Kingdoms to have come from a more exotic realm where dreamtheft is commonplace.

Advanced Skill: Dreamtheft (POW)

The skill of Dreamtheft is an advanced skill. It combines formal teaching and natural, magical aptitude. It does not rely on any pacts or any language. Through the use of the skill, the Dreamthief, aided by the crook of his profession (which is inherently magical), merges with the body and dreaming mind of the dreamer, their bodies and souls becoming entwined, joined by the power of the crook. The thief then enters the dream state of the dreamer, locates the dream and steals it.

To successfully bind with the dreamer the Dreamthief matches his Dreamtheft skill against the dreamer's Persistence in an opposed test. Success allows the Dreamthief access to the dream state of the dreamer. A critical success allows the Dreamthief access, but with a stronger mental fortification: increase the Dreamthief's available Magic Points by half (rounding up) to use in capturing the dream sought. A fumble of the Dreamtheft roll means the Dreamthief is repelled by the strength of the dream, and also loses a number of Magic Points equal to the dream's intensity.

The Seven Dream Realms

Dreamthieves have named seven different dream realms, which roughly equate to the kinds of dreams most experience. By naming these realms, they can more easily identify and thus capture a dream.

1. Sadanor – The Land of Dreams in Common
2. Marador – The Land of Old Desires
3. Paranor – The Land of Lost Beliefs
4. Celador – The Land of Forgotten Love
5. Imador – The Land of New Ambition
6. Falador – The Land of Madness
7. The seventh realm is unnamed. Dreams from here are in the true province of Chaos.

Each realm produces dreams of a different intensity and depth. The dreams of Sadanor, which all of us share, are the fleeting dreams where the day's events are ordered and stored – as is common to every human. These are relatively weak dreams, and easily made tangible by the Dreamthief. As one progresses through the realms, the dream intensity strengthens and it becomes more difficult for the Dreamthief to mould and steal them. Each realm is stronger than the last, and the seventh, unnamed realm is the strongest of all. It contains and generates dreams that not only defeat Dreamthieves, but consume them. This is the fate seemingly suffered by Alnac Kreb when

he tried to heal Varadia, the holy daughter of Raik Na Seem of the Barrudim in *The Fortress of the Pearl*.

Dream Characteristics

Dreams have two characteristics: *Intensity* and *Persistence*. Intensity measures the strength of the dream and how much magical resource is needed to capture it. Persistence measures the resistance the dream offers to capture.

The dream realm's number (see 'The Seven Dream Realms' above) indicates the strength and type of the dream it produces. The number indicates the number of four-sided dice rolled to determine the dream's Intensity. The name of the realm defines its content. Thus, dreams from Celador all have an Intensity of 4D4 and concern forgotten, old, and unrequited love.

The dream's Intensity is the number of Magic Points the Dreamthief needs to expend to bind and steal it. A dream of Sadanor is relatively weak, requiring no more than 4 Magic Points. Those of Falador, Land of Madness, range from an intensity of 6 through to 24; quite simply, some dreams of madness are so powerful that even the most skilled Dreamthief cannot deal with them.

A dream's Persistence is its Intensity multiplied by five. Thus, a dream of Sadanor with an intensity of 2 has a Persistence of 10%. When capturing a dream the Dreamthief matches his Dreamtheft against the dream's Persistence in an opposed roll. If successful, the dream is captured and it costs the Dreamthief Magic Points equal to the dream's Intensity. If the opposed test fails, the dream eludes capture and the Dreamthief loses 1 Magic Point. If the test is fumbled, the full Intensity in Magic Points is lost. If the test critically succeeds, the cost is half the dream's Intensity, rounded up.

Dreamtheft Backlash

If, in the course of trying to capture a dream, the opposed test against the dream's Persistence is fumbled, *and the dream's Persistence roll succeeds critically*, backlash occurs. The Dreamthief loses twice the dream's Intensity in Magic Points and this manifests itself as a physical wasting of the Dreamthief's soul and body. The Dreamthief suffers a number of points of physical damage to each hit location equal to every point of the dream's Intensity. The damage appears as a physical wasting away of the body, as though all energy has been sucked from every muscle, nerve and sinew. In extreme cases, as is the case with Alnac Kreb, the Dreamthief may end-up literally spluttering out their wasted internal organs before dying.

DreamQuests

A dreamquest is an adventure in itself, akin to Elric's quest for Varadia's freedom and the Fortress of the Pearl. Such quests are not undertaken lightly and only in pursuit of the strongest, most powerful dreams.

✳ A dreamquest frequently involves dealing with the dreamer's own dreamscape which intersects with, but is discrete from, the dream realms. The Dreamthief wanders a landscape of the dreamer's own mind, encountering dream-forms of the dreamer's acquaintances, friends, lovers and enemies, and these may be oddly skewed versions of the real people with very different forms of behaviour and intent.

✳ Dreams defy logic: whilst in a dreamer's dreamscape the participants in the dreamquest might find they can fly, take on different characteristics or appear as different people (or an amalgamation of several different individuals in one body).

✳ The dreamscape reflects the dreamer's personality and view of the world. Familiar sites and places might be presented in odd or curious ways.

✳ If the dreamer is unaware of the intrusion, or hostile to it, he might unconsciously send other dream elements to expel the intruders. These take physical form so combat takes place as normal, although death results in the Dreamthief and companions being expelled from the dreamer's mind and possibly suffering psychological damage.

✳ The dreamquest might require a number of separate tasks, or stages, to be completed before the Dreamthief can move to the next. These obstacles might be social encounters, combat situations, puzzles, or love affairs requiring a certain resolution or outcome that fits with the dreamer's own psyche before progress continues.

✳ Whilst a dreamquest might take a few minutes or hours in physical time, dreamtime is vastly different. The questers might spend days, weeks or months – or time may not appear to pass at all – in completing their quest.

✳ As is evident from the above, a Dreamthief can undertake a dreamquest with companions. It costs the Dreamthief 1 Magic Point for every companion taken into the dreamscape. These Magic Points are not regenerated whilst in the dreamscape, and

Dreamstaffs

At her belt was a sword, and cradled above her left shoulder was a hooked staff of gold and ebony, a more elaborate version of the one which lay on the carpet beside Alnac's corpse.
– The Fortress of the Pearl

A Dreamthief's staff is a symbol of their profession and skill, and a conduit for the Dreamthief's natural abilities to enter and steal dreams. A typical staff is about a metre in length and curved like a shepherd's crook at one end. No Dreamthief can complete their work without the aid of their staff, and they are fiercely protected. They may be as ornate as Oone's, inlaid with gems or wrought with precious metals, or more utilitarian in appearance. Ostentation typically denotes the expertise of the Dreamthief, but this is not always so.

The staff contains the dreams the Dreamthief steals. It can hold any number of stolen dreams which are then sold at the Dream Bazaar; however, once stolen by the thief, and committed to the staff, the Dreamthief cannot access the inherent power of the dream; that is forbidden by the Dreamthief's code, and no Dreamthief would ever attempt to use a captured dream to boost their own power or abilities.

companions cannot actively steal dreams – although they can interact with, and fight, anything the dreamer throws at them, using their normal, mundane abilities.

* Demons and elemental allies cannot enter the dreamscape. Adventurers with such pacts and alliance have no magical help, save for any weird logic the dreamscape itself imparts.

The Dream Bazaar and the Guild of Dreamers

Dreamthieves sell their stolen dreams at the Dream Bazaar, which is held in a realm known only to Dreamthieves and those who work on their behalf, the Dream Traders. Dream Traders are able to tread the Moonbeam roads with the same ease as a Dreamthief, but they are not thieves themselves. Rather they act as brokers between the customer and supplier, negotiating the price, agreeing the terms and arranging the transfer of the dream. Dream Traders are sometimes retired Dreamthieves, or thieves who have discovered a higher aptitude for selling rather than stealing.

Twice a year Dreamthieves step through the planes to the Dream Bazaar – a magical place thronged with Dream Traders clad in garish styles and colours representing hundreds, if not thousands, of styles from across the Multiverse. They frequent the opulent taverns and cafes that line the immense marble-floored market square, interviewing Dreamthieves with wares for sale,

negotiating prices and making payments. Dream Traders always take a percentage of the sale and the best command as much as 50% of the deal. Payment takes many forms: hard cash, gems, rare spices, silks or clothes from hard-to-reach planes. They know who wants a particular dream, who can get it, or who wants rid of one.

Once a deal is agreed the Dream Trader provides the details of the customer and arranges the time for the dream to be transferred. The Dreamthief travels to the agreed location and transfers the dream in the reverse of the process used to capture it. Once transfer has been made, the Dream Trader pays the Dreamthief, less his percentage.

All Dreamthieves and Dream Traders are members of the Guild of Dreamers which regulates and monitors all engaged in this enterprise. New Dreamthieves who have completed their apprenticeship, and Dream Traders, must swear an oath to the guild and agree to abide by its code. This requires no particular test although the guild elders, which consists of the best and most experienced Dreamthieves and Traders, can inherently sense if a potential applicant is unsuited to the business and deny membership. Likewise the network of thieves and traders is so extensive that the guild elders quickly become aware of any transgressions of the code and take action – including the breaking of a Dreamthief's staff and expelling them from the guild.

THE SEVENTH DARK

This chapter offers advice and some rules options for Games Masters running *Elric of Melniboné* campaigns. The Elric stories have a unique style and atmosphere, and whilst it is not essential to replicate the doom and torment of the albino, capturing the atmosphere of the saga definitely lends authenticity. It also contains a synopsis of the Elric saga, although this is no substitute for reading these fine stories and it is hoped that the synopsis will encourage new readers to seek out the tales, and old readers to revisit them.

Adventurer Improvement

An adventurer improves his skills, characteristics and learns new powers, through experience improvement and training. Improvement can be a slow and gradual process, or it can be attained through adventuring and all the risks accompanying it. There are two ways to improve a character – through *improvement rolls*, or through *training*.

In an average *Elric of Melniboné* game, each adventurer should receive three improvement rolls. This can be modified by the Games Master if the adventurer performed particularly poorly or heroically, giving a range of between one and five improvement rolls. Improvement rolls are always made at the end of an adventure, not during it.

Training, on the other hand, takes time, and is best suited for gaps between adventures, otherwise known as 'downtime'.

Improvement Rolls

A player can choose to spend one improvement roll to attempt to increase one known skill.

✳ Select the skill to be increased and roll 1D100.
✳ If this 1D100 result is *greater* than the skill's current score, the skill increases by 1D4+1 points.
✳ If this 1D100 result is *equal to or less* than the skill's current score, the skill only increases by one point.
✳ There is no limit to the score a skill can reach.

Resilience and *Persistence* work slightly differently – those skills only increase by one point if the 1D100 result is *greater* than the skill's current score, and do not increase at all if the roll is less than the skill's current score.

Training

Practising or researching a skill generally takes one day per 10% the character already possesses in the skill. Once this training period is complete, the character may attempt to improve that skill, using the same system as an improvement roll. Most cults offering training charge a fee for their services, reflecting the upkeep of equipment, retention of teachers, mentors, and so forth. See page 94 in the *Lords of Million Spheres* chapter for the general cult training costs.

Practice

All skills may be learnt through practice, except for Lore skills.

Research

The following skills can be increased through research: Craft, Engineering, Evaluate, First Aid, Healing, Language, Lore, Mechanisms and all Sorcery skills.

Characters may apply a +10 modifier to the skill test when attempting to learn the skill through research. This is an addition to the roll, not the skill.

Mentors

A mentor must have a score in the skill being taught that is at least double his student's score. The mentor must be present with the student for the entire practising or research period. Before the student makes their skill test to improve the skill, the mentor makes a skill test for the taught skill. If the mentor's skill test is a failure, then the student makes their test as normal. If the mentor's skill test is a success, then the student makes their skill test and applies a positive modifier to the roll equal to the mentor's *critical success range* with the skill. Note that this is an addition to the roll, not the skill. In addition, if the student's improvement roll results in a gain of 1D4+1 points, this gain is instead increased to 1D6+1 points.

Learning New Advanced Skills

In order to learn a new Advanced skill, the character must either be able to research it (in that it is both researchable and the relevant research material is to hand) or they must be taught it by a mentor.

It costs two improvement rolls to attempt to learn a new Advanced skill. The adventurer immediately gains the new Advanced skill at the base score determined by the appropriate Characteristics. The adventurer may now increase the skill normally through practice or research.

Improving Characteristics

A player can choose to spend *three* improvement rolls to attempt to increase one Characteristic by one point.

* Multiply the Characteristic to be increased by five. Then roll 1D100.
* If this 1D100 result is *greater* than the Characteristic x 5, the Characteristic increases by one point.
* If this 1D100 result is *equal to or less* than the Characteristic x 5, the Characteristic does not increase. However, one skill that the character already possesses is increased by one point. One of this skill's derived Characteristics must be the same as the Characteristic which was not improved.
* A roll of 96 to 00 on this roll always results in the Characteristic increasing.
* SIZ may never be increased using improvement rolls.
* If the adventurer has a Pact, any POW gained through a characteristic improvement is not dedicated to the patron deity – unless the adventurer wishes to dedicate, of course.

The maximum for a human characteristic to is 21, with the exception of POW, which has no upper limit. For non-humans, the maximum for a Characteristic is equal to the maximum possible starting score for the Characteristic plus three.

Hero Points

In an average story, each character should receive a Hero Point at its conclusion. Games Masters are encouraged to reward heroic acts or poignant role-playing with extra Hero Points.

Hero Points can be used in a variety of ways. One Hero Point is deducted form the character's total every time one of the following options is taken.

Second Chance: A character can re-roll any dice roll that affects his character. This can be a skill test, damage roll or anything else that has some effect on him. He can even force an opponent to re-roll an attack or damage roll made against him.

Glancing Blow: A character who suffers a Major Injury may spend a Hero Point and downgrade that injury to a Serious Injury. This simultaneously reduces the damage so that it is at a negative score equal to the location's starting hit points.

Luck of the Heroes: A Hero Point may be spent to alter the storyline of the current scenario in some minor way. This may only be done with the approval of the Games Master and allows a character to become truly lucky for a short period of time. For example, a character who surrenders and is then taken hostage may spend a Hero Point to be granted a chance of escape. The player may decide he is unlocked from his chains by a slave looking for revenge on his masters, that he finds a wire to pick locks with on the floor of his cell or the chains are corroded and may yield to his brute strength. The suggested course of action should always be plausible in the situation.

Legendary Abilities: The character may spend Hero Points to acquire a Legendary Ability he has qualified for.

Legendary Abilities

In order to gain a Legendary Ability, a character must meet the requirements listed for it and then spend the required number of Hero Points.

Armoured Titan

Requirements: STR 15 or higher, any close combat Weapon skill at 90% or higher.
Hero Points: 4

The adventurer is especially skilled at fighting in heavy armour. Reduce the penalty from armour by 20%, to a minimum of 20%.

Battle Fury

Requirements: CON 15 or higher, any close combat Weapon skill at 90% or higher.
Hero Points: 6

The adventurer can enter a Battle Fury as a Combat Action. While in a Battle Fury, the following effects take place:

* STR and CON are both considered to be 5 points higher, but only for the purposes of determining Damage Modifier.
* All close combat Weapon skill tests, including Unarmed and Martial Arts, receive a +50% bonus.
* All your Persistence and Resilience skill tests receive a +50% bonus.
* The adventurer may not parry, dodge or dive for cover.

The adventurer remains in Battle Fury for a number of rounds equal to his CON. Upon leaving Battle Fury, he automatically gains three levels of Fatigue.

Born to the Saddle

Requirements: POW 15 or higher, Riding 90% or higher.
Hero Points: 4

While riding, the following effects take place:

* Any penalty to the Riding skill is reduced by –20 %. For instance, if the driving rain and slippery ground would normally apply a –40% penalty to the Riding test, the penalty is reduced to –20%.

* The adventurer may use 2H Weapon skills, Polearms and Staffs.
* The adventurer may treat all animals he rides as trained for combat.
* The adventurer may use the Riding skill instead of the Dodge skill when dodging.

Dead Eye

Requirements: DEX 15 or higher, any ranged Weapon skill at 90% or higher.
Hero Points: 5

Pick any single ranged weapon (with at least 90% skill). While using this weapon, the following effects take place:

* Increase the weapon's Range by 50%.
* Increase the weapon's damage by +2 (only to targets within Range).
* Precise attacks with the weapon only suffer a –20% penalty.

Decapitating Swing

Requirements: STR 15 or higher, either 2H Sword or 2H Axe skill at 90% or higher.
Hero Points: 6

This ability can only be used with a 2H Axe or 2H Sword and only against an opponent whose SIZ is within ten of the adventurer's SIZ.

Decapitating Swing is declared before a precise attack, targeting the opponent's head, is started. Any attempt to dodge or parry this precise attack gains a +20% bonus. As long as the attack inflicts at least a Minor Wound, the attack is converted to a Major Injury that decapitates the target.

Devilish Charm

Requirements: CHA 15 or higher, Influence 70% or higher.
Hero Points: 4

The adventurer has a roguish charm and daring that is irresistible, and puts others off their guard. He may use the Influence skill even on his worst enemies – for example, trying to Influence someone just after trying to kill them, by spinning some specious and elaborate argument masking the true facts.

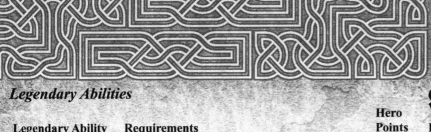

Legendary Abilities

Legendary Ability	Requirements	Hero Points
Armoured Titan	STR 15+, close combat Weapon skill 90%+	4
Battle Fury	CON 15+, close combat Weapon skill 90%+	6
Born to the Saddle	POW 15+, Riding skill 90%+	4
Dead Eye	DEX 15+, ranged Weapon skill 90%+	5
Decapitating Swing	STR 15+, 2H Sword or Axe skill 90%+	6
Devilish Charm	CHA 15+, Influence skill 90%+	4
Disease Immunity	CON 15+, Resilience skill 70%+	4
Duellist	DEX 15+, 1H Weapon or Rapier skill 90%+	5
Empathic Wound	POW 15+, Healing skill 90%+	5
Heroic Aura	CHA 15+, Influence skill 90%+	6
Jouster	STR 15+, Riding skill 90%+, Spear 90%	4
Linguist	INT 15+, two non-native Language skills 50%+	4
Loremaster	INT 15+, four Lore skills 50%+	5
Madness of Purpose	POW 15+, Insanely driven in pursuit of a goal	2
Poison Immunity	CON 15+, Resilience skill 70%+	4
Scientific Genius	INT 15 or higher, Mechanisms 50% or higher, Engineering 50% or higher	6
Skin of the Bear	CON 15+, Resilience skill 90%+	5
Slaying Touch	POW 15+, Martial Arts skill 90%+	6
Tireless	CON 15+, Athletics skill 90%+	4
Wall Leaping	DEX 15+, Acrobatics skill 90%+	5

Disease Immunity

Requirements: CON 15 or higher, Resilience 70% or higher.
Hero Points: 4

The adventurer is immune to all normal diseases. Magical diseases will still affect him although he gains a +20% bonus to tests to resist them.

Duellist

Requirements: DEX 15 or higher, 1H Weapon skill or Rapier skill at 90% or higher.
Hero Points: 5

While using a selected weapon the following effects take place:

✳ The adventurer may parry one additional attack per Combat Round (over and above the normal Reaction allowance).

✳ The adventurer gains a +10% bonus to the Weapon skill when parrying.

✳ Increase the weapon's damage by +1.

Empathic Wound

Requirements: POW 15 or higher, Healing skill at 90% or higher.
Hero Points: 10

Empathic Wound, allows the adventurer to offset the injuries a companion has sustained by transferring the hit point damage to himself. For instance, if a companion has been wounded in the Leg for four hit points of damage, the adventurer can take one, two, three or four of those hit points upon himself, instantly healing a like number of hit points in the companion's Leg. A wound appears on the adventurer's body at the same hit location as the companion's (in the case of different species with different hit locations, the Games Master should assign the damage to the most appropriate location). One hit point of damage may be transferred each Combat Round, during which neither patient nor healer may move or perform other Combat Actions.

Transferring damage with Empathic Wound is one of the most gruelling endeavours in the world. Each Combat Round, the adventurer must make a Resilience test with a −40% penalty or take one level of Fatigue (see page 79). Empathic Wound is incapable of restoring or reattaching severed limbs or resurrecting a character.

Heroic Aura

Requirements: CHA 15 or higher, Influence skill at 90% or higher.
Hero Points: 6

All allies within the adventurer's CHA in metres will be heartened by his presence, gaining his CHA as a bonus to any Persistence or Resilience tests they are called upon to make.

In addition, the adventurer may make take a Combat Action to encourage nearby allies, requiring an Influence test. If this is successful, they gain his CHA as a bonus

to all Weapon skills for the remainder of the Combat Round.

Jouster

Requirements: STR 15 or higher, Riding skill at 90% or higher, Spear skill 90% or higher.
Hero Points: 4

When using a lance from horseback, the adventurer may double the damage from his and the mount's Damage Modifier for the purposes of calculating Knockback. Furthermore, the adventurer may make an opposed Riding test with his foe if he tries using his Riding skill to add the SIZ of his mount for avoiding Knockback – if the adventurer wins this test, then the opponent cannot add his mount's SIZ to his own score.

Linguist

Requirements: INT 15 or higher, two Language skills (aside from your native tongue) at 50% or higher.
Hero Points: 4

In order to use this ability, the adventurer must either converse with a speaker of a strange language for one hour, or simply hear the language being spoken for two or more hours. He then automatically gains the Language skill in that language at its basic score.

A successful improvement roll when improving a Language skill doubles the skill points gained (roll 2D4+2 rather than 1D4+1).

Loremaster

Requirements: INT 15 or higher, four Lore skills at 50% or higher.
Hero Points: 5

Any time a Lore skill test is failed, the adventurer is entitled to make an immediate Persistence test (with the same modifiers as the original Lore test) to see if he can recall some shred of knowledge germane to the subject at hand.

Madness of Purpose

Requirements: POW 15 or higher. Pan Tangians get this ability for free, and waive the POW requirement.
Hero Points: 2

The adventurer's utter disregard for the worth of all things, including his life and the lives of others, allows

him to risk his life in an insane fashion if it furthers his goals. The adventurer may succeed automatically at one Resilience or Persistence test per day, with the exception of tests made to resist sorcery.

Poison Immunity

Requirements: CON 15 or higher, Resilience 70% or higher.
Hero Points: 4

The adventurer is immune to all normal poisons. Magical poisons will still affect him, though he gains a +20% bonus to tests to resist them.

Melnibonéans are naturally immune to all known poisons. All Melnibonéans gain this ability irrespective of the core requirements.

Scientific Genius

Requirements: INT 15 or higher, Mechanisms 50% or higher, Engineering 50% or higher.
Hero Points: 6

The adventurer's research into the arts of Arkyn has allowed him to understand the basic principles behind mechanical science. The adventurer can build automata in half the usual time, although the Magic Point cost to power it is still the same.

Skin of the Bear

Requirements: CON 15 or higher, Resilience 90% or higher.
Hero Points: 5

Skin of the Bear gives one Armour Point of natural armour on all hit locations. This stacks with equipped armour.

Slaying Touch

Requirements: POW 15 or higher, Martial Arts 90% or higher.
Hero Points: 6

Slaying Touch is declared before a precise attack is started (the type of precise attack is up to the adventurer, though if the target is wearing armour, it will have to be bypassed). As long as the attack inflicts at least a Minor Wound, the attack is considered a Slaying Touch. The target must immediately succeed at a Resilience test with a –40% penalty or die.

Tireless

Requirements: CON 15 or higher, Athletics 90% or higher.
Hero Points: 4

The adventurer may engage in medium activity for a number of minutes equal to his CON x 10 before risking Fatigue. The time between subsequent Fatigue tests for continuing to engage in medium activity is likewise his CON x 10 in minutes.

He may engage in heavy activity for a number of Combat Rounds equal to his CON score before risking Fatigue. The time between subsequent Fatigue tests for continuing to engage in heavy activity is likewise his CON score in Combat Rounds.

The adventurer also recovers from each level of Fatigue in half the normal time (one level for every two hours of light activity or one hour of complete rest).

Wall Leaping

Requirements: DEX 15 or higher, Acrobatics 90% or higher.
Hero Points: 5

The adventurer may only use Wall Leaping if not Overloaded, Exhausted or Debilitated. The entirety of his movement in a Combat Action may be made along a vertical surface, allowing you to bypass an obstruction that might otherwise block his path or even climb a wall at lightning speed. This can result in running up a wall with one Combat Action, attacking an enemy with a second Combat Action, and then returning to the floor with a third Combat Action.

However, the adventurer cannot continue moving along a vertical surface from Combat Round to Combat Round – he must reach level ground (or a suitable perch) by the end of the last Combat Action in a round or fall.

Crafting an Elric of Melniboné Campaign

There is no reason why a campaign should follow the Elric saga's events. Having the adventurers die along with the world does not have to be the ultimate fate of a campaign. Games Masters and players may not always enjoy such a conclusion.

Playing *Elric of Melniboné* allows the direction of the Elric saga to be reconfigured or even retold completely. For example, instead of Chaos destroying the world, the campaign might climax with Chaos defeated, but only at great cost. A campaign could be set years before Elric comes to the throne, giving the Games Master plenty of time to build the campaign up to a vivid climax. In such a campaign the adventurers may still die as the world does, but only after a long life, be it happy or ruined, bitter, tragic or sorrowful. Or you could allow the adventurers to flee to an alternate Young Kingdoms where Law or the Balance triumphs, for in the Multiverse there are endless worlds and endless possibilities. If the campaign is to end as the Young Kingdoms ends, with Chaos conquering and dissolving the world, it is going to be a long time coming, which means that the campaign might possibly last for years. Throughout that long story arc is the space for many long tales to be told, an individual but intertwined campaign for each of the adventurers.

Character-Driven Plots

In character-driven campaigns the Games Master develops plots out of adventurers' backgrounds and actions. Character-based background stories can be played out over many years. Try not to rush the story. Hints and revelations for the adventurer can be scattered out among a collection of adventures, and only slowly merge into the main story or sequence of stories. Frequent or constant revelations mean their impact will be lessened. Plot ideas for character-driven scenarios often come when the player first generates his adventurer, and players should try to generate backgrounds allowing the Games Master plenty of leeway where plot ideas are concerned. Games Masters should ideally always participate in an adventurer's creation in order to assist with, and take secret notes on, possible plot seeds.

An example of a character-driven plot is the lost or amnesiac adventurer whose only possession, when first starting out as an adventurer, is a ring bearing a strange heraldic device or insignia. After many adventures they come across an ornate key bearing that very same sign. The key brings sporadic dreams of a curious door in an unknown city. One day, years later, the adventurer sees that door. It is unlocked by the key. What lies behind it; another world where the adventurer is king? Stairs

Alternative Eras
Birth of Melniboné

Taking its cue from '*Elric: The Making of a Sorcerer*' comics, this campaign is based at the time of Melniboné's earliest presence in what will be the Young Kingdoms. The world is dominated by many barbarian tribes, such as the Grome-worshipping Pukwadji of the area later to be known as the Silent Lands, or the ambitious Falkryn barbarians from the western continent, sworn enemies of the emerging empire. At this time Melniboné's rule is benevolent and open; the Lords of Chaos are not yet worshipped and have almost no influence in the world. Imrryr and Myyrrhn are the elder civilizations and both have enjoyed an alliance in the past. The continents of these Old Kingdoms are unexplored territories where the Elemental Lords dominate. Imrryr is steadily becoming the most gleaming jewel at the heart of the world, inspiring others to greater civilisation.

Bright Empire's Height

Melniboné rules the world through her pacts with Chaos and the elementals. The continents have been carved into provinces ruled by Melnibonéan nobles who subjugate the human tribes and clans through a mixture of military might, magical terror and the threat of dragon venom. The tribes of the west – the Rijorian Confederacy, the Terkesians and the Shakurians – are either apologists for, or enemies of, the provincial lords depending on the degree of integrity or corruption of their rulers. The first great cities, inspired by Imrryr, are being raised through sorcery: Gromoorva; Lashmar; Dhakos; Bakshaan. In the north Quarzhasaat is beginning to form an empire of its own and the tradition of the sorcerer-adventurers is beginning. The Il'm barbarian tribe battles the Bilmirites whilst Melniboné watches with wry amusement, occasionally meddling with one side or the other simply to see what will happen. At this time humans are considered slaves to work for Melniboné's selfish gain and little else. Life is at its hardest and has little value. Battlebarges, not merchant ships, patrol the seas. And, on a blasted, semi-vitrified island known as Barbarian Island, a swarthy race of humans called, in their guttural tongue, Mabden, arrives from another plane, sullen unloved, and savage. They take a look around them, see that this place has opportunities and rename the island Pan Tang.

The Dharzi Wars

A thousand years before Elric the Dharzi swept in from the east, scouring the Il'm and Bilmirites, crossing the Pale Sea in their sea-monster-drawn galleys, and carving deep into the heart of the Bright Empire with their beast-drawn chariots. These 'beast-men' commanded pacts with certain Beast Lords that challenged even the Bright Empire's relationships, and against their armies of mutated creatures – hybrids of natural creatures, bred to slaughter – the Bright Empire is forced to defend her territories. Some humans welcome the Dharzi onslaught, hoping they will be freed from oppression. But the Dharzi are every bit as ruthless as Melniboné and humans are forced to fight with Melnibonéans against the monstrous invader. The Dharzi wars last decades and are fought on many fronts. New kingdoms form as each front yields a victory: Lormyr in the south, followed by Filkhar. In the west the Dharzi are pushed deep into the Silent Lands where the Chaos Engines of Cran Liret are turned upon them, unleashing hellish magics and living spells that consume the souls of those they control. Every resource of Melniboné is poured into making the Dharzi pay, and the Dharzi lords are hunted by their own hunting hounds while hordes of baying Melnibonéan nobles gallop behind, thrilling to the chase. By the time the war with the Dharzi has ended, the world is different. Humans have achieved a measure of independence they will not readily concede. Lormyr and Filkhar are granted limited self-rule for their efforts against the Dharzi. Exhausted Imrryrian nobles return to their dream couches, leaving the Il'm to occupy their gleaming cities of Karlaak and Bakshaan. And on Pan Tang, which harboured several Dharzi sorcerers whilst it marvelled at the forces of Chaos being unleashed around it, the Mabden create a theocracy and start to plot their future.

leading to a crypt and forgotten treasures? What are its implications? Plots within the alien court and invasion by another nation? a dread curse that slays all those dear to him? Theft or loss of either key or ring could form additional adventures. Such side-plots can often be used to tie in with another adventurer's background scenarios.

Epic Elric Sagas

Adventurers' stories should be epic in scope, just as the Elric saga itself. Epic stories are ones in which:

✱ The adventurers battle armies and win (or overturn) kingdoms.

✱ Overthrows tyranny, be it Law or Chaos; rules wisely and well, until their beloved consort, (who has been built up from the start of the campaign and is a trusted, and much-loved Non-Player Character) takes a secret lover, (perhaps with good reason, if the adventurer were forever disappearing for months on end) plots to kill the adventurer, and he is forced to execute or exile her.

✱ The adventurer comes from a humble background, travelling the world in his youth with a pack of rough and ready adventurers; gradually develops an allegiance to one power or another; eventually rising to rule whatever church they are faithful to, only to discover, with the help of his old friends, that the church he so loved is riddled with corruption and treachery. Does he destroy the institution he once revered? Set up a rival church? Turn his back upon the church to live as a hermit?

✱ The adventurer becomes a great and famous foe of Pan Tang. As a youth he defends his village from a pirate attack; goes on to take a Pan Tangian galley while fishing at sea; defeats a minor Demon Isle fleet and is immortalised in a popular ballad, only to face eventual capture and slavery upon Pan Tang; there discovering the only true love of the adventurer's life, and tragically loosing her to sharks or Pan Tangians in the final, dramatic escape from Hwamgaarl.

✱ The adventurer gains love at bitter cost, perhaps the death of a close friend or family member (the king's soldiers discover the adventurer's old father sheltered the outlaw-princess he loved, and kill her; a favourite brother is slain helping the adventurer rescue a farming community plagued by raids from a

gang of murderous bullies through some clumsiness of the adventurer) or even the death of a whole tribe, village, city or nation.

Moorcock's works tend towards grand scenes and the cataclysmic. *Elric of Melniboné* campaigns should follow in this tradition.

From Plot Threads to Tapestries

Interweaving the separate stories with the deeds of the Elric saga itself, can be a challenge. Character-driven plots can be easily linked: the killer of one adventurer's parents plays some despicable role in the betrayal of another to enemy forces; one adventurer's sorcerous foe turns out to possess a grimoire giving clues to another adventurer's amnesiac past. Take care to think such links through before introducing them. Often it can be wise to create a plot lynchpin even before the adventurers are created. Telling the players that they will all be family members, or from the same nation or city, can all be the point on which the plots hang. It is better to have only a few strong and believable plot links rather than too many that are too trite.

Events from the saga can be added to campaigns with little difficulty. This book notes pertinent historical details as they unfold through the campaign years. They are written in such a way that Games Masters can base scenarios and campaigns incorporating the Elric saga into play.

Alternatively, you may find brief references in the books inspiring whole campaigns. A Games Master could use the Sack of Imrryr, in which almost everybody dies save Elric and his adopted crew, as the devastating finale to a long chronicle involving pirates, Straasha and the sea as its theme. Another Games Master might want to set an entire campaign in the Weeping Waste, with the adventurers superstitious, spiritually aware tribesmen. Virtually anything is possible in the Young Kingdoms.

What About Elric?

Elric's doom should cast its shadow across the adventurers' lives from time to time, but it is wise not to allow the characters to become too close to the crimson-eyed albino, nor to allow Elric, as a character, to dominate the game. Remember that the adventurers are the heroes, not Elric himself. Adventurers should be given plenty of opportunity to learn about Elric, and develop their own opinions of him as a character in a game, as opposed to a character in a book which has entertained the player, before they meet him. Gossip concerning Elric of Melniboné constantly circulates through the Young Kingdoms, and has since his coronation. The adventurers will have heard ballads, rumours and outrageous lies long before they finally encounter the proud Prince of Ruins himself.

Sooner or later however, the Games Master is sure to want to introduce Elric directly to the campaign. When Elric finally appears make sure not to cheapen the air of menace and mystery that surrounds the tragic hero. A meeting with Elric will have more impact if it occurs as part of a pivotal or climactic moment in the campaign, rather than as a random encounter. No matter when an encounter with Elric occurs, the event should always be dramatic and memorable. Passing through a city such as Bakshaan in Elric's wake is a good way of illustrating his effect upon the Young Kingdoms. It also allows the adventurers to encounter Elric's destiny without the risk of having to meet him personally. Stormbringer, after all, is notoriously hungry for souls; even brief acquaintances of Elric tend to have regrettably short lives.

From Plane to Shining Plane

For heroes, travel between the planes of existence is common place and in countless ways. The devices used to move between planes need not – indeed should not – be explained: planar gates, mysterious rings, shared dreams, the Black Ship, or even simply turning a corner and finding oneself in a completely different realm. The adventurers are heroes and the higher powers, be it Law, Chaos or the Cosmic Balance, always finds a use for them elsewhere in the Multiverse. Some suggestions for plane-shifting mechanisms are offered below.

However, if adventurers are to travel the Multiverse, the conceit should be controlled and used sparingly. Moving from plane to plane is usually only possible when the Cosmic Balance decrees it, and frequent shifts to parallel realms will quickly pale. The Young Kingdoms have plenty of opportunities for adventure and has imminent perils of its own. Moving from one plane to another should be an occasional diversion and a treat; not a regular commute.

Dreams. The adventurers share a common dream in which they undertake a form of dreamquest. This may be at the behest of a Dreamthief or directed by the higher

powers. Or perhaps, after the sacking of Imrryr, a dream couch comes onto the market. Dream couches seem to possess similar abilities to those of Dreamthieves, allowing the sleeper to project into a dream realm. Users of a dream couch should find themselves participating in the mythical and semi-mythical events of the world's past, such as assisting Earl Aubec to carve new worlds from Chaos or to assist the ancient heroes Bisrana, queen of the Shazaar, Thokor of the Jharks and Ralyn of the Dhars in their struggles against the emergent Bright Empire.

The Black Ship sails the Multiverse, piloted by its blind captain and mute helmsman, but is this the only form the ship takes? On some occasions it might be a wagon or carriage controlled by female versions of the captain and steersman. On others the same people might be posing as beggars of Nadsokor who, for a fee, claim to be able to guide adventurers to a particular treasure or locale (once they have completed the otherworld task, of course).

Innate Ability. Many individuals demonstrate the ability to move through the planes at will. Dreamthieves are one example, but there are others, and certain adventurers might demonstrate this ability either as a gift/compulsion as part of a Pact, or as something they are simply born with. The ability might only allow the adventurer to shift to one particular plane, or it might be involuntary. Quite often certain conditions within the Multiverse have to be right for plane shifts to occur, but as the Multiverse is infinite, the configuration of various spheres and realms happens continually, so the right conditions need never be far away. How this innate ability manifests needs to be carefully considered by the Games Master; even Melnibonéans do not regularly display such talents. Furthermore, the ability to shift to another plane should never be demanded by a player. It is not a right, and the Games Master is always the final arbiter on such matters.

The Will of the Gods. The gods have many agendas and quite often they are concerned with events beyond the Young Kingdoms. The Sword Rulers, for instance, occupy a very different hierarchy of power in the Fifteen Planes of Corum's world than they do in that of the Young Kingdoms. Faithful servants and cult members may be called upon – or even compelled – to act on the god's behalf in some other realm. This is a keen opportunity to reveal something of the true nature of the Cosmic Struggle that may lead to the adventurers questioning their faith. Even the Lords of Law, who portray themselves in the

Young Kingdoms as the White Lords, may prove to be clothed in shades of grey in other realms, where Chaos is actually the tempering and moderate force. Acting on the fiat of a god should be reserved for those who have attained at least initiate status within the cult; gods seek faithful and capable people, and lay worshippers are likely to be ignored completely.

Synopsis of the Elric Saga

The Elric saga spans short stories, novels and comics. Michael Moorcock wrote the stories out of chronological sequence, filling-in more details on the albino's adventures on and off over the course of 40 years. Space simply does not permit an absolute bibliography of every Elric reference and appearance, but the core elements of the saga, presented in a roughly chronological order, are given below.

Elric: The Making of a Sorcerer (Graphic Novel)

This series of four graphic novels tells the story of the earliest days of the Bright Empire, before its fateful pacts with Chaos were established. Elric, in preparation for his role as Emperor, undergoes four separate dreamquests using the dream couches of Melniboné, re-enacting the events that lead to the pacts formed with the four Elemental Lords, in the guise of 'White Crow'. In the process of these quests he encounters both Arioch and the Black Blade for the first time, and inadvertently permits Chaos to enter the world. Throughout the dreamquests he is opposed by his jealous cousin, Yyrkoon, who covets the Ruby Throne himself. Elric prevails, and is named by his father, Sadric, as the true successor to the Bright Empire.

Elric of Melniboné (Novel)

This novel describes how Elric is betrayed by Yyrkoon and must go in search of Stormbringer to defeat him. In the process of his adventures he is cast into the sea and left to drown following a battle with Young Kingdoms pirates; gains the use of the Ship Which Sails on Sea and Land from Lord Grome; summons Arioch for the first time, and eventually locates Stormbringer on the plane of Ameeron. At the story's conclusion Elric decides to spend a year exploring the Young Kingdoms so he might expand his knowledge of the outside world and become a more effective emperor.

The Sailor on the Seas of Fate (Short Story Collection)

Set during Elric's wanderings, this short story collection tells of the albino's adventures with three other versions of the Eternal Champion – Corum, Erekosë and Hawkmoon – in their bid to defeat the sentient city-entities Agak and Gagak. Later he confronts a Melnibonéan lord from his past, Earl Saxif D'aan, who mistakes a simple girl as his long-lost love. In the course of these adventures he meets Count Smiorgan Baldhead of the Purple Towns, and journeys with Duke Avan Astran to R'lin K'ren A'a, where he discovers Stormbringer's preference for the souls of his friends above all others.

The Fortress of the Pearl (Novel)

Again set during his year of wandering, Elric is sick and close to death in Quarzhasaat. He is engaged by Lord Gho Faazi, and a rival, Manag Iss, to retrieve the Pearl in exchange for his life, which has been threatened by Lord Gho. In the course of his quest he ventures to the Kasbeh Moulor Ka Riiz meeting Alnac Kreb, a Dreamthief, who dies trying to save Varadia, the daughter of Raik Na Seem, who holds the key to the Pearl's location. Shortly after he is joined by Oone, the Dreamthief, who teaches Elric some of her skill, and guides him through the dream realms in search of the eponymous castle.

Elric at the End of Time (Short Story Collection)

This short story collection concerns Elric in only one story. Having defeated the krettii of Sorcerers' Isle, Elric is 'kidnapped', for want of a better word, by the Dancers at the End of time; Mistress Christia, Una Persson and Lord Jagged. This pastiche reflects on the thesis that any sufficiently advanced technology is indistinguishable from magic, and Elric at first believes that the Dancers – who are possessed of such technologies – are the Lords of Chaos themselves.

The Weird of the White Wolf (Short Story Collection)

This short story collection recounts the fateful sacking of Imrryr, where Elric returns from his wanderings to find Yyrkoon has usurped the Ruby Throne and placed Cymoril in a sorcerous sleep. Elric leads the Sea Lords

of the Young Kingdoms against Imrryr, and battles Yyrkoon who possesses Mournblade, Stormbringer's brother runesword. In the battle Cymoril awakens and is accidentally slain by Elric. The Sea Lords are purged by dragon fire as they flee Melniboné and Elric, wracked with guilt for the death of his cousin and the destruction of his homeland, attempts to rid himself of Stormbringer – only to find himself more reliant upon it than ever. Later stories in the collection detail Elric's search for the Dead God's Book where he meets Moonglum for the first time, and their long friendship is established. Elric learns more about the battle between Law and Chaos and his melancholy deepens. His first encounter with Theleb K'aarna occurs when he aids Queen Yishana of Jharkor against Balo's incursion into the world. Jealous that Yishana finds Elric preferable to himself, the sorcerer sends the chaotic butterfly to attack them, becoming Elric's sworn enemy thereafter.

The Vanishing Tower (Short Story Collection)

Elric encounters Myshella, Empress of the Dawn, whilst hunting for Theleb K'aarna in Lormyr. Having roused Myshella from one of K'aarna's spells, Elric faces the Kelmain Host and witnesses some of the dreadful power of Law when the hideous 'noose of flesh' is deployed against the Kelmain. Rejecting Myshella's entreaties, Elric and Moonglum head to the northern continent where he travels to Nadsokor, manipulated by Theleb K'aarna's wiles, and assists in the defeat of King Urish. From there he seeks refuge in Tanelorn, which he finds, but cannot gain, contentment. Whilst there he finds himself whisked to another plane where he joins with two further incarnations of the Champion, returning in time to save Tanelorn from an attack led by Theleb K'aarna. But, despite his best efforts, the Pan Tangian escapes once more and this time slays Myshella. With the last bastion of Law gone, Chaos increases its grip on the world.

The Revenge of the Rose (Novel)

Elric is entreated by the ghost of his father, Sadric, to find the rosewood box that contains his soul. Elric embarks on an adventure, accompanied by the poet Wheldrake, that takes him into other planes where he encounters the Gipsy Nation, a vast caravan of wheeled cities. He also meets Prince Gaynor the Damned for the first time, and is forced to fight this new nemesis in spite of Arioch's inability to assist. In the course of this adventure Elric manages to save his own soul to some extent from his Melnibonéan heritage and learns more from a reluctant Arioch about the nature of the Cosmic Struggle.

The Bane of the Black Sword (Short Story Collection)

A collection of short stories in which Elric is engaged to assassinate Nikorn of Ilmar, a prosperous Bakshaani merchant, by jealous rivals. Elric learns that Nikorn's bodyguard is none other than Theleb K'aarna, his old enemy, and in the course of the ensuing battle to take Nikorn's palace – aided by the

mercenaries of Melniboné – Dyvim Tvar, Elric's cousin, is killed through K'aarna's sorcery. But the Pan Tangian's magic saps his mind and Elric's revenge is found in the gibbering, semi-human madman that was once a powerful magician. The collection also details Elric's saving of Zarozinia Voashoon of Karlaak, whilst travelling through Org, and she becomes the second love of his life. Elric returns with her to Karlaak and there finds peace for the final time.

Stormbringer (Novel)

Stormbringer chronicles the last of Elric's adventures and tells how Jagreen Lern brings Chaos to the world in the final battle between Law and Chaos. Kidnapping Zarozinia from Karlaak, Elric is forced to wield Stormbringer once more and venture across the Young Kingdoms, Moonglum at his side, combating Chaos at every turn. In the course of this last, tragic adventure, Elric meets again with Queen Yishana of Jharkor, aiding her in the battle for the western continent. He is captured by Jagreen Lern and Lord Pyaray as he attempts the rescue of Zarozinia, and discovers his beloved wife has been mutated into a dreadful form by the power of Chaos. Directed by the Lords of Law for the first time, he ventures into Mordaga, the Sad Giant's castle, in search of the Chaos Shield, one of the weapons designed to defeat Chaos, and thence to a plane where he confronts Roland, who protects the Horn of Fate, which, when blown, heralds the start of our own cycle of time. One by one Elric's enemies and loved ones fall, including Rackhir and Dyvim Slorm, Elric's kinsman who helps awake the dragons of Melniboné for their last flight. Finally Elric kills Jagreen Lern, denying Stormbringer the theocrat's soul, but finds that Moonglum must sacrifice his own to the Black Blade if Elric is to have the strength to blow the Horn of Fate. Stormbringer's final treachery is revealed as a new cycle of time is ushered in and the Cosmic Balance attains equilibrium; its final worlds, *'Farewell, friend. I was a thousand times more evil than thou!'* are some of the most famous and chilling in fantasy literature.

The Dreamthief's Daughter (Novel)

Von Bek and Elric intertwine in this story that sees Von Bek betrayed by his cousin, Prince Gaynor von Minct, who desires the family sword, Ravenbrand, to aid the schemes of the Nazis. Whilst tortured, Von Bek starts to gain some sense of his kinship with Elric, and the latter's personality comes to the fore. Escaping captivity Von Bek/Elric travels into the mythical realm of Off-Moo, and then back to the Young Kingdoms to act against the schemes of Miggea of Law and Prince Gaynor the damned as they prepare to assault Tanelorn.

The Skrayling Tree (Novel)

Further chronicles of the Von Bek family, Ulrik von Bek, now living in Canada with Oona, is plagued by mysterious and disconcerting events: he is visited by a strange albino version of himself and, when Oona is abducted by a group of Native Americans, Ulrik trails them using The Skrayling Oak. His adventures take him across mythical landscapes, which include incarnations of White Crow and Hiawatha. The dual existence of Von Bek/Elric re-emerges, with a section of the story concerning Elric's dream questing whilst held captive by Jagreen Lern during the events described in *Stormbringer*. Finally the hero discovers that Gaynor the Damned, now ruling over a mob of outcasts, is behind Oona's abduction.

The White Wolf's Son (Novel)

Told chiefly through the eyes of Oonagh von Bek, Elric's great-granddaughter, Prince Gaynor once again threatens the Multiverse through trying to capture the Runestaff, the symbol of the Cosmic Balance. Elric, Oona and other versions of the Eternal Champion, travel the Multiverse to save Oonagh and the Runestaff, eventually reaching a resolution in the Granbretan of Hawkmoon's Tragic Millennium.

The Seventh Dark

CREATURES

These creatures are all drawn from the Elric saga, as well as a series of more mundane animals that *Elric of Melniboné* adventurers might be expected to encounter on their travels. Creatures found in *RuneQuest Monsters* may be used in Elric games, or substituted for those here (or vice-versa). The Elric saga draws on many familiar beasts from myth and legend, and the key is imagination. Monsters figure heavily in the saga, so the more the better!

Creatures & Intelligence

Some of the creatures listed in this book have randomly determined INT, whilst others have only a single number listed as their INT, or *fixed INT*. A creature with a randomly determined INT is considered sapient – it is a rational creation capable of logical thought and self-determination. A creature with a fixed INT is sentient but not sapient. Fixed INT creatures operate solely on instinct rather than logic or intuition. Creatures with a very large fixed INT have rudimentary reasoning abilities, as well as a set of complex and finely-honed instincts.

Creatures of Chaos

These are monsters, demons and the products of chaotic experiments. Thankfully they are rare, and most Young Kingdoms people will never encounter them. But *Elric of Melniboné* adventurers are not most people. Like other Chaos creatures, these beasts determine characteristics using an 8, rather than a 6, sided dice.

Clakars

Silently descending were three massive ape-like creatures, borne on great leathery wings. Shaarilla recognised them and gasped. 'Clakars!' Moonglum shrugged as he hurriedly drew his sword –

'A name only – what are they?' But he received no answer for the leading winged ape descended with a rush, mouthing and gibbering, showing long fangs in a slavering snout.

– The Bane of the Black Sword

Thought to be the primeval ancestors of the Myyrrhn (who, themselves are considered the oldest race in the world), clakars are winged primates, akin to gorillas, and aggressive, attacking anyone straying into their territory. They are rarely found singly, being most commonly encountered in groups of up to 15.

Characteristics

STR	3D8	(14)
CON	3D8	(14)
DEX	4D8	(18)
SIZ	3D8	(14)
INT	2D8	(9)
POW	3D8	(14)

Clakar Hit Locations

D20	Hit Location	AP/HP
1-2	Right Leg	3/6
3-4	Left Leg	3/6
5-6	Abdomen	3/7
7-8	Chest	3/8
9-11	Right Wing	3/6
12-14	Left Wing	3/6
15-17	Right Arm	3/5
18-19	Left Arm	3/5
20	Head	3/6

Weapons

Type	Weapon skill	Damage
Bite	40%	1D8+1D2
Claw	60%	1D10+1D2

Special Rules

Combat Actions:	3
Strike Rank:	+14
Movement:	4m on the ground, 6m in the air
Skills:	Dodge 65%, Perception 45%, Persistence 40%, Resilience 60%
Typical Armour:	Thick hide (3 AP, no Skill Penalty)

Creatures of Matik

Created by Matik of Melniboné, these 5 metre tall hybrids of vulture and lion stalk the borders of the Earth and Chaos. They are immense predators that can be commanded by their summoner. They seem to especially hate the Hunting Dogs of the Dharzi and may have been a chief weapon against them during Melniboné's war with the Beast Folk a millennia ago.

Characteristics

STR	5D8+16	(39)
CON	5D8+8	(32)
DEX	2D8+8	(17)
SIZ	5D8+24	(47)
INT	1D8	(5)
POW	3D8	(14)

Creature of Matik

D20	Hit Location	AP/HP
1-2	Tail	4/16
3-4	Right Hind Leg	4/16
5-6	Left Hind Leg	4/16
7-10	Hindquarters	4/17
11-14	Forequarters	4/18
15-16	Right Front Leg	4/16
17-18	Left Front Leg	4/16
19-20	Head/Neck	4/16

Like demons, the creatures of Matik take only half damage from normal weapons.

Weapons

Type	Weapon skill	Damage
Bite	55%	1D8+2D10
Claw	45%	1D6+2D10

Special Rules

Combat Actions:	3
Strike Rank:	+11
Movement:	12m
Skills:	Dodge 35%, Perception 30%, Resilience 50%, Tracking 35%

Dragons

Melnibonéans claimed direct kinship with the Phoorn dragons. In another age they had shared the same names, the same quarters, the same power. In ancient history, it was said dragons had ruled Melniboné as kings. Whatever the truth, Elric and his kind could drink dragon venom, which killed most other creatures. The venom was so powerful that it ignited in the air as soon as it spewed from the dragons' mouths.

Their names were simple, like most names given to them by men –Blacksnout and Whitesnout. Their names for themselves were long, complicated and utterly unpronounceable, detailing ancestry and where they had journeyed.
– The Dreamthief's Daughter

Nothing – simply *nothing* – conveys the majesty of Melniboné than the dragons, and Melniboné's ability

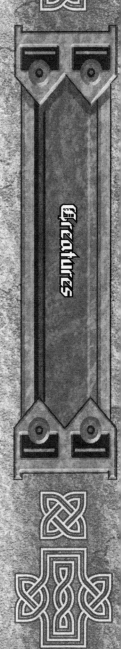

to command them. Immense, serpentine, intelligent and utterly awe-inspiring, the dragons *are* Melniboné.

There are many breeds; two are mentioned in the Elric saga. The *Phoorn* are long-snouted and graceful, with black and white rings around the snout and tail that fade with maturity. The *Erkanian* are stockier and snub-snouted. Regardless of species, all dragons share similar characteristics.

* Dragons enjoy indefinite life spans. Dragons were already present on Melniboné when it was first colonised, and were ancient even then.
* Dragons do not breathe fire. Rather their venom is combustible when mixed with air. It has reserves to make up to three attacks when awake.
* Dragons need sleep to recharge both their energy and venom reserves. A mature dragon typically sleeps for 10 years for each full day of activity. Younger dragons and dragons of different species may require less sleep, but sleep is essential to them and they cannot be roused unless they are ready.
* Dragons are highly intelligent and form a psychic and empathic bond with their riders. Flamefang and Elric, for example, share a deep and loving trust.
* Using the shoulder-located membrane known as the *skeffla'a*, dragons can travel between planes of existence, although this seems to be an infrequent occurrence. Perhaps travel of this kind requires far greater periods of regenerative sleep.
* Dragons are found only on Melniboné where they sleep in the vast dragon caves beneath the island's surface.

The body of a dragon is serpent-like with a graceful, slender, whip-like tail. The scales are iridescent, and patterned with subtle and rich purples, scarlets, golds and dark greens.. Their limbs are also graceful but still exceedingly powerful; there is nothing fragile about a dragon. The wing span of a Phoorn is at least 10 metres, and the natural indentations along the creature's spine allow up to three riders, although only one is common – and even then, an empathic bond is essential.

The characteristics below are for a Phoorn dragon of reasonable maturity. Older dragons will be bigger, stronger and faster.

Characteristics

STR	6D8+40	(67)
CON	12D8+16	(70)
DEX	2D8+8	(17)
SIZ	10D8+24	(69)
INT	3D8+8	(22)
POW	3D8+8	(22)
CHA	3D8	(14)

Dragon Hit Locations

D20	Hit Location	AP/HP
1-2	Tail	12/28
3-4	Right Hind Leg	12/28
5-6	Left Hind Leg	12/28
7-8	Hindquarters	12/29
9-10	Forequarters	12/30
11-12	Right Wing	12/27
13-14	Left Wing	12/27
15-16	Right Front Leg	12/28
17-18	Left Front Leg	12/28
19-20	Head	12/28

RIDING A DRAGON

Only Melnibonéans can ride a dragon. It requires an opposed Persistence roll to gain the dragon's trust first, and then a number of months of patient training, meditation, and interaction with the dragon's dreams (using a dream couch) equal to the dragon's POW. Once this has been accomplished a Pact is formed between rider and dragon; treat this as a Pact skill equal to POW+CHA at its starting value. Attempting to awaken a dragon from sleep requires an opposed roll between the Pact and the dragon's Persistence.

Riding a dragon is treated using the Pact skill. No test is needed for routine tasks, but ordering a dragon to perform complex aerial manoeuvres always requires a Pact test.

Dragon riders who achieve a Pact skill of 70% or higher are allowed to bear the title 'Dyvim', meaning 'Dragon Lord' in Low Speech.

Weapons

Type	Weapon skill	Damage / AP
Bite	65%	1D10+3D12 / 4
Claw	70%	1D8+3D12 / 6
Tail	30%	1D10+3D12 / 8
Venom	80%	1D6+4*

*Dragon venom combusts with air creating a stream of flame that causes 1D6+4 points of damage each round to every hit location of anything caught in the blast radius, equal to the dragon's CON in metres. A single burst of venom lasts for 10% of the dragon's CON in Combat Rounds. Fires caused by dragon venom cannot be extinguished with water.

Special Rules

Combat Actions:	3
Strike Rank:	+19
Movement:	6m, 10m when flying
Skills:	Athletics 120%, Evaluate +100%, Influence 150%, Lore (Million Spheres) 80%, Persistence 100%, Resilience 120%, Tracking 110%,
Typical Armour:	Dragon Scales (AP 12, no Skill Penalty)

Elenoin

These flame-haired, female-bodied warriors are beast-like in their ferocity and appetite for slaughter. Hailing from the 8th Plane they are cannibalistic and are known to pause in the intensity of battle to eat their slain enemies. Elenoin adopt a particular combat style: first a high-pitched keening song accompanied by a wild, dervish dance, followed by a rapid charge against their foe, greatswords whirling above their heads. Their hair falls to their knees and writhes with a life of its own, reaching out to snare opponents. There is a POW x3% chance for an elenoin to pause over a fallen opponent and start to eat, offering a potential opening for the quick-witted.

Characteristics

STR	4D8+8	(26)
CON	4D8+8	(26)
DEX	2D8+8	(17)
SIZ	2D8+8	(17)
INT	1D8	(5)
POW	3D8+8	(22)

Elenoin Hit Locations

D20	Hit Location	AP/HP
1-3	Right Leg	–/9
4-6	Left Leg	–/9
7-9	Abdomen	1/10
10-12	Chest	1/11
13-15	Right Arm	1/8
16-18	Left Arm	1/8
19-20	Head	1/9

The hair of the elenoin acts as 1 point of armour across the upper body. Like demons, they take only half damage from normal weapons.

Weapons

Type	Weapon skill	Damage / AP
Keening Song	90%	Paralysis, see below
Greatsword	60%	2D8+1D8 / 4
Fanged Bite	40%	1D6+1+1D8
Hair	30%	Entangle

The keening scream-song requires all who hear it to make a Persistence test versus its potency of 60% to avoid being paralysed for 1D8 Combat Actions. Once they start combat, elenoin cease using their scream-song ability. The elenoins' hair moves with a life of its own. For every Combat Action spent attacking, the hair gains an additional, simultaneous attack. If it strikes, it wraps around the opponent reducing all combat and manoeuvre skills by –40%.

Special Rules

Combat Actions:	3
Strike Rank:	+11
Movement:	4m
Skills:	Athletics 60%, Dodge 60%, Persistence 60%, Resilience 60%

Firebeetles

Immense beetles, their backs spouting flame, burrow deep beneath the Sighing Desert appearing only occasionally when compelled to do so in pursuit of food. The beetle's carapace is armoured so heavily that even Stormbringer cannot do very much damage, although Elric finds that the beetles are vulnerable on the underside of the body.

Characteristics

STR	6D6+20	(41)
CON	4D6	(14)
DEX	3D6+4	(15)
SIZ	6D6+20	(41)
INT	4	(4)
POW	3D6	(11)

Weapons

Type	Weapon skill	Damage / AP
Mandibles	50%	1D8+2D10 / 15
Fire Spill*	25%	1D6+2

*The beetles can spill pools of blazing oil onto opponents beneath. The sticky oil clings to any hit location it splashes inflicting damage each round until extinguished. Armour Points are effective against fire spill damage.

Firebeetle Hit Locations

D20	Hit Location	AP/HP
1	Right Leg 1	8/11
2	Right Leg 2	8/11
3	Right Leg 3	8/11
4	Right Leg 4	8/11
5	Right Leg 5	8/11
6	Right Leg 6	8/11
7	Left Leg 1	8/11
8	Left Leg 2	8/11
9	Left Leg 3	8/11
10	Left Leg 4	8/11
11	Left Leg 5	8/11
12	Left Leg 6	8/11
13-14	Forequarters Carapace	15/13
15-16	Hindquarters Carapace	15/12
17	Forequarters Underside	4/13
18	Hindquarters Underside	4/12
19-20	Head	15/13

Special Rules

Combat Actions:	3
Strike Rank:	+9
Movement:	6m
Skills:	Athletics 75%, Dodge 40%, Perception 50%, Resilience 75%, Tracking 40%
Typical Armour:	Carapace (AP 15 on top, AP 8 on legs, no Skill Penalty)

Ghouls of Org (and elsewhere)

'All about the foot of the monstrous barrow swarmed the leprous-white ghouls who sensed the presence of Elric, the folk of Org's sacrifice to them. Now Elric understood. These were the things that Org feared more than the Gods. These were the living-dead ancestors of those who now revelled in the Great Hall. Perhaps these were actually the Doomed Folk. Was that their doom? Never to rest? Never to die? Just to degenerate into mindless ghouls?'
– The Bane of the Black Sword

The ghouls of Org are cannibalistic and vampiric, draining the life-force of a victim and helping to subdue it. These were clearly once human, or human-like, and there is no explanation for how they degenerated to this state. A spell perhaps? A curse?

The characteristics below represent the ghouls of Org, but larger, meaner types doubtless exist.

Characteristics

STR	3D8+4	(18)
CON	2D8+8	(17)
DEX	1D8+2	(7)
SIZ	2D8+4	(13)
INT	1D8	(5)
POW	1D8	(5)

Ghoul Hit Locations

D20	Hit Location	AP/HP
1-3	Right Leg	–/6
4-6	Left Leg	–/6
7-9	Abdomen	–/7
10-12	Chest	–/8
13-15	Right Arm	–/5
16-18	Left Arm	–/5
19-20	Head	–/6

Weapons

Type	Weapon skill	Damage
Bite	35%	1D8+1D4
Grasp	25%	Vampiric Touch, drains 1D3 CON per round

Special Rules

Combat Actions:	2
Strike Rank:	+6
Movement:	3m
Skills:	Athletics 15%, Dodge 20%, Perception 20%, Resilience 25%

Grahluk

Supposedly the kin of the elenoin and thus hailing from the 8th Plane also, the bestial, ape-like grahluk exist only to slaughter elenoin and can only be summoned to counter an elenoin attack. When that task is complete, they have no further reason for living and fall upon the discarded greatswords of their ancient foes.

The summoning spell for the grahluk is rare, even by Melnibonéan standards and is contained in only one grimoire belonging to Emperor Sadric 86th, Elric's father.

Characteristics

STR	4D8+16	(34)
CON	4D8+16	(34)
DEX	4D8	(18)
SIZ	3D8+8	(22)
INT	1D8	(5)
POW	3D8+8	(22)

Hit Locations

D20	Hit Location	AP/HP
1-3	Right Leg	–/12
4-6	Left Leg	–/12
7-9	Abdomen	–/13
10-12	Chest	–/14
13-15	Right Arm	–/11
16-18	Left Arm	–/11
19-20	Head	–/12

Like demons, grahluk take only half damage from normal weapons.

Weapons

Type	Weapon skill	Damage	AP/HP
Fanged Bite	60%	1D6+1D12	
Net*	60%	Entangle	2/10
Round Shield	65%	1D6	8/12

*If the net strikes, it wraps around the location struck, immobilising it if a limb, or forcing the opponent to fall over if it is the head, chest or abdomen. Parrying the net with a weapon or shield causes that object to be snared instead, rendering it ineffective until it is ripped free. Breaking free of the net requires an opposed test of Athletics (Brute Force).

Special Rules

Combat Actions:	3
Strike Rank:	+12
Movement:	4m
Skills:	Athletics 60%, Dodge 45%, Perception 30%, Persistence 50%, Resilience 50%

Hit Locations

D20	Hit Location	AP/HP
1-2	Tail	1/6
3-4	Right Hind Leg	1/6
5-6	Left Hind Leg	1/6
7-10	Hindquarters	1/7
11-14	Forequarters	1/8
15-16	Right Front Leg	1/6
17-18	Left Front Leg	1/6
19-20	Head/Neck	1/6

Special Rules

Combat Actions: 3
Strike Rank: +11
Movement: 6m
Skills: Dodge 35%, Perception 30%, Persistence 30%, Resilience 40%, Tracking 65%

Mist Giant (Bellbane)

Now he could make out some of its saliencies. Two eyes, the colour of thin, yellow wine, were set high in the thing's body, though it had no separate head. A mouthing, obscene slit, filled with fangs, lay just beneath the eyes. It had no nose or ears that Elric could see. Four appendages sprang from its upper parts and its lower body slithered along the ground, unsupported by any limbs. Elric's eyes ached as he looked at it. It was incredibly disgusting to behold and its amorphous body gave off a stench of death and decay.
– The Weird of the White Wolf

Elric remarks that the hunting grounds of the Mist Giant, Bellbane, are far to the west of the Marshes of the Mist, indicating that Bellbane (and possibly others of his kind) are not native to the marshes – although that is where Bellbane is encountered. The Mist Giant's origins are a mystery, but it is clearly a creature of legend for it has a name – although whether it is a creature of Law or Chaos is unclear. Naturally, the latter is presumed because Elric invokes the name of several minor Chaos Lords as he battles Bellbane, and this has some kind of impact on the creature.

Hunting Dog of the Dharzi

A hybrid of dog and eagle, Dharzi hunting dogs are a relic of the Dharzi lords and were once used both for hunting prey as sport and foes in war. Fast and tenacious, with vile breath and vicious claws, they are keen and tireless trackers.

Characteristics

STR	2D8+8	(17)
CON	2D8+8	(17)
DEX	2D8+8	(17)
SIZ	1D8+8	(13)
INT	1D8	(5)
POW	3D8	(14)

Weapons

Type	Weapon skill	Damage
Bite	50%	1D6+1D2
Talons	45%	1D6+1+1D2

Mist Giants ignore the effects of Major Wounds as their bodies are only semi-corporeal. They can also regenerate lost hit points, making them formidable foes. Each damaged hit location regenerates 1 HP per round.

Characteristics

STR	6D8+8	(35)
CON	6D8+8	(35)
DEX	2D8+8	(17)
SIZ	2D8+12	(21)
INT	1D8	(5)
POW	4D8	(18)

Mist Giant Hit Locations

D20	Hit Location	AP/HP
1-8	Gaseous Body	–/13
9-10	Right Lower Tendril	–/10
11-12	Left Lower Tendril	–/10
13-14	Right Upper Tendril	–/10
15-16	Left Upper Tendril	–/10
17-20	Head	–/12

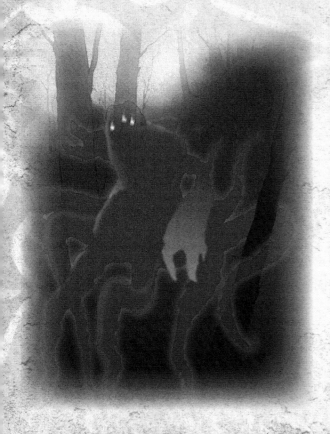

Like demons, Mist Giants take only half damage from normal weapons.

Weapons

Type	Weapon skill	Damage
Mist Tentacle*	35%	See below
Bite	60%	1D6+1D12

*Mist Giants have four semi-corporeal tentacles that are used to grasp an opponent and move it towards the maw. Escaping the grasp of the tendril requires an Athletics (Brute Force) test.

Special Rules

Combat Actions:	3
Strike Rank:	+11
Movement:	4m
Skills:	Dodge 20%, Perception 35%, Persistence 35%, Resilience 100%

Olab

The things were essentially reptilian but with feathery crests and neck wattles, though their faces were almost human. Their forelegs were like the arms and hands of men, but their hind legs were incredibly long and stork-like. Balanced on these legs, their bodies towered over the water. They carried great clubs in which slits had been cut and doubtless these were what they used to hurl the crystalline discs. Staring at their faces, Elric was horrified. In some subtle way they reminded him of the characteristic faces of his own folk – the folk of Melniboné. Were these creatures his cousins? Or were they a species from which his people had evolved?'
– *The Sailor on the Seas of Fate*

Tenacious and ferocious, the Olab are the guardians of the jungles leading to mythical R'lin K'ren A'a. They are cunning warriors, attacking from ambush by hurling their razor sharp, crystalline discs from slotted clubs. They are extremely accurate with this method of attack and no less effective in hand-to-hand combat. Olab do not retreat from small groups of intruders and attack in waves until all opponents retreat or are dead. They ignore the effects of Major Wounds, effectively fighting until they drop.

Clearly Elric sees something in the Olab that reminds him of his own people. How they came to be this way – or how Melnibonéans descended from their bizarre appearance – is unanswered.

Characteristics

STR	2D8+8	(17)
CON	4D8+8	(26)
DEX	2D8+8	(17)
SIZ	2D8+6	(15)
INT	2D8+2	(11)
POW	3D8	(14)

Olab Hit Locations

D20	Hit Location	AP/HP
1-3	Right Leg	1/9
4-6	Left Leg	1/9
7-9	Abdomen	1/10
10-12	Chest	1/11
13-15	Right Arm	1/8
16-18	Left Arm	1/8
19-20	Head	1/9

Weapons

Type	Weapon skill	Damage	AP/HP	Range
Club	60%	1D6+1D4	2/4	
Discus (Club)	65%	2D10+1D4	2/3	50m
Discus (Thrown)	60%	2D10+1D4	2/3	30m

Special Rules

Combat Actions: 3
Strike Rank: +14
Movement: 4m
Skills: Athletics 55%, Dodge 60%, Perception 70%, Persistence 60%, Resilience 90%, Tracking 80%
Typical Armour: Scaled bodies and feathered wattles (1 AP, no Skill Penalty)

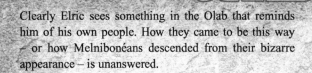

Oonai

In their native form Oonai resemble bloated, black-skinned, pig-like creatures. Once they were servants of Chaos but Chaos deserted them leaving them stuck with their grotesque forms. So sickened by this betrayal the Oonai have forsaken Chaos and now serve Law (indeed Myshella, Empress of the Dawn, summons the Oonai to fetch Elric to Kaneloon). To escape their own disgusting appearance Oonai constantly shift their shape, adopting ever more grotesque combinations of beasts such as the dragon-shapes and multicoloured, fanged swans Elric and Moonglum witness in the wilds of Lormyr. Oonai typically assume the forms of winged creatures, so the hit locations below are based on such a configuration. When summoned they retain no single form for longer than one Combat Round before changing again.

Characteristics

STR	8D8	(36)
CON	8D8	(36)
DEX	3D8	(14)
SIZ	4D8	(18)
INT	2D8	(9)
POW	3D8	(14)

Hit Locations

D20	Hit Location	AP/HP
1-2	Tail	*/11
3-4	Right Hind Leg	*/11
5-6	Left Hind Leg	*/11
7-8	Hindquarters	*/12
9-10	Chest/Forequarters	*/13
11-12	Right Wing	*/10
13-14	Left Wing	*/10
15-16	Right Front Leg	*/11
17-18	Left Front Leg	*/11
19-20	Head	*/11

Once creatures of Chaos, Oonai sustain only half damage from normal weapons.

* The Armour Points of the Oonai change with each form they take. Assume a value of 1D8 for each random form.

Weapons

Oonai employ a variety of natural weapons based upon the form they assume. Below are some possible variations.

Type	Weapon skill	Damage
Tentacles	40%	1D8+1D12
Fangs	40%	1D6+1+1D12
Talons	55%	1D8+1+1D12

Special Rules

Combat Actions:	3
Strike Rank:	+12
Movement:	6m
Skills:	Dodge 35%, Perception 30%, Persistence 30%, Resilience 40%, Tracking 45%

CREATURES OF LAW

MASTODON

Mastodon roam the Weeping Waste and were used by the Melnibonéans in times past to pull their great war-chariots. A few Waste tribes breed and ride these immense beasts, believing them to be one of Lord Grome's most beloved creations.

Mastodon are fur-covered, like woolly mammoths, and similar in height but their skulls are larger and flatter with a stockier and more robust build. The tusks of the mastodon can exceed five metres in length, and are almost horizontal, unlike those of mammoth which tend to be curved.

Characteristics

STR	10D6+30	(65)
CON	4D6+21	(35)
DEX	3D6	(11)
SIZ	10D6+30	(65)
INT	6	(6)
POW	2D6+6	(13)
CHA	5	(5)

Mastodon Hit Locations

D20	Hit Location	AP/HP
1-2	Right Hind Leg	9/20
3-4	Left Hind Leg	9/20
5-8	Hindquarters	9/21
9-12	Forequarters	9/22
13-14	Right Front Leg	9/20
15-16	Left Front Leg	9/20
17	Trunk	9/19
18-20	Head	9/20

Weapons

Type	Weapon skill	Damage
Trample	50%	5D12
Tusk	55%	1D12+2D12

Special Rules

Combat Actions:	2
Strike Rank:	+9
Movement:	6m
Skills:	Athletics 80%, Perception 45%, Resilience 65%

Typical Armour: Thick Hide (AP 9, no Skill Penalty)

SABRE-TOOTH TIGER (SMILODON)

The sabre-toothed tigers of the Weeping Waste and southern Pikarayd are pack-animals, stalkers of the plains. Stocky and powerful over short distances, their favoured tactic is to ambush their prey from a high point, leaping onto the back and stabbing down with their dreadful sabre-curved fangs. Pan Tang prizes these beasts, with regular hunting parties sent to the Wastes and Pikarayd to capture live specimens for use in the Tyger regiments of Hwamgaarl.

Characteristics

STR	6D6 + 10	(31)
CON	3D6 + 6	(17)
DEX	3D6 + 3	(14)
SIZ	4D6 + 15	(29)
INT	5	(5)
POW	3D6	(11)

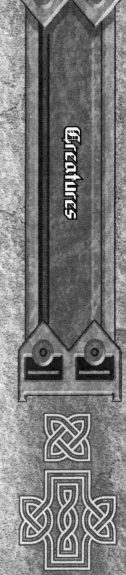

Creatures

D20	Hit Location	AP/HP
1–2	Right Hind Leg	3/9
3–4	Left Hind Leg	3/9
5–7	Hindquarters	3/10
8–10	Forequarters	3/11
11–13	Right Front Leg	3/9
14–16	Left Front Leg	3/9
17–20	Head	3/9

Weapons

Type	Weapon Skill	Damage
Stab	75%	1D10+1D12
Bite	45%	1D8+1D12
Claws	50%	1D6+1+1D12

Special Rules

Combat Actions:	3
Strike Rank:	+10
Movement:	6m
Skills:	Athletics 75%, Dodge 50%, Persistence 40%, Resilience 60%, Survival 50%, Tracking 80%
Typical Armour:	Hide (AP 3, no Skill Penalty)

Snake, Venomous

Another common reptile, venomous snakes are found across the Young Kingdoms. In Dorel, the legendary black serpents possess the deadliest venom known. The statistics given below are for one of the more famous varieties of venomous snake – the Melnibonéan cobra. Other vipers can be created by varying the STR and SIZ Characteristics, as well as the Potency of the snake's poison. For example, a Dorel Black Serpent's Characteristic SIZ and STR are reduced by a D6 each.

Characteristics

STR	2D6+6	(13)
CON	2D6	(7)
DEX	3D6+18	(29)
SIZ	2D6	(7)
INT	3	(3)
POW	2D6+6	(13)
CHA	3	(3)

Melnibonéan Cobra Hit Locations

D20	Hit Location	AP/HP
1–6	Tail	1/3
7–14	Body	1/5
15–20	Head	1/3

Weapons

Type	Weapon skill	Damage
Bite	60%	1D2–1D2+poison

Special Rules

Combat Actions:	4
Strike Rank:	+15
Movement:	4m
Skills:	Athletics 35%, Dodge 75%, Stealth 95%
Typical Armour:	Scales (AP 1, no Skill Penalty)

Melnibonéan Cobra Venom

The cobra bite causes horrific hallucinations, sometimes ending in madness.

Type: Injected or Smeared
Delay: 1 Combat Round
Potency: 55
Full Effect: –1 penalty to victim's INT, every *five minutes*. At zero the victim goes insane
Duration: 6D10 minutes

Dorel Black Serpent Venom

The most lethal snake of the Young Kingdoms, its venom is almost invariably fatal.

Type: Injected
Delay: 1 Combat Round
Potency: 70
Full Effect: 1 hit point damage to all locations, every *minute*
Duration: 6D10 minutes

HEROES & VILLAINS

This chapter presents information on characters appearing in the Elric saga, including Elric and his notorious sword, Stormbringer. As most of the personalities presented here are likely to be encountered only rarely (although some, such as Duke Avan Astran, might be patrons of adventurers), full game statistics are not provided with the exceptions of Elric, Moonglum, Prince Gaynor and Yyrkoon. All of these may act as protagonists in one form or another and thus require a degree of game definition.

Personalities
Duke Avan Astran

Duke Avan was a man about forty, with a square, handsome face. He was dressed in a gilded silver breastplate, over which was arranged a white cloak. His breeches, tucked into black, knee-length boots, were of cream-coloured doeskin. On a small sea-table at his elbow rested his helmet, crested with scarlet feathers…

…'He's Avan Astran of Old Hrolmar,' grunted Count Smiorgan from the other side of the huge ham-bone. 'He's well known as an adventurer-explorer-trader. His reputation's the best. We can trust him, Elric.'
– The Sailor on the Seas of Fate

A seasoned traveller, explorer and trader, with a reputation for being just and fair, Duke Avan Astran is respected throughout the Young Kingdoms. His city, Old Hrolmar, is the most liberal in Vilmir, partly due to his influence and his exploits across the Young Kingdoms and into the Unknown East, which have brought both it, and Astran, wealth and renown.

Astran meets his doom when he seeks R'lin K'ren A'a and he is slain by Stormbringer – one of the first of many trusted companions perishing by Elric's unwilling hand. But in campaigns set before or during Elric's year of wandering, prior to the sack of Imrryr, Astran can be freely encountered, perhaps even acting as a patron for a group of worthy adventurers.

Dyvim Slorm

'Our knowledge is ancient,' Dyvim Slorm agreed, 'yet, so old is it that it has little relation to present events, I think. Our logic and learning are suited to the past…'
– Stormbringer

The son of Dyvim Tvar, Slorm is Elric's final surviving kinsman at the final battle with Chaos, and before that, leader of the Melnibonéan mercenaries as they wander the Young Kingdoms after the sacking of Imrryr. Even though he is a Dragon Lord, Slorm seems wise and pragmatic despite the fate of his people, and he is loyal to Elric until the end.

Dyvim Tvar

Dyvim Tvar signed to the guards and suddenly there were two ranks of armoured men between Yyrkoon and the throne. Yyrkoon glared back at the Lord of the Dragon Caves. 'You had best hope you perish with your master,' he hissed.

'This guard of honour will escort you from the hall,' Dyvim Tvar said evenly. 'We were all stimulated by your conversation this evening, Prince Yyrkoon.'
– Elric of Melniboné

One of Elric's most trusted and loyal kinsmen, Dyvim Tvar is responsible for the dragon caves of Imrryr and thus one of the highest ranking of the imperial court. He trusts Elric as both emperor and friend, and, even though Elric's actions force Tvar and the rest of the warriors of Melniboné into being wandering mercenaries, he still retains a certain trust and respect for the albino.

Tvar dies in the attack on Nikorn of Ilmar's fortress. Up until then he might be encountered abroad in the Young Kingdoms following the fall of Imrryr, either accompanied by his mercenaries, or alone, engaged on some mission to secure work for his people.

Prince Elric, 428ᵗʰ Emperor of the Ruby Throne

It is the colour of a bleached skull, his flesh; and the long hair which flows below his shoulders is milk-white. From the tapering, beautiful head stare two slanting eyes, crimson and moody, and from the loose sleeves of his yellow gown emerge two slender hands, also the colour of bone, resting on each arm of a seat which has been carved from a single, massive ruby. The crimson eyes are troubled and sometimes one hand will rise to finger the light helm which sits upon the white locks: a helm made from some dark, greenish alloy and exquisitely moulded into the likeness of a dragon about to take wing. And on the hand which absently caresses the crown there is a ring in which is set a single rare Actorios stone whose core sometimes shifts sluggishly and reshapes itself, as if it were sentient smoke and as restless in its jewelled prison as the young albino on his Ruby Throne.
—Elric of Melniboné

Proud prince of ruins, slayer of kin, a pirate, a reaver, a sorcerer, a murderer, and the final champion of the Cosmic Balance. Elric, 428ᵗʰ emperor of the Dragon Isle, is an albino and deficient of iron in his blood, lending him the ghostly pallor that is part of his legend. Considered unfit to rule by even his father, Sadric the 86ᵗʰ, Elric has had to fight for his position, and is constantly under challenge from Prince Yyrkoon, who sees himself as the rightful heir to the Ruby Throne.

Despite being of pure Melnibonéan blood, and thus cruel and vengeful by nature, Elric is capable of love and compassion, deep guilt and self-loathing. Whilst contemptuous of humans, he understands that Melniboné's future lies in understanding them, not oppressing them – heretical ideas in the eyes of such as Yyrkoon. When Elric decides to spend a year studying the Young Kingdoms, learning from them, Yyrkoon usurps him and helps trigger the fateful events leading to the world's destruction.

As a wanderer Elric is almost totally reliant on Stormbringer, and the two form a symbiotic relationship that Elric loathes yet cannot break. Most of those whom Elric loves die because of this relationship, and this weird drives Elric into a deep, sustained depression that is only occasionally lifted.

As a sorcerer, Elric is the most powerful in the Young Kingdoms, though most of his magic, taught him by his father, is based on the ancient pacts with the elemental and Beast Lords. Despite serving Chaos, he is a reluctant champion and summoning Arioch both disgusts and fascinates him. As his understanding of the nature of the struggle between Law and Chaos deepens, so does his distrust of his patron demon, and, eventually, Elric turns to the service of Law, deserting Chaos as it threatens to engulf the world.

As a man, Elric is a loyal friend and caring lover. He is capable of developing considerable affection for those he adventures with, especially humans (more so than his kinsmen, it seems), and it is not in his nature to ignore such loyalties – again, a curious trait in a Melnibonéan emperor.

Elric can be encountered anywhere in the Young Kingdoms but his presence should be used sparingly, his appearances echoed in deeds, rumours and hearsay in the taverns and inns. Elric's doom is legendary, and most choose to avoid the complications it brings.

The characteristics below are based on Elric as he is when not relying on Stormbringer for vitality. The figures in parentheses are his normal values when sustained by herbs and drugs. His characteristics change when the runesword is feeding him the strength of stolen souls.

Characteristics: STR 5 (13), CON 6 (13), DEX 11 (15), SIZ 16, INT 24, POW 40 (8 POW dedicated to Arioch, 1 POW dedicated to Flamefang), CHA 18
Skills: Athletics 62%, Command 100%, Courtesy 99%, Dodge 110%, Dreamtheft 30%, Evaluate 90%, First Aid 90%, Healing 75%, Influence 120%, Language (Common) 110%, Language (High Speech) 110%, Language (Low Speech) 130%, Lore (Animal) 90%, Lore (Dragon) 106%, Lore (Plant) 107%, Lore (Imperial Court) 180%, Lore (Beast Lords) 102%, Lore (Chaos) 95%, Lore (Elements) 110%, Lore (Law) 75%, Lore (World) 94%, Lore (Melniboné) 120%, Perception 95%, Persistence 95%, Resilience 20% (60)%, Riding (Dragon) 130%, Riding (Horse) 110%, Shiphandling 70%, Sing 75%, Stealth 84%, Streetwise 75%, Survival 90%, Tracking 70%, Throwing 88%, Unarmed 65%, Witch Sight 80%

Armour & Hit Points

D20	Hit Location	AP/HP
1-3	Right Leg	–/5 (6)
4-6	Left Leg	–/5 (6)
7-9	Abdomen	7/6 (7)
10-12	Chest	7/7 (8)
13-15	Right Arm	–/4 (5)
16-18	Left Arm	–/4 (5)
19-20	Head	7/5 (6)

Half Melnibonéan Plate: –6% skill penalty

Weapons

Type	Weapon skill	Damage	AP/HP
Stormbringer	see page 156		
Kite Shield	120%	1D6(+1D2)	10/18
Bone Bow	100%	2D8(+1D2)	2/9

Special Rules: *Combat Actions:* 2 (3), *Strike Rank:* +18 (+20), *Magic Points:* 31, *Movement:* 5m

Pacts and Summonings: Pacts with all Elemental Lords at 90%, Pacts with all Beast Lords at 80%, Pact (Arioch) 90%, Pact (Dragon) 95%

Summoning Rituals: Gnome 100%, Salamander 80%, Sylph 110%, Undine 100%, Creatures of Matik 75%, Grahluk 80%

Elric's Pacts with the elementals and beasts are as a result of his wearing of the Actorios, Ring of Kings, and thus he does not need to dedicate POW to them. Due to his intensive sorcerous training, Elric could, in theory, summon any demon given time, space and concentration. However he is always reticent to do so. If required, during the course of a game, assume he has a Summoning Ritual skill for all demon types of 80%.

Gifts and Compulsions: Stormbringer

PRINCE GAYNOR THE DAMNED

The leader stepped forward out of the press. He wore a silvered mirror helm. I had seen it before. I knew him. And something in me, however terrified, knew the satisfaction of confirmed instinct. My instincts had been right. Gaynor the Damned was abroad again.

If I had not recognized him by his helm I would have known him by that low, sardonic laughter.
'Well, well, Cousin. I see our friend heard the sound of my horn. He seems to have inconvenienced you a little.' He held up the curling bull's horn, covered in ornate copper and bronze, which hung at his belt. 'That was the second blast. The third will bring the end of everything.'
– The Skrayling Tree

Just as there is an Eternal Champion, so is there an Eternal Enemy: Prince Gaynor is that enemy, taking on many guises and many allegiances. In many ways Gaynor is a pawn of fate in the same way as Elric, but they differ in a crucial way. Prince Gaynor actively and consciously chases his power, believing that in doing so he will be rewarded by whomever he serves. He is therefore a willing participant in the Cosmic Struggle, a reliable agent for the forces of Law and Chaos to use to serve their agendas. Gaynor has served both Law and Chaos, and is a devout enemy of the Cosmic Balance. In various guises he has served Mabelode, Count Mashabak of Chaos and Miggea of Law. He has, in turn, been a sorcerer, a knight, and a nobleman. His damnation comes from his conscious seeking of unattainable power, his soul utterly forfeit to whichever deity his current incarnation is allied with.

In the Young Kingdoms he is allied with Duchess Miggea and leads her armies against Tanelorn, but he might equally be found serving Mabelode or Mashabak, or any of the Higher Powers. In most cases he always appears fully helmed, speaking in a sinister, sonorous tone. The helmet often hides a hideous, malformed countenance or even none whatsoever. Whatever form he takes, he is always allied closely with a much higher power and actively working on its behalf. His schemes are elaborate and cunning, conducted with relish and utter disregard for the consequences.

Prince Gaynor might thus be freely encountered anywhere in the Young Kingdoms, and serving any of the major Lords of Law or Chaos. For this reason alone he makes an excellent major protagonist for a campaign, establishing many smaller schemes through others (such as Klosterheim, a favoured henchman) that slowly involve the adventurers, leading, finally, to an encounter with the Eternal Enemy himself.

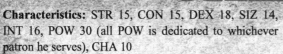

Characteristics: STR 15, CON 15, DEX 18, SIZ 14, INT 16, POW 30 (all POW is dedicated to whichever patron he serves), CHA 10

Skills: Athletics 70% , Courtesy 90%, Dodge 90%, Evaluate 90%, Influence 90%, Lore (Chaos or Law) 90%, Lore (World) 70%, Lore (Million Spheres) 70%, Mechanisms 65%,Perception 80%, Persistence 78%, Resilience 80%, Riding 100%, Sleight 60%, Stealth 60%, Survival 90%, Throwing 75%, Unarmed 60%

Armour & Hit Points

D20	Hit Location	AP/HP
1-3	Right Leg	6/6
4-6	Left Leg	6/6
7-9	Abdomen	6/7
10-12	Chest	6/8
13-15	Right Arm	6/5
16-18	Left Arm	6/5
19-20	Head	6/6

Full Plate: Gaynor appears to suffer no skill penalties

Weapons

Type	Weapon skill	Damage	AP/HP
Longsword	110%	1D10+1D2	4/10
Shortsword	99%	1D6+1D2	3/8
Long Bow	99%	2D8+1D2	2/7
Kite Shield	99%	1D6+1D2	10/18

Special Rules: *Combat Actions:* 3, *Strike Rank:* +17, *Movement:* 4m

Pacts and Summonings: Pact (Lord of Law or Chaos) 100%

Gifts and Compulsions: Gaynor has no magic as such, but he always has Gifts equalling 30 POW, and at least 3 Compulsions, relevant to whomever he serves. One of his gifts is always Eternal Life as Gaynor is, effectively, immortal although he remains vulnerable to sorcerous weapons.

Seeks own obliteration, Insanely ambitious, Craves Stormbringer, Must betray own patron

Jagreen Lern

The leaders headed their army, banners of dark silk rustling above their helms. King Sarosto and his thin ally, aquiline Jagreen Lern in glowing scarlet armour that seemed to be red hot and may have been. On his helm was the Merman Crest of Pan Tang, for the claimed kinship with the sea-people.
– Stormbringer

Jagreen Lern is Pan Tang's latest theocrat – the head of both church and state – and is as close to true evil as it is possible to get in the Young Kingdoms.

Jagreen Lern is typical of Mabden humans; swarthy, with a stern complexion and jet-black, oiled hair. His thin face holds narrow, intense eyes filled with ambition, cunning, cruelty and hatred. Jagreen Lern rules through fear: fear of his own, dreadful nature and of the pacts he has forged with the major Dukes of Hell. He is totally a servant of Chaos and completely bent to its will. His naïve belief is that Pan Tang will emerge as the new imperial power

administering the word of Chaos once Law has been vanquished. He is committed to achieving this goal irrespective of the consequences, and quite prepared to use every imaginable atrocity as a result.

Characteristics: STR 13, CON 10, DEX 13, SIZ 14, INT 19, POW 34 (10 dedicated to Chardros, 10 dedicated to Xiombarg), CHA 12

Skills: Athletics 55%, Command 85%, Dodge 77%, Influence 100%, Language (Common) 100%, Language (High Speech 75%), Language (Low Speech) 90%, Language (Mabden) 100%, Lore (Animal) 80%, Lore (Chaos) 100%, Lore (Million Spheres) 58%, Lore (World) 85%, Perception 84%, Resilience 84%, Survival 56%, Throwing 51%, Unarmed 50%

Armour & Hit Points

D20	Hit Location	AP/HP
1-3	Right Leg	6/5
4-6	Left Leg	6/5
7-9	Abdomen	6/6
10-12	Chest	6/7
13-15	Right Arm	6/4
16-18	Left Arm	6/4
19-20	Head	6/5

Full Plate: (−42%)

Weapons

Type	Weapon skill	Damage	AP/HP
Great Axe	95%	2D6+2+1D2	3/10
Dagger	98%	1D4+1+1D	4/6
Kite Shield	90%	1D6+1D2	10/18

Special Rules: *Combat Actions:* 3, *Strike Rank:* +16, *Magic Points:* 14, *Movement:* 4m

Legendary Abilities: Born to the Saddle, Madness of Purpose

Pacts and Summonings: Pact (Chardros) 100%, Pact (Xiombarg) 100%

Summoning Rituals: Salamander 75%, Demon of Combat 68%, Demon of Knowledge 75%, Demon of Protection 54%

Gifts and Compulsions: Endurance, Animal Familiar, Horde, Slave, Poison Immunity

Morbid fascination with death. Paranoid. Jealous. Obsessed with creating a chaotic empire.

Moonglum

Lately, since Elric had near-permanent residence in his wife's city of Karlaak, Moonglum had continued to travel and had been in command of a small mercenary army patrolling the Southern marches of Pikarayd, driving back the barbarians inhabiting the hinterland of that country. He had immediately relinquished this command when Elric's news reached him and now, as the tiny ship bore them towards a hazy and peril-fraught destiny, savoured the familiar mixture of excitement and perturbation which he had felt a dozen times before when their escapades had led them into conflict with the unknown supernatural forces so closely linked with Elric's destiny. He had come to accept as a fact that his destiny was bound to Elric's and felt, in the deepest places of his being, that when the time came they would both die together in some mighty adventure.

– Stormbringer

Small, red-haired, ugly, and blessed with courage, mischief and an innate good humour, Moonglum is the most loyal of all Elric's companions. He comes originally from Elwher, which he believes is the finest city in the world, and was an experienced mercenary in his home lands where he fought in the battle of Eshmire Vale alongside Rackhir of Phum. He is a pure adventurer at heart, forever restless, forever seeking good food, good wine and good entertainment. He is not above petty theft, but neither is he villainous or selfish; merely adaptable and practical.

Moonglum frequently acts as Elric's conscience and, whilst it is not always acknowledged, Elric listens to, and accepts, the Eshmirian's worldly wisdom.

There is every chance of Moonglum being encountered before the sack of Imrryr as he is widely travelled in the Young Kingdoms. Following Elric's marriage to Zarozinia, Moonglum takes to wandering once more, eventually becoming a commander of the mercenaries in Pikarayd.

He is loyal to Elric until the very end of time, willingly offering his soul so give Elric enough energy to blow the Horn of Fate, the final act of ultimate friendship.

Heroes & Villains

Characteristics: STR 16, CON 16, DEX 20, SIZ 8, INT 13, POW 16, CHA 17

Skills: Acrobatics 60%, Athletics 95%, Dodge 98%, Evaluate 95%, First Aid 78%, Language (Common) 100%, Language (Low Speech) 15%, Language ('pande) 100%, Lore (Animal) 65%, Perception 90%, Resilience 89%, Riding 80%, Sing 75%, Sleight 90%, Stealth 90%, Streetwise 90%, Survival 90%, Throwing 97%, Unarmed 75%

Armour & Hit Points

D20	Hit Location	AP/HP
1-3	Right Leg	1/5
4-6	Left Leg	1/5
7-9	Abdomen	6/6
10-12	Chest	6/7
13-15	Right Arm	1/4
16-18	Left Arm	–/4
19-20	Head	–/5

Plate Breastplate, Leather Trews: –15%

Weapons

Type	Weapon skill	Damage	AP/HP
Longsword	115%	1D10	2/10
Scimitar	120%	1D6+1	4/10
Shortsword	111%	1D6	6/8

Special Rules: *Combat Actions:* 4, *Strike Rank:* +16, *Movement:* 4m.

Mordaga

Mordaga was as tall as two men, but his back was slightly stooped. He had long, curling black hair and was clad in a deep blue smock, belted at the waist. Upon his great feet were simple leather sandals. His black eyes were full of a sorrow such as Moonglum had only seen before in Elric's eyes. Upon the sad giant's arm was a round shield which bore upon it the eight amber arrows of Chaos. It was of a silvery green colour and very beautiful. He had no other weapons.

'I know the prophecy,' he said in a voice that was like a lonely, roaring wind. 'But still I must seek to avert it. Will you take the shield and leave me in peace, human? I do not want death.'
– Stormbringer

Once a god, Mordaga dared to challenge his fellows and even the authority of the Cosmic Balance. As punishment he was banished to the Earth, cursed to mortality, and to live with the knowledge that, one day, 'four men of fate' will come to take the Chaos Shield and his life. Mordaga is therefore a sorrowful, fearful, pathetic and doomed creature, testament – if any were needed – of the cruelty of the god realms.

His castle is hidden in the far north of the Young Kingdoms, a secret from even the nomads of the Sighing Desert. It lies at the top of a mountain, reached by stairs spiralling towards its summit. The castle has two lines of defence. The first, near the gates, is an ancient, semi-sentient tree capable of releasing its leaves to attack intruders. The leaves flood forth in waves, seeking out the living, and attach themselves. Every leaf causes a hit point of damage, if it contacts bare skin, and also drains a point of POW. The tree can send forth a wave of 1D20 leaves per combat round, which hang lazily in the air, as if being blown by a gentle wind. The leaves have an attack ability of 40% and can be parried. The second defence is more predictable: 150 human warriors, mercenaries perhaps, recruited to protect Mordaga from the 'four men of fate'. These warriors, compelled by whatever remains of Mordaga's godhood, fight with little mercy.

Those who penetrate Mordaga's defences are greeted by the sorrowing giant. He is likely to heap any number of rewards on those who come to kill him, and it can be presumed, perhaps, that his castle is well-stocked with treasures that will persuade even the hardest heart. Should adventurers come seeking Mordaga and try to kill him, they will find he resists their blows. His destiny is to be slain only by the men of fate – and the man who delivers the fatal blow is Moonglum, who understands that fate cannot be denied.

Myshella, Empress of the Dawn

She was standing there, her black hair curling over her shoulders, her scarlet gown clinging to her body. Her lips curved in a smile of irony and her eyes regarded him steadily. She was the woman he had seen in the castle. The sleeping woman. Was this part of the dream?
'I am called Myshella. …'
'Empress of the Dawn?'

She smiled again. 'Some have named me that. And others have called me the Dark Lady of Kaneloon.'

'Whom Aubec loved? Then you must have preserved your youth carefully, Lady Myshella.'

'No doing of mine. It is possible that I am immortal. I do not know. I know only one thing and that is that Time is a deception...'

– The Vanishing Tower

The last true Champion of Law, Myshella dwells far from humankind in the castles of Kaneloon and Ashaneloon, in the south of the Young Kingdoms. Immensely beautiful, and courted by many over the millennia, she guards against the incursions of Chaos from the formless stuff that eddies at the edge of the world. Those who seek her are persuaded into her service by promises of their heart's desire, made real by Kaneloon's strange properties. Her lovers – heroes all – have been many, and their devices and standards adorn the castle walls.

Myshella is doomed to be killed by Theleb K'aarna, but before that time she may very likely reveal herself in dreams or other ways to attract potential agents to her service. As can be seen from the quotation, she can enter dreams almost like a Dreamthief, though she is not of their kind, and is a most persuasive patron when the designs of Law are threatened.

Oone

'Then I will tell you what I know and what I desire of you,' said Oone. She linked her free hand in his arm and led him further into the groves of palms and cypress. 'A dreamthief,' she began, 'does exactly what the title implies. We steal dreams. Originally our guild were true thieves. We learned the trick of entering the worlds of other peoples' dreams and stealing those which were most magnificent or exotic. Gradually, however, people began to call upon us to steal unwanted dreams, or rather the dreams which entrapped or plagued friends or relatives. So we stole those. Frequently the dreams themselves were in no way harmful to another, only to the one who was in their power...'

– The Fortress of the Pearl

A master Dreamthief, Oone acts as Elric's tutor and guide in the ways of dreamtheft and into the dream realms in search of the Fortress of the Pearl. She is not a native of the Young Kingdoms, but seems to visit the plane often enough.

She and Elric are lovers, briefly, and, unbeknown to Elric, she bears his children: twins, a boy and a girl...

Rackhir

'I am Rackhir,' said the man. 'Called the Red Archer for, as you see, I affect scarlet dress. It is a habit of the Warrior Priests of Phum to choose but a single colour to wear. It is the only loyalty to tradition I still possess.' He had on a scarlet jerkin, scarlet breeks, scarlet shoes and a scarlet cap with a scarlet feather in it. His bow was scarlet and the pommel of his sword glowed ruby-red. His face, which was aquiline and gaunt, as if carved from fleshless bone, was weather-beaten, and that was brown. He was tall and he was thin, but muscles rippled on his arms and torso. There was irony in his eyes and something of a smile upon his thin lips, though the face showed that it had been through much experience, little of it pleasant.

– Elric of Melniboné

A renegade from the Unknown East, Rackhir has turned his back on Chaos and seeks peace in Tanelorn – a city which he eventually finds and saves from the ravages of the beggar army raised by Narjhan. He is a past lover of scheming Sorana, and a companion to Elric on several adventures, although he meets a tragic end by Stormbringer as he, Elric, Moonglum and Dyvim Slorm, battle to reach Mordaga's hidden fortress.

As a Warrior Priest of Phum his patron Lord of Chaos was Vezhan, Lord of the Wings.

Count Smiorgan Baldhead

Meanwhile the man from the Purple Towns, unaided by sorcery, put axe and sword to good work and dealt with three more of his one-time comrades, exulting in work as if he had nursed a taste for it for some time. 'Yoi! But this is worthwhile slaughter!' cried the black bearded one.

– The Sailor on the Seas of Fate

Elric first meets Smiorgan Baldhead in the strange lands beyond the Crimson Gate. Betrayed by a crew of pirates, Smiorgan uses cunning to win their confidence (and his survival) before assisting Elric in their slaughter. From then on, the two men are firm friends, up until Smiorgan's death in the aftermath of the sack of Imrryr.

Smiorgan is the owner of a fleet of merchant ships in Menii, the Purple Towns' capital. He has wandered the

Heroes & Villains

world and clams to have sailed to the Unknown East, navigating the feared Roaring Rocks. He accompanies Elric on several adventures, including the exploration of R'lin K'ren A'a and is presumably instrumental in gathering together the Sea Lords when Elric decides to take the ultimate revenge on Yyrkoon.

STORMBRINGER & MOURNBLADE

It was heavy, yet perfectly balanced, a two-handed broadsword of prodigious size, with its wide crosspiece and its blade smooth and broad, stretching for over five feet from the hilt. Near the hilt, mystic runes were engraved and even Elric did not know what they fully signified. 'Again I must make use of you, Stormbringer,' he said as he buckled the sheath about his waist, 'and I must conclude that we are too closely linked now for less than death to separate us.'
– *Stormbringer*

Stormbringer and Mournblade are more than just swords. They are more than just demon swords; they are, in fact, agents of fate in the same way the Cosmic Balance is an arbiter of it. Both swords, brother and sister, are certainly sentient, and whilst forged to destroy a race of gods, they are, perhaps, closer to being gods themselves. These are unique weapons, and only a Melnibonéan of the royal line can wield them. They are treacherous, vampiric and parasitic, draining the souls of those they kill and passing the power to the wielder who quickly grows dependent on the surging strength of the Black Blade. Sapient souls are preferred, and the souls of loved ones and companions the sweetest tasting of all.

Both swords are capable of independent action. This is usually confined to stirrings and shiftings, low moans and rumbles. But in the midst of carnage, drunk on souls, they scream with an unearthly delight and guide the hand of the user to even greater carnage.

Standard weapon statistics are redundant for Stormbringer and Mournblade. Use these special rules instead – but note that only Melnibonéans can use these weapons. Normal mortals attempting to do so are likely to find themselves as the victims. For, as Stormbringer utters, *'I was a thousand times more evil than thou!'*

✴ The runeswords are not forged of earthly metals, although they have the appearance of black iron. Neither sword can be damaged or broken by any mortal force, and are so hard that they automatically damage any weapon which tries to parry them.

✴ Although heavy, neither weapon adds to fatigue.

✴ Each sword adds 100% to the attack percentage of the wielder.

✴ Every hit inflicts 3D8 points of damage.

✴ Every hit that penetrates armour drains 1D100 POW from *sapient* creatures.

✴ Every 10 points of POW drained raises the STR *and* CON of the wielder by 1 point. These temporary points are lost at the rate of 1 per Combat Round.

✴ The swords are capable of flight, manoeuvring of their own freewill at a speed of 4m per round.

✴ The swords do not normally fight on their own, but can turn in the hand of the wielder and make a single attack of their own volition.

✴ At any time in a battle, Stormbringer and Mournblade will be aware of the wielder's companions and loved ones. At an opportune moment the blade will lunge at a companion, aiming to take their soul. The wielder must make an Athletics (Brute Force) test to stay the Black Blade's attempt.

Ultimately, neither Stormbringer nor Mournblade should ever fall into the hands of adventurers. These are unique and immensely powerful weapons that would have an enormous impact on any campaign.

THELEB K'AARNA

Theleb K'aarna tittered. It was an obscene sound, coming as it did from the throat of a sorcerer of no mean skill. It did not fit with his sombre, black-bearded countenance, his tall, scarlet-robed frame. It was not a sound suited to one of his extreme wisdom.
– *The Bane of the Black Sword*

The love-sick and jealous sorcerer of Pan Tang is Elric's sworn enemy for many reasons. In the course of his career he tries to kill Elric and Moonglum numerous times, besieges Kaneloon, enchants Myshella, attacks Tanelorn, and his actions result in the deaths of both the Empress of the Dawn and Elric's kinsman, Dyvim Tvar. Pushing the boundaries of his knowledge just too far, Theleb K'aarna eventually goes completely insane, having used the last of his power and sanity to fuel his spells.

Yishana is a capricious and scheming woman who enjoys the attentions of powerful men and their subsequent manipulation through her considerable charms. She is the lover to both Elric and Theleb K'aarna, and has doubtless taken many previous lovers only to discard them later when bored or their usefulness has expired.

Yishana fights alongside Elric at the final battle for the world, struggling against the advancing forces of Pan Tang, aided by the mercenaries of Melniboné and the Knights of Shazar. For all her scheming she is resourceful, brave and genuinely cares for her country.

Whether or not she is possessed of eternal youth is a rumour, but certainly Theleb K'aarna had such things in his command, so there may be some truth in it.

Prince Yyrkoon

His dark features, at once handsome and saturnine, are framed by long black hair, waved and oiled, and his expression, as ever, is sardonic while his bearing is arrogant. The heavy brocade cloak swings this way and that, striking other dancers with some force. He wears it almost as if it is armour or, perhaps, a weapon. Amongst many of the courtiers there is more than a little respect for Prince Yyrkoon. Few resent his arrogance and those who do keep silent, for Yyrkoon is known to be a considerable sorcerer himself. Also his behaviour is what the court expects and welcomes in a Melnibonéan noble; it is what they would welcome in their emperor.
– Elric of Melniboné

Usurper prince of the Ruby Throne, Yyrkoon represents the Bright Empire's dark heart; its cruelty and desire to dominate. Maddened by Elric's rule and his love for Cymoril, Yyrkoon is driven to ever greater lengths to depose his cousin. He opposes him via the dream couches, attempting to manipulate the myths of Melniboné so Elric might die; he engineers Elric's betrayal in a battle against pirates. In later atrocities he robs men of their memories and contests Elric for the possession of the Black Blades,

Theleb K'aarna is truly evil. Vain, selfish and desperate for power at any cost, he is a highly skilled sorcerer – almost Elric's match – with numerous pacts and bargains made with all sorts of supernatural beings.

Queen Yishana

Her long hair was black and shone around her head. Her breasts were large and her hips broader than Elric remembered. 'Good morning, wolf,' said she with a half-smile that was at once sardonic and provocative. 'My scouts reported that you were riding with your countrymen. This is pleasant. Have you forsaken your new wife to return to subtler pleasures?'
'No,' he said. 'Good morning, Yishana. You do not change. I've half a suspicion that Theleb K'aarna gave you a draught of the waters of Eternal Life before I killed him.'
'Perhaps he did. How goes your marriage?'
– Stormbringer

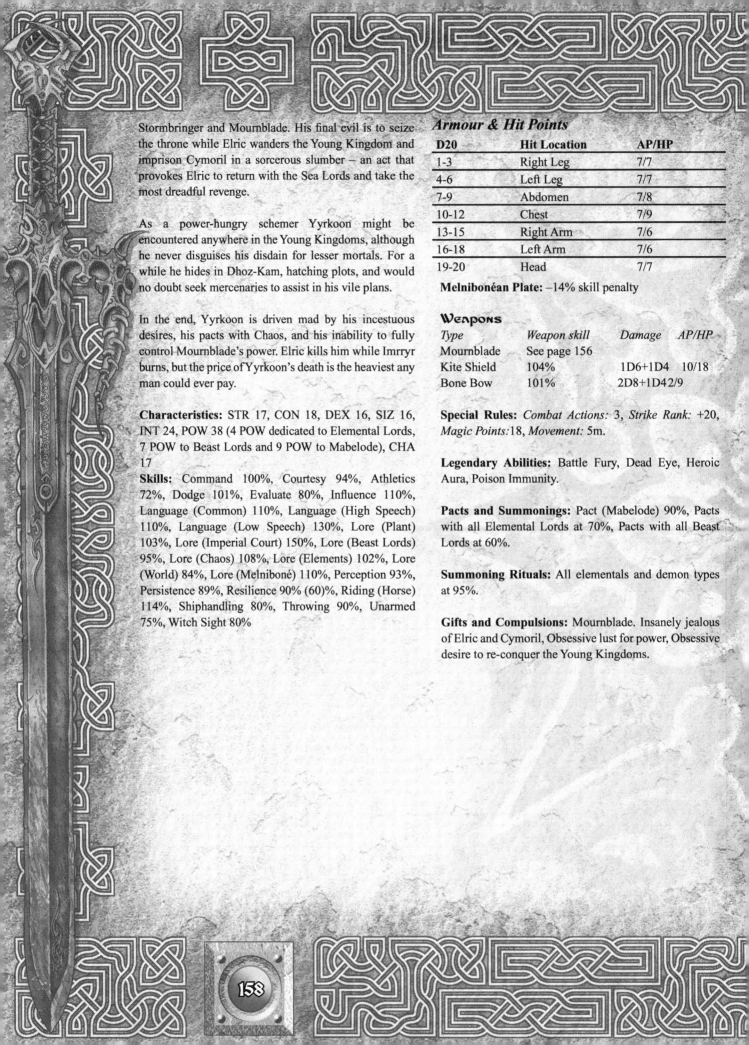

Stormbringer and Mournblade. His final evil is to seize the throne while Elric wanders the Young Kingdom and imprison Cymoril in a sorcerous slumber – an act that provokes Elric to return with the Sea Lords and take the most dreadful revenge.

As a power-hungry schemer Yyrkoon might be encountered anywhere in the Young Kingdoms, although he never disguises his disdain for lesser mortals. For a while he hides in Dhoz-Kam, hatching plots, and would no doubt seek mercenaries to assist in his vile plans.

In the end, Yyrkoon is driven mad by his incestuous desires, his pacts with Chaos, and his inability to fully control Mournblade's power. Elric kills him while Imrryr burns, but the price of Yyrkoon's death is the heaviest any man could ever pay.

Characteristics: STR 17, CON 18, DEX 16, SIZ 16, INT 24, POW 38 (4 POW dedicated to Elemental Lords, 7 POW to Beast Lords and 9 POW to Mabelode), CHA 17

Skills: Command 100%, Courtesy 94%, Athletics 72%, Dodge 101%, Evaluate 80%, Influence 110%, Language (Common) 110%, Language (High Speech) 110%, Language (Low Speech) 130%, Lore (Plant) 103%, Lore (Imperial Court) 150%, Lore (Beast Lords) 95%, Lore (Chaos) 108%, Lore (Elements) 102%, Lore (World) 84%, Lore (Melniboné) 110%, Perception 93%, Persistence 89%, Resilience 90% (60)%, Riding (Horse) 114%, Shiphandling 80%, Throwing 90%, Unarmed 75%, Witch Sight 80%

Armour & Hit Points

D20	Hit Location	AP/HP
1-3	Right Leg	7/7
4-6	Left Leg	7/7
7-9	Abdomen	7/8
10-12	Chest	7/9
13-15	Right Arm	7/6
16-18	Left Arm	7/6
19-20	Head	7/7

Melnibonéan Plate: −14% skill penalty

Weapons

Type	Weapon skill	Damage	AP/HP
Mournblade	See page 156		
Kite Shield	104%	1D6+1D4	10/18
Bone Bow	101%	2D8+1D4	2/9

Special Rules: *Combat Actions:* 3, *Strike Rank:* +20, *Magic Points:* 18, *Movement:* 5m.

Legendary Abilities: Battle Fury, Dead Eye, Heroic Aura, Poison Immunity.

Pacts and Summonings: Pact (Mabelode) 90%, Pacts with all Elemental Lords at 70%, Pacts with all Beast Lords at 60%.

Summoning Rituals: All elementals and demon types at 95%.

Gifts and Compulsions: Mournblade. Insanely jealous of Elric and Cymoril, Obsessive lust for power, Obsessive desire to re-conquer the Young Kingdoms.

INDEX

Character Name:

Player Name:

Race:

Cultural Background:

Profession:

Characteristics

Characteristic	Current Score
STRength	
CONstitution	
DEXterity	
SIZe	
INTelligence	
POWer	
CHArisma	

Attributes

Attribute	Current Score
Combat Actions	
Damage Modifier	
Hero Points	
Magic Points	
Movement	
Strike Rank	

Basic Skills

Basic Skills	Characteristic(s)	Current Score
Acrobatics	DEX	
Athletics	STR+DEX	
Boating	STR	
Dodge	10+DEX–SIZ	
Driving	10+POW	
Evaluate	INT	
First Aid	INT	
Influence	10+CHA	
Lore (Animal)	INT	
Lore (Plant)	INT	
Lore (World)	INT	
Perception	INT+POW	
Persistence	30+CHA+POW	
Resilience	30+CON+POW	
Riding	DEX+POW	
Sing	CHA	
Sleight	DEX	
Stealth	10+DEX–SIZ	
Throwing	DEX	
Unarmed	STR	

Weapon Skills

Weapon Skills	Characteristic(s)	Current Score
Basic Close Combat	STR+DEX	
Basic Ranged	DEX	

Advanced/Sorcery Skills

Advanced Skills	Characteristic(s)	Current Score

Favoured Close Combat Weapons

Weapon	Skill Score	Damage	ENC	AP/HP	Special Notes

Favoured Ranged Weapons

Weapon	Skill Score	Damage	Range	Load	ENC	AP/HP

Hit Locations

D20	Hit Location	Armour Points	Hit Points
1–3	Right Leg		
4–6	Left Leg		
7–9	Abdomen		
10–12	Chest		
13–15	Right Arm		
16–18	Left Arm		
19–20	Head		

Equipment

Item	ENC	AP/HP	Special Notes

Total ENC: **Current Fatigue:**

Michael Moorcock's Elric of Melnibonē

Legendary Abilities

Ability	Effect

Cults

Cult Name

Pact Skill

Rank

Gifts

Compulsions

Cult Name

Pact Skill

Rank

Gifts

Compulsions

Sorcery

Summoning Ritual	Value

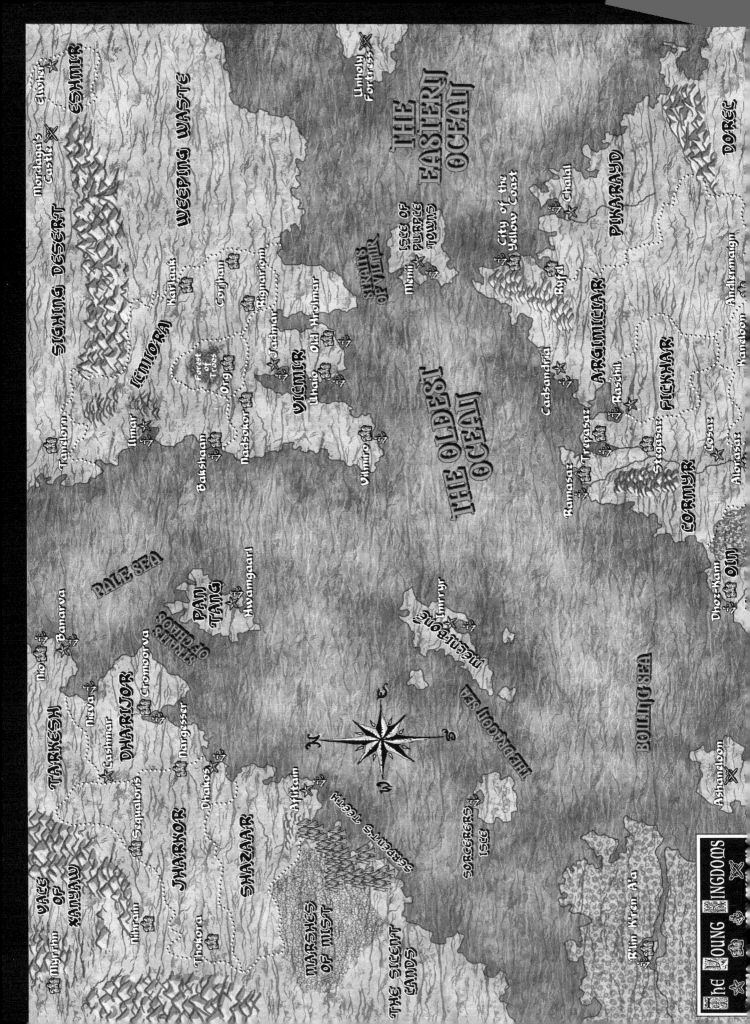